Ernest Mandel

NLB

Revolutionary
Marxism Today

Edited by Jon Rothschild

ילר

First published, 1979
© Ernest Mandel, 1979

NLB, 7 Carlisle Street, London W1

Typeset in English Times by
Red Lion Setters, London WC1

Printed by Lowe & Brydone Printers,
Thetford, Norfolk

Bound at Kemp Hall Bindery, Oxford

ISBN   0 86091 022 9 (cloth)
ISBN   0 86091 024 5 (paper)

Contents

Introduction

Jon Rothschild

Ernest Mandel is probably best known in the English-speaking world as one of the most innovative Marxist economists since the Second World War. His *Late Capitalism* (NLB, 1975), simultaneously an analysis of the long post-war economic boom and a history of the capitalist mode of production in the twentieth century, was the first major synthesis produced by the revival of Marxist economic theory in the late sixties and early seventies. This work, whose conclusions were initially greeted with some scepticism, predicted the end of the period of rapid growth and argued that 'late capitalism' would ultimately prove unable to eradicate the fundamental contradictions of capitalism, a prediction largely confirmed since the outbreak of the 1974-75 international recession.

Late Capitalism was itself the culmination of nearly two and a half decades of research and was preceded by a number of other works which have since become classics of modern economic analysis. Mandel's *Marxist Economic Theory* (Merlin, London, 1968), originally drafted in 1962, was the first comprehensive restatement of the principles of Marx's *Capital* as they apply to twentieth-century reality; it also contained a systematic attempt to bring the Marxist method of analysis to bear on the economies of the Soviet Union and the East European countries. His *Formation of the Economic Thought of Karl Marx* (NLB, 1971) traced the development of Marx's economic categories from the early philosophical writings to *Capital*. *Europe Versus America* (NLB, 1970) examined the rise of the Common Market and the intensification of inter-imperialist competition as absolute American hegemony over the world market began to fade. More recently, in *The Second Slump* (NLB, 1978), Mandel presented a meticulous account of the 1974-75 recession and its aftermath, locating that recession in the context of the history and theory of capitalist crises. *The Long Waves of Capitalist Development: A Marxist View* (CUP, forthcoming) based on the Alfred Marshall Lectures given by Mandel at the University of Cambridge in 1978, represents a further development of his theoretical and empirical research into the functioning and prospects of the capitalist economies of the West.

Only relatively recently, however, has the English-speaking public become aware of Mandel's stature as a political leader, one of the foremost theoreticians of the Fourth International (FI), the world organization founded by Leon Trotsky and his supporters in 1938 to begin the reconstruction of an international movement whose revolutionary spirit had been extinguished by the bureaucratic degeneration of the Soviet Union and the Third (Communist) International under Stalin. Mandel has been an activist in this movement since his early youth. Born in 1923, he became a revolutionary in 1939 and joined the Trotskyist movement in his native Belgium in 1940, helping to rebuild an underground group there after the Nazi invasion. He has been a member of the Central Committee of the Belgian revolutionary organization continuously since 1941. He was active in the Resistance throughout the occupation. Twice arrested by the Nazis, he escaped the first time; when re-arrested, he was formally 'tried' before a Nazi court and deported to a prison camp in Germany in 1944. Early that year, between his first and second arrests, he had participated in the first European conference of the underground sections of the Fourth International. In 1946, when the Second World Congress of the FI reassembled those European militants who had survived the war and their comrades around the world, Mandel was elected to the leadership body of the International. He has remained on it ever since, serving as the reporter on international politics at each of the World Congresses held since the mid-fifties. With the growth of the political impact and membership of the International since 1968, Mandel has become one of the leading public figures of the Trotskyist movement, defending its views against both criticisms from other currents of the workers' movement and attacks from the representatives of the capitalist class. He has thereby established a reputation as a consummate polemicist, clashing with such opponents as Shirley Williams of the British Labour Party, Santiago Carrillo of the

Communist Party of Spain, John Kenneth Galbraith, and others. The most recent fruit of this aspect of his activity is the book *From Stalinism to Eurocommunism* (NLB, 1978), a comprehensive critique of the evolution of the Communist parties of Western Europe in the seventies.

While the FI has been the centre of Mandel's political activity, he has had significant influence in other domains as well. During the fifties and sixties, when the Belgian Trotskyists were active within the Socialist Party, he was deeply involved in the trade-union movement, as a member of the economic studies commission of the FGTB, the Belgian national union federation. In that capacity he was co-author of the report on the concentration of economic power adopted by the special congress of the FGTB in 1956. He was also editor of the weekly *La Gauche*, organ of the Socialist Party left wing, whose members were expelled from the party in 1965 for their systematic opposition to the official policies of coalition with the Christian Social Party and to the anti-strike legislation enacted by that coalition in 1962.

For more than twenty years he has been an active participant in trade-union and workers' seminars throughout Europe, helping to educate thousands of activists both inside and outside the FI. The pamphlet *Introduction to Marxist Economics*, based on his presentation at one such session, has been translated into many languages and has sold more than 400,000 copies. *From Class Society to Communism* (Ink Links, 1978), a subsequent general introduction to Marxist theory as a whole, seems likely to achieve similar levels of diffusion. Even *Late Capitalism*, a difficult theoretical work, has been published in ten languages and has sold nearly 70,000 copies. Mandel's pamphlets cover nearly every aspect of revolutionary politics, from the Leninist theory of party organization to the nature of bureaucracy in the labour movement. In all, his writings have been published in a total of thirty languages.* The bourgeoisie has responded to this political work in its own way: at one time or another, Mandel has been barred from entering the United States, France, West Germany, Switzerland, and Australia, to mention only

---

*Flemish (his native tongue), French, English, German, Spanish, Italian, Portuguese, Swedish, Norwegian, Danish, Icelandic, Finnish, Greek, Turkish, Kurdish, Persian, Arabic, Hebrew, Hindi, Gujarati, Bengali, Tamil, Sinhala, Chinese, Japanese, Russian, Polish, Czech, Serbo-Croat, and Hungarian.

the 'liberal-democratic' countries whose rulers have deemed his presence deleterious to their 'national security'.

Mandel is therefore uniquely qualified to present a comprehensive synopsis of the Fourth International's analysis of the contemporary world scene and the opportunities it affords for a revolutionary breakthrough to socialist democracy. This is the purpose of *Revolutionary Marxism Today*. The interviews assembled here, although taken at various times and supplemented by additional questions, have been edited so as to present a systematic view of world politics.* The first deals with the strategy of proletarian revolution in the advanced capitalist countries, with special reference to Western Europe. The second examines the Trotskyist theory of permanent revolution and the strategy it implies for the anti-imperialist and democratic struggle in the dependent capitalist countries of the 'third world', arguing that the tasks of that struggle can be accomplished only through socialist revolution. The third explores the nature of the societies in which capitalism has already been overthrown but in which a privileged bureaucracy commands a monopoly of political power; Mandel emphasizes the transitional nature of these societies and the prospects for anti-bureaucratic political revolution as the only means of attaining full proletarian democracy within them. The final interview focuses on the evolution of world politics since the Second World War, considering such difficult issues as the character of the war itself, the reasons underlying the Sino-Soviet dispute, and the peculiar features of the labour movement in the United States and Japan; it concludes with a discussion of the organizational precepts and political prospects of the Fourth International and its view of what a socialist society should be like.

All the various interviewers in these discussions—Denis Berger, Robin Blackburn, Quintin Hoare, Jon Rothschild, and Henri Weber—are themselves members of the Fourth International. But the interviews are not at all catechistic in form. This is not only because the individual questioners deliberately strove to pose critical and challenging issues. More important, it reflects one of the features of the FI itself. Although the members of the various

---

*Earlier versions of parts of these discussions appeared in the journal *Critique Communiste* (Paris) and in English in *New Left Review* (London).

national sections of the International hold common views on what they consider the pivotal principles of revolutionary Marxism, there are significant differences of opinion among them on a broad range of particular issues and also on some, far from inconsequential points of theory and interpretation. This unique combination of unanimity on an array of programmatic tenets affecting nearly every phase of the worldwide struggle for socialism and vigorous, often profound disagreements on how these principles should be understood and applied today is one of the hallmarks of the International. The members of the FI, provided they adhere to the practical decisions of the organization, are fully entitled to express their differences and to organize to fight for their views within the International. No other current of the labour movement has shown itself capable of such an expansive approach to politics, and none has succeeded in accommodating such a diversity of views within an inclusive unity of principle. In this sense, the interviews, while they express the personal views of Ernest Mandel on particular issues (views with which other members of the Fourth International might disagree), may also be regarded as representative of the general outlook of the International itself. No sector of the Left can claim a monopoly of political insight today, and the limitations and imperfections of the interview as a form need little emphasis. Nevertheless, the question can legitimately be asked: has so wide a geographical and thematic range of problems facing the socialist movement across the world ever before been dealt with in a single compass?

To the Memory of
JABRA NICOLA
Pioneer Arab Marxist & Palestinian Trotskyist
the most impressive internationalist
I ever met.

1

Socialist Strategy in the West

The Trotskyist movement has long been identified with the concept of world revolution, which it has counterposed not only to the theory of 'socialism in one country' but also to all similar theses, such as the notion that any particular country or region constitutes the key arena or 'centre' of international political struggle. In recent years, however, much of the theoretical production of the Fourth International has been concentrated on one part of the world: Western Europe. Discussions about the strategy of proletarian revolution in the contemporary world tend rapidly to become discussions of the revolutionary process in Europe. What is the reason for this? Does it reflect a deeply rooted 'Eurocentrism' that inflects Trotskyist analysis in a certain direction despite the theory of world revolution?

World revolution is an objective process that has dominated the history of the twentieth century. But the world revolution, like the world economy to which it corresponds, develops unevenly. Up to now, socialist revolutions—overturns involving the action of masses of people in the elimination of capitalism, even if that action was bureaucratically controlled to a large extent—have occurred in relatively underdeveloped countries: Russia, Yugoslavia, China, Vietnam, Cuba. With the exception of Russia, the major participants in these revolutions have been forces other than the urban proletariat—and even in Russia this class was socially weak, despite the leading political role it played. The main forms of revolutionary struggle and the central features of the states that emerged from these revolutions have been decisively influenced by these factors.

While revolutionary Marxists should—indeed, must—explain the causes of this course of development, under no circumstances should they suggest that the specific course of world revolution was pre-determined for structural reasons. Such an interpretation would condemn as hopeless utopians Marx, Engels, Lenin, Trotsky, Luxemburg, and the founders of the Third and Fourth Internationals, all of whom, at various times, had the highest expectations of short-term revolutionary advances in quite a number of advanced, industrialized countries. It would also tend to justify *a posteriori* all the reformist misleaders of the Western working class whose counter-revolutionary policies during revolutionary crises were basically motivated by a profound disbelief in any real possibility of socialist revolution in the imperialist countries. (I am leaving aside those labour bureaucrats who were—and remain—consciously opposed to socialist revolution for reasons of material self-interest, even, or rather especially, when they believe revolution to be quite possible.) More to the point, however, such an interpretation would be incompatible with reality, with the actual history of revolutionary struggles in the imperialist countries.

The Fourth International is convinced that this historic detour of world revolution through the less developed countries is gradually nearing its end; the trend clearly shifted with the general strike and massive crisis in France in May 1968. We are firmly convinced that the urban proletariat will play—*is* playing—an ever more predominant role in the world revolutionary process. This contention should not be seen as a purely 'geographic' observation. It is not only that there will be revolutionary explosions in highly industrialized, imperialist countries; in a number of semi-colonial countries and in many of the bureaucratized workers' states, the proletariat has now emerged (or is rapidly emerging) as the absolute majority of the active population and will therefore provide the main combatants in the process of permanent revolution in the underdeveloped countries and of anti-bureaucratic political revolution in the workers' states.

The features of socialist revolutions centred primarily on the urban working class will differ widely from those of revolutions in relatively less developed countries, and in delineating those features we must base ourselves on real historical experiences if we want to avoid falling into pure speculation. Up to now, however, such revolutions, even if they were defeated, have occurred mainly in Europe, the only possible exception being the Chilean experience of the early seventies. Thus, to discuss the main features of revolutionary strategy largely in terms of their application to Western Europe today is not at all to fall victim to any sort of 'Eurocentrism', but is simply to strive to make the discussion as concrete as possible. The historical laboratory of urban-based proletarian revolutionary struggle has been Europe, and the countries in which objective conditions and the level of working-class consciousness make the prospects for socialist revolution most immediate are also in Europe, particularly southwestern Europe.

It is for this reason that much of the theoretical work of the Fourth International in recent years has been concentrated on Europe. It must be kept in mind, however, that our analysis—and the strategy based on it— is applicable not only in Europe, but also in North America, Japan, Australia, and the more industrialized under-developed countries, such as Brazil, Argentina, Mexico, and South Korea. We are quite convinced that coming years will see pre-dominantly proletarian revolutions not only in Europe, but also outside it. In that sense, a discussion of revolutionary strategy centred on Europe is not at all 'Eurocentric', for its objective is to refine a strategy of struggle that will also be indispensable else-where. But if that strategy is to be scientific—in other words, based on real experience—the discussion that produces it must hinge on reality itself, and that means a discussion about Western Europe in the first place.

The 'Model' of October

This raises a closely related question. You mentioned that even the Russian revolution provides only a partial exception to the observation that all revolutions so far have occurred in relatively backward countries. One of the accusations frequently made against the revolutionary Left, and especially the Fourth International, is precisely that it mechanically superimposes onto the reality of the advanced capitalist countries of Western Europe a 'model' derived from the Russian revolution: breakdown of the state, rise of soviets, dual power, marginalization of reformists, and development of the clash between soviet power and bourgeois power to the point of insurrection. However, the argument runs, the social formations in question are in reality so different that it is as senseless to superimpose this Bolshevik schema as it would be to apply a Maoist model of protracted guerrilla warfare, or a Guevarist or Vietnamese model. Hence, the specificity of the capitalist societies of Western Europe requires an equally specific and different strategy for the conquest of power. What do you think of this?

There are several questions mixed up here. We must start by distinguishing between what is specifically Russian and what is universal in the 'schema' or 'model' of the Russian revolution. What was specifically Russian was not the duration of the revolutionary crisis, nor the soviet form of self-organization of the masses, nor the tactics utilized by the Bolsheviks to win a majority in the soviets, nor the concrete form of the decomposition of the bourgeois state. This is not a dogmatic assertion, but a conclusion drawn from the historical experience of more than half a century. All the features I have just listed, and quite a few others, can be found in the German revolution of 1917-23, in the Spanish revolution of 1936-7 and—in a more embryonic form—in the Portuguese revolutionary process of 1974-5. Early signs of their development can be seen too in the Italian events of 1920, in the revolutionary upsurge in Italy at the end of the Second World War, and even in May '68 in France. That is why we consider these to be the most likely forms of revolutionary crisis in Western Europe.

Similarly, the extent of decomposition of the Tsarist/bourgeois state apparatus in Russia between February and October 1917 is not at all peculiar to the Russian social formation. It is a phenomenon that recurred in all the revolutionary crises in Western Europe that I have mentioned—perhaps in different forms, but with the same, and sometimes with an even more pronounced dynamic. Thus, during 1975, the repressive forces in Portugal were more paralysed and the bourgeois state apparatus was in a more advanced stage of decomposition than was the Tsarist/bourgeois state apparatus at any time between February and October. Of course, I am not here denying the obviously far greater *intrinsic* strength and stability of the bourgeois state and social order in the West, *in normal times*. But, precisely, that strength is itself dependent upon the maintenance of that 'normality'. When social 'peace' is shattered, as in May '68 in France, for instance, that apparent strength is replaced by an evident vulnerability.

What was, indeed, peculiar to Russia was not the *ease* with which the Bolsheviks were able to seize power, but on the contrary the much greater *difficulties* they faced on the eve and above all on the morrow of the seizure of power—compared with the possibilities in the advanced capitalist countries of today. I am not trying to advance a paradox. Truly, the most striking feature of the critiques levelled against revolutionary Marxists by anti-Leninists and centrists is their attempt to ignore or blot out this obvious fact. The peculiarity of Russia lay above all in the limited weight of the working class in the total active population. This meant that the Bolsheviks could hold an absolute majority in the soviets, whilst remaining a political minority in the country—a situation which is unthinkable in an advanced capitalist country. In England, France, or Italy it would be impossible for a party to have 65 per cent of the votes in workers' councils elected in every town by universal suffrage, and at the same time to have only 20 or 30 per cent of the votes of the whole population. What would be the social basis of such a disparity? What was also peculiar to the Russian social formation was the existence of a huge peasant hinterland, which served as the rural base for the reconstruction of a counter-revolutionary army and for its attempts to reconquer the towns. The social structure of most West European countries makes this unthinkable as well.

Another peculiarity of the Russian social formation was the much lower degree of technical, cultural, and political preparation of the working class for the direct exercise of political and economic power than exists in the advanced capitalist countries. Yet another specific feature was the world context of the Russian revolution. International capitalism was then incomparably stronger than it is today: it had at its disposal infinitely greater economic, social, political, and even ideological resources, as well as an incomparably more extensive and secure international system of supports and credits. Thus, the Russian revolution was from the outset threatened with submergence by a counter-revolution basing itself on the passivity of the majority of the population and on an active minority not much smaller than the minority that supported the revolution. In addition, an armed international counter-revolution was ready to undertake an almost immediate military intervention, invading Russia with armies from six, seven, or eight different countries. Today, such operations are a little more difficult! In 1975 there was no 'descent' on Portugal by the Spanish regular army—let alone the French, German, or American regular armies. Nor do I think that a victorious revolution in Spain, Italy, or France will have to face anything of that kind in the first three or six months. The world has changed a great deal since 1917. Lenin himself said many times that the Italian, German, and British workers would do much better than the Russian. And in all the writings of the founders of the Third International, we find a constant concern to distinguish what was programmatic, theoretical, and universal in the October Revolution from what was conjunctural, determined by the difficult and unfavourable circumstances in which the Russian October occurred.

My own conclusion from the historical balance-sheet, then, may sound paradoxical: the 'Leninist schema', or what I see as the essence of Leninism—namely, the strategy that combines *State and Revolution*, the documents of the first four congresses of the Communist International, and what is valid in *Left-Wing Communism*—is much more applicable in the advanced capitalist countries of Europe than it ever was in Russia. In all likelihood, that strategy, which was not applied in its entirety or even to a very great extent in Russia, will be fully applied for the first time in Western Europe.

Revolutionary Crisis and Bourgeois Democracy

In contrast to all gradualist strategies, the revolutionary Marxist conception attributes a key role to the notion of revolutionary crisis. However, not all crises of bourgeois society are revolutionary, or even pre-revolutionary. Can you explain exactly what you understand by a revolutionary crisis in an advanced capitalist country? Could June '36 in France be characterized in that way? Or the Liberation? Or May '68?

There is a certain lack of precision in the relevant concepts used by the Marxist classics, and, despite the modest theoretical gains of recent years, the Fourth International has still not entirely eliminated this imprecision. Your question then is very much to the point. My answer will be only an approximation, since we still lack the

practical references that would allow us to settle the matter definitively. Let me begin by referring to the essential point developed by
Lenin. An impetuous rise of the mass movement does not in itself
create a revolutionary crisis. Such an upsurge gives rise to a *pre-
revolutionary* situation (or process), which may go a long way without developing into a revolutionary situation. A *revolutionary*
situation or crisis (the lack of precision is evident in our identification of the two for the time being) requires the combination of the
impetuous rise of the mass movement with the real inability of the
possessing class, the bourgeoisie, to rule. In Lenin's brilliant formulation, a revolutionary crisis breaks out 'when the "lower classes"
no longer want to be ruled in the old way, and when the "upper
classes" cannot carry on ruling in the old way'.

We must obviously interpret the expression 'cannot carry on
ruling' not in the general historical, but in the conjunctural sense
that the 'upper classes' lose the material possibility of exercising
power. Let me illustrate this by a very 'provocative' example (which
has long been the subject of a debate amongst revolutionaries). In
May '68, there was not a really revolutionary situation, since the
Gaullist regime was not so paralysed that it could not go on ruling.
At no point did De Gaulle lose the capacity for political initiative. He
was thrown off course and temporarily immobilized by the changed
relation of forces. He was shrewd enough not to take on the
extremely powerful mass movement with a frontal assault—which
could have provoked a revolutionary situation! But he never lost the
capacity for political manoeuvre and initiative. He waited for his
hour (or almost the exact minute) to strike, and when this came it was
clear at once that—due to the complicity of the reformist leadership
of the French Communist Party—he was in a position to assert his
power throughout the country.

A revolutionary crisis appears when the bourgeoisie loses this
capacity for initiative and assertion of its political authority.
Whence does it derive? This is the real problem. It is difficult for us
today, with so rich an experience behind us, to reduce all the major
instances of revolutionary crisis in Europe—Russia 1917, Germany
1918-19, Hungary 1919, Spain 1936-7, Yugoslavia 1941-4, perhaps
even Portugal 1975, and the list is not exhaustive—to a single
common denominator. However, we can isolate two or three basic
factors.

First, a highly advanced stage of decomposition of the repressive apparatus of the state machine. This is an altogether decisive element in the loss of authority and initiative by the bourgeoisie. It may be due to a war or to the disintegrating effects on important sections of the army of a partially miscarried coup d'état, as in Spain. Or it may be the result of a general strike or workers' uprising of such great moral and political power that it disintegrates the army from within, as happened in the days following the Kapp putsch in Germany in 1920. *Second* (the positive side of the same coin), a generalization or at least broad development of organs of workers' and popular power to the point where a regime of dual power exists, with the same impact on the repressive apparatus. The bourgeois state apparatus is obviously completely paralysed once the workers' and people's councils are strong enough for a major part of the public services to identify with them. If the staff of the banks reject the orders of the finance minister or of the governor of the Central Bank in favour of the workers' council of the banking sector, then the whole administration is paralysed. It is the same with the transport sector, and so on. If the phenomenon is widely extended, to include even sectors of the police, it is clear that what is involved is a total paralysis of the bourgeois state apparatus and of the bourgeoisie's capacity for centralized political initiatives.

However, it is the *third*, politico-ideological dimension to the mounting crisis which interests us most, because it has hitherto been so neglected. *There must be a crisis of legitimacy of the state institutions in the eyes of the great majority of the working class.* Unless this majority identifies with a new, rising legitimacy, then a revolutionary development of the crisis is highly unlikely. I do not say that it is ruled out, for the uneven development of class consciousness can give rise to some strange and surprising combinations. However, if we use the term 'legitimacy' in its most general sense, then the mere fact that the masses no longer recognize themselves in a government elected by universal suffrage—and perhaps reflecting a majority of two or three years, or even six months previously—does not suffice to create a revolutionary crisis. It is a governmental or ministerial crisis, or at most a crisis of the regime, but it is not yet a genuinely revolutionary crisis. For that there must be a further ideological, moral dimension whereby the masses begin to reject the legitimacy of the institutions of the bourgeois state. And that can come about only through profound experiences of struggle and a very sharp—though not necessarily violent or bloody—clash between these institutions and the immediate revolutionary aspirations of the masses.

The way in which a revolutionary crisis appears is closely linked to such phenomena. Look, for example, at the extremely complex French situation in June 1936, about which Trotsky's judgements were not false, but rather incomplete. (No doubt I will be accused of revisionism on this score, but that does not bother me—Marxism is a science, and this kind of question must be discussed scientifically and not dealt with peremptorily by appeals to authority.) Can one say that the masses unreservedly supported the Popular Front government? Of course not. If that had been the whole story, there would have been no general strike and the masses would have entrusted the Socialist Prime Minister Léon Blum with the application of his programme. The launching of the general strike expressed a clear element of mistrust: for some it was just a question of giving the Blum government 'a helping hand', a push from behind, but that push took on such force that it called into question the whole time-scale, and even the will of the newly elected ministers to apply the programme. Was there an objective tendency for the leaderships of the Socialist Party, the Communist Party, and the trade unions to be outflanked? Clearly the occupation of the factories, expressing a spontaneous rejection of the capitalist system, went far beyond the programme of the Popular Front—a programme which in any case was more moderate than that of today's Union of the Left, as far as its challenge to private property was concerned.

However, all that I have just said, which can be found in Trotsky's analyses, is still rather incomplete, since it leaves untouched the undeniable fact that June '36 not only came off, but was also *over-come* with baffling ease. When you see millions of workers occupy their factories, objectively posing the eradication of private property and of the bosses' rights over the means of production, and then you see the way in which after the Matignon agreements they nearly all accepted a mere combination of immediate economic reforms with the implementation of the Popular Front programme, you need a further explanation of this retreat. What was absolutely decisive were the parliamentary and electoralist illusions and the lack of an alternative political solution with any real credibility. The spontaneous action of the workers developed by leaps and bounds; but the partial development of consciousness was not enough to lead them to question the legitimacy of the institutions of bourgeois democracy and oppose to them institutions created by the working class itself. Thus it is no accident that there was no generalization of soviets in June '36. (Those who try automatically to identify strike committees, often set up by the trade unions, with soviets are making a big mistake. They are confusing what could have been the embryo of a movement of workers' councils with the culmination of that movement; a preliminary, preparatory stage with a situation of generalized dual power.)

Well, that is my not altogether satisfactory attempt at an analysis. Our concepts are still rather imprecise, even if we are approaching a greater rigour. Once again, all this must be studied in the light of the historical experiences in Western Europe since 1917 and a thorough balance-sheet drawn up, categorizing, classifying, and comparing the revolutionary and pre-revolutionary situations. I think that it is by this historico-genetic method that we will succeed, rather than by an abstract attempt to work out concepts that may well be challenged by the next historical experiences. It is only the balance-sheet of history and revolutionary practice that will teach us to think more correctly.

So you think that when Trotsky wrote of June '36 'the French revolution has begun', he was hopelessly wide of the mark?

Trotsky himself revised his judgement when he later said of June '36 that it was a mere caricature of the February revolution in Russia. So his first assessment was certainly incomplete. We know ourselves from May '68 that when a pre-revolutionary situation arises, revolutionaries are faced with a dual obligation and a dual task. On the one hand, they must analyse what is happening in as cool and objective a way as possible. On the other hand, they are obviously not passive spectators—they intervene in the situation in order to change it. Any self-respecting revolutionary organization which is more than a mere sideline sect has to attempt to change the pre-revolutionary situation into a revolutionary one. It strives to develop the potential for workers' councils and other forms of self-organization inherent in the situation.

Of course, there is a certain contradiction between this organizational and political task and the job of the analyst and historian. The former is a dynamic attempt to unblock and change the situation, whereas the latter is descriptive, purely analytic, and thus more static. When Trotsky said 'The French revolution has begun', he was not just saying 'I really hope the French revolution has begun', but also 'Revolutionaries are able to and must intervene in this kind of general strike in order to transform it into a revolution'. We completely agree with that position: it was possible to do that in June '36 as it was in May '68. We therefore accuse the reformists, Stalinists, and centrists of not having done that—they who had infinitely greater resources than us in the existing political and organizational balance of forces. Their failure to do it does slightly modify our later assessment of what took place; but one cannot conclude from the fact that the French revolution had not begun that it was not possible. For us, the uneven development of class consciousness does not have a purely spontaneous aspect, independent of the intervention of the subjective factor; it also involves a whole area of possibility, determined by the political forces of the workers' movement, the relation of forces between the traditional leaderships and the revolutionary minorities, and the responsibility of those who are in a position to push forward events but do not do so. We do not dissolve that responsibility in over-objectivist analyses.

What about the Liberation?

That is a more complex question. First of all, you cannot place under a single general heading—'the Liberation'—the experiences in Yugoslavia, Greece, Italy, France, and Belgium, not to mention Denmark, Holland, and other countries. The differential development of the resistance movements gave rise to widely varying relations of forces. Second, Marxists must take great care in assessing the level of consciousness of the masses—the extreme complexity and unevenness of which can lead dogmatic thinkers to lose their bearings. It is true—and I know this from my own experience of debates with Social Democrats and centrists during the occupation—that it was difficult to call upon the working masses of Western Europe to rise up immediately against the allied imperialist powers. The treacherous policy of the Social Democratic and

Stalinist leaders, and of the leaders of the reconstituted trade-union federations, had been firmly within the ideological framework of the alliance of 'democratic nations' against the 'totalitarian countries'; they had thus induced a degree of identification between Anglo-American and French imperialism and the democratic cause, or even the cause of some kind of transition to socialism. However, it is also the case that the broad-based, intense mobilizations in some countries—especially Yugoslavia, Greece, and Italy, and to a slightly lesser extent France—possessed an inner logic that made it possible to challenge capitalism and the bourgeois state, and above all to take initiatives in the construction of a popular power from below. Such initiatives could have led to the generalization of revolutionary situations of dual power.

I do not think that an immediate struggle for power was possible in countries like France as soon as the Nazi front collapsed. Nor do I think that we can treat as insignificant the presence of American troops, which has been held up as the sole, irrefutable argument by the Stalinists and which revolutionaries have tended to dismiss a little too lightly. The nearest we can get to a correct formulation is this: during the liberation struggles, it was possible to develop factory occupations and take-overs, to form local organs of popular power, and above all to bring about the general arming of the masses, in such a way as to generalize situations of dual power and open up the possibility of a subsequent seizure of power.

We should not forget that the presence of American troops was limited in time and that the American soldiers brought strong pressure to bear for their return. Moreover, even without any pre-existing situation of dual power, the fluctuations in the political conjuncture brought about highly explosive crises. The most important of these was in Italy in 1948, when, in response to the attempted assassination of Togliatti on 14 July, the masses went well beyond a general protest strike and occupied factories, railway stations, electric power stations, etc., thus demonstrating that they instinctively posed the question of power. If workers' councils had already existed and if a part of the proletariat had been armed, then July 1948 could have opened up an extremely deep revolutionary crisis in Italy. Such a development would have been possible in France as well—but of course with the aid of 'ifs' one can rewrite the whole of world history!

It has been argued that what was decisive in this period was the weight of international factors, of US imperialism, and that even if a situation of dual power had arisen in a strategically more important country of Western Europe, it could only have ended in a heavy defeat of the working class.

I am not at all sure of that. There are obviously so many unknown factors underlying that kind of question that it is difficult to give an entirely satisfactory answer—we enter the realm of speculation and counter-speculation. However, I think that people who were in the Communist Parties at that time (and who have a guilt complex which they certainly need to assuage) generally underestimate the following factors: the crisis, reaching the point of mutiny, within the US Army; the desire of the American soldiers to go home as quickly as possible; the pressure of the war in the Pacific, which was not yet over; the necessity for US imperialism to establish complete control over the Pacific and Japan in order to assure its world hegemony, which meant that it could not keep the bulk of its troops in Western Europe.

I think the enormous prestige of the Soviet Union and of the Red Army is also underestimated, as well as the extreme political, military, and moral weakness of the European bourgeoisie. I repeat, the question of whether or not it was possible to seize power is for me a false question. *What is clear is that the relationship of forces could have been infinitely more favourable to the workers' movement if there had been a communist leadership that was not prepared to liquidate the gains of the mass resistance, to reconstruct the bourgeois state, and to capitulate before the exigencies of bourgeois economic reconstruction.* Had such a leadership existed, a situation of dual power would have been created which could well have borne fruit at a later stage: 1947, 1948, or 1949, it is hard to say exactly when.

The responsibility of the Stalinist leadership in 1944-7 is therefore overwhelming, even if we abstract from the mood of the masses. In fact, the real 'ultra-leftists' play into the hands of the Stalinists when they argue that a working class that was so patriotic and nationalist was in any case incapable of struggling for power. At bottom such arguments allow the CP leaders to escape their responsibilities. 'Priority to production'; 'the strike is the weapon of the trusts'; the calls of Maurice Thorez, leader of the French Communist Party, for 'one army, one state, one police force'; the disarming of the partisans; participation in government—it was this whole criminal policy of the CP leaderships in France, Italy, or Belgium which liquidated the clear possibilities of revolutionary development inherent in the very deep crisis of the bourgeois order. The objective crisis of the bourgeoisie was much more profound in 1944 than it is today. Western Europe was a grouping of economically disorganized countries which had been bled dry and where nothing worked properly. Today it is very hard to imagine that. It was much more similar to Germany in 1918-19 than to present-day Europe. Of course, I am not saying that such a crisis is the 'most useful' in bringing on a revolutionary situation and a 'classical' seizure of power by the working class, but the depth of the crisis should not be forgotten. If there had been an adequate and bold revolutionary leadership, it could have compensated for a lower level of consciousness and preparation of the working class than exists today.

In every advanced capitalist country, the masses have shown a strong attachment to bourgeois representative democracy, to 'formal democracy'. It is exactly as if the popular masses had themselves taken over the bourgeois precept: 'The democratic republic may be an abominable regime, but it is surely the least abominable of them all'. This attachment is especially strong in France, where the parliamentary regime and the democratic gains were not concessions shrewdly granted to the masses, but the result of revolutionary popular struggles. This adherence of the masses to the principles of bourgeois representative democracy, and even to the institutions and procedures which embody it, constitutes a serious obstacle on the road to the destruction of the bourgeois state and the establishment of socialist democracy. Can you explain the roots of these democratic illusions amongst the masses, and how they can be overcome?

There is an ambiguity in bourgeois parliamentary democracy which the bourgeoisie has succeeded in exploiting to the full, with the obvious and indispensable complicity of the reformist leaderships, who thus bear an overwhelming historical responsibility. Little by little, this ambiguity has been converted into one of the main ideological props of bourgeois domination in those countries where the working class has become the great majority of the nation. The ambiguity consists in the following. In most cases after the First World War, and sometimes even later in the 1930s or 1940s, the masses began to identify their *democratic freedoms*—which are an absolute gain that we aim not merely to defend but to consolidate and deepen within the workers' state—with *bourgeois-democratic, parliamentary state institutions*. Although it is true that reformist leaderships bear overwhelming responsibility for this, they could nevertheless not have had the effect they did without a specific conjunction of historical circumstances. Of major importance was the experience of fascism; so too was that of Stalinism, both through the reformist turn of the Comintern in 1934 and through the repulsive example of the regimes of Eastern Europe and the USSR.

Also significant has been a certain political maturing of the workers' movement, which now faces a changed and enriched political problematic. It is no longer preoccupied solely with demands for the reduction of the working day and for protection against unemployment and sickness, or with the general question of universal suffrage and freedom of association. The organized workers' movement and important sections of the working class today take up a wide range of questions concerning commercial and financial policy, infrastructural development, employment, education, etc. At the same time, since the movement has increasingly neglected the problems of education of the working class and proletarian democracy, bourgeois politics has stepped in to fill the vacuum and thus articulated the choices and alternative policies that confront and concern the masses. This has made little difference in a country like the United States, where the masses are not very concerned with politics. But in countries where there is a much higher level of mass interest, since it is only in the bourgeois political arena of parliament and elections that these questions can be raised and decided upon, this politicization has undoubtedly contributed to the process of identification we mentioned earlier.

I have stressed elsewhere the negative side of this. The characteristic feature of bourgeois democracy is the tendency towards atomization of the working class—it is individual voters who are counted, and not social groups or classes who are consulted. Moreover, the economic growth of the past twenty-five years has brought into the heart of the working class consumption habits—most clearly symbolized by the automobile and the television—that serve to reprivatize leisure activity and thus to reinforce the atomization of the class. The time has gone when political questions were discussed *collectively* in the *Maisons du Peuple*—as was still the case in the thirties; or when working-class newspapers were read and discussed collectively. Of course, this reprivatization of leisure activity can lead by a historical detour to a higher level of class consciousness. Workers, especially young workers, read much more and have a higher level of culture. Future possibilities of real proletarian democracy may thus be strengthened. But for a long period this reprivatization has assisted the identification between bourgeois democracy and the defence of democratic freedoms. Herein lies the basic source of ambiguity.

This answer to your first question clears the ground for the second: how can we overcome this obstacle? Generally speaking, we must seek to bring about a radical break between, on the one hand, the defence of the democratic freedoms and self-activity of the working class—everything that is, to the greatest extent possible, free, broad, spontaneous, and self-determined activity of the masses—and, on the other hand, the institutions of the bourgeois state. There is, of course, something of the chicken and the egg in this, for it is precisely the revolutionary situation that can make this break not only possible, but even relatively simple and inevitable. That is the lesson of the Portuguese revolutionary process of 1975, and it will be similarly affirmed in the coming revolutions in Spain, Italy, and France.

It is irresponsible—even criminal—for revolutionaries to seek to oppose the concept of 'dictatorship of the proletariat' or 'people's power' to democratic freedoms. On the contrary, any tactic or initiative of revolutionaries that allows the masses to learn, through their own experience, *that the extension of their own freedom conflicts with the restrictive institutions of bourgeois democracy* is not only extremely useful but even indispensable. The most symbolic and synthetic example is that of freedom of the press; it is here that the Portuguese revolution was blown off course and that there was great confusion which the bourgeoisie and Social Democracy were able to turn to their advantage.

What lessons should we draw from initiatives such as those of the *República* or *Radio Renascença* workers? Certainly not that we want to suppress the right of any political party to publish its own papers in a regime of soviet democracy. There can be absolutely no question of that. What is at issue is the *broadening* of the freedom of the press to include print-shop workers, radio-station workers, as well as workers' commissions and groups within every workplace. They too need the right to express themselves freely in the press—even if they do not have the means to express themselves with the same regularity as political parties. In other words, our aim is to *break the monopoly* of private ownership, and even of political party ownership, not in the sense of taking away anyone's present right of expression, but in the sense of extending that right to others. Thus, despite all the errors committed by the centrist and ultra-left leaderships in these two experiences, it remains an extremely positive and democratic achievement that there was a broadcasting station able to report all the workers' struggles and publicize the demands and resolutions of any working-class group without being controlled by the censorship of the government or of a party headquarters. This pointed in the same direction as the paper *Izvestia* created during the Russian revolution—which, after all, was initially simply an organ in which all the soviets could freely express themselves, irrespective of their political affiliation or majority composition.

Considerable political skill and the authority of a vanguard party are required to use examples of this kind to show the masses in practice that the revolution extends democratic freedoms; to show that it is the defenders of private property, the absolute authority of parliament, and the monopoly position of political parties who in fact seek to restrict these freedoms and to prevent the masses from gaining a greater degree of liberty, political weight, and power than they have in a bourgeois-democratic republic. The conclusive demonstration of this can take place only in a fairly long period of dual power, during which such experiences enter the consciousness of the masses and are, so to speak, internalized by a sufficient number of workers. However, once this is achieved, then what we referred to as a possible break becomes a reality. This is not at all a utopian blue-print, but the concrete way a soviet legitimacy will be created that is more deeply rooted in the convictions and consciousness of the masses than bourgeois-democratic legitimacy.

Only a real experience, going beyond resolutions, newspaper articles, and propaganda speeches, can accomplish this. Thousands upon thousands of workers must grasp, on the basis of their own experience, that the practice of proletarian democracy cannot be confined within the limits of bourgeois democracy. That brings us back to the question of the duration of dual power, and here the historical record forces us to regard the Russian experience as exceptional. A period of six or seven months is much too short for a proletariat like that of Western Europe to progressively abandon the legitimacy of bourgeois democracy in favour of the new, higher legitimacy of proletarian democracy. *A longer period of dual power will probably be needed, which may be partial and discontinuous and may stretch over several years.* In Germany, for example, the workers' councils lasted only a few months as organs of political power, whereas the factory councils partially survived for several years with powers going beyond those of the legal authorities. And in 1923 the German communists were almost unanimous in considering this remnant of 1918-19 to be the main organ of development of class consciousness during the revolutionary upsurge; they also thought that it would be around these organs that it would become possible once again to place the seizure of power by the German working class on the order of the day. The industrially advanced countries of Western Europe will probably throw up a whole range of such variations and combinations.

Finally, I would like to stress the absolutely decisive importance here of workers' control. Although the relation between proletarian and bourgeois democracy—in other words, the problem of the state—appears to revolutionaries and Marxist theorists as a supremely political problem, in fact the everyday mediations of real pedagogic value for the working class are not purely political. Even the freedom of the press has never been a pure political abstraction for the working class. It is the freedom to say things of immediate interest to the workers. This nearly always revolves around their immediate preoccupations, their daily lives, their demands, struggles, and experiences. Such 'freedom of the press' is not an absolute, abstract freedom to say whatever comes into one's head, but the concrete freedom to *give an account* of concrete things—of struggles, demands, and fighting goals. This is related to the key role of workers' control in a period of dual power, since it trains the class for the exercise of power.

Of course, we are neither Economists nor spontaneists, and we understand the embryonic, fragmented, inadequate, and thus almost utopian character of workers' control. Nevertheless, it constitutes an invaluable *practical training*. Workers' control is not concerned merely with the minutiae of the firm; once it is extended to certain vital sectors, in particular to the public services, its revolutionary potential becomes enormous. Workers' control over the banks, public transport, power stations, and television—just to give four examples—will shake to its foundations the whole daily life of a modern nation. It is through this kind of apprenticeship that the workers will continually run up against the restrictive and repressive authority of the bourgeois-democratic state, even if it is 'governed' by workers' parties, and that they will learn the limits of this bourgeois democracy and the need to replace it.

The Portuguese far left let slip an enormous ideological opportunity. After all, it is no accident that when Soares, the one-time frenzied agitator for the freedom of the press, dropped his mask, he had to start attacking 'anarcho-populism' or 'anarcho-spontaneism' —in other words the initiatives of the masses. He began to preach the strengthening of discipline and state authority or, to call things by their right name, *repression*. In a revolutionary situation, the workers must learn that the real debate is not between democracy and dictatorship, but between the limited and repressive character of bourgeois democracy and the extension of democratic freedoms by the initiative and authority of the masses. Once that debate is won, the break of the masses with bourgeois institutions no longer seems as difficult and unrealizable as it did at first. But for that to happen, revolutionaries have to apply intelligent tactics, and not engage in senseless, ultra-left attacks against 'social-fascism'.

The Experience of Soviet Democracy

Perhaps another reason for these democratic illusions is that the superiority of direct soviet democracy over representative bourgeois democracy has never been convincingly demonstrated in the eyes of the workers—either in propaganda or in practice. We are prone to speaking of soviet democracy as 'a thousand times higher than the most democratic forms of bourgeois democracy' (Lenin), but that can often seem to be begging the question. In what way does our critique of the formal character of bourgeois democracy not also apply, mutatis mutandis, to soviet democracy—since, so long as some kind of social and technical division of labour exists, it necessarily entails forms of representation and delegation? What emerges from a clear analysis of the first months of the Russian revolution is 1. that the rank-and-file delegates became very rapidly alienated from the general assemblies of the main soviets, including that of Petrograd (look, for example, at the constant appeals in the Soviet press for delegates to attend assembly meetings); 2. that power underwent an enormous concentration in the executive bodies at the top. One could list a whole series of indications that a system of soviet democracy based on such a form of delegation of power also lends itself to the political expropriation and manipulation of the masses and to the usurpation of power. To what extent is the Fourth International aware of these dangerous, formal aspects of such a system of soviet democracy, and how does it seek to guard against them and assure as real a democracy as possible?

First of all, the argument that the superiority of soviet democracy 'has never been shown in practice' is slightly anachronistic. Of course, the present generation of workers has had no such experience, and it can sometimes seem artificial to juxtapose what exists, however imperfect it may be, with what has not appeared before one's eyes. Nevertheless, we should keep in mind that the international working class has lived through several highly developed experiences of direct democracy, which has stood up to the test of practice and demonstrated its superiority over bourgeois democracy. Let me mention just one of many examples. Between July 1936 and May 1937, the Spanish and especially Catalan committees developed the experience of direct democracy beyond the limits of the bourgeois regime in numerous fields—in particular, in local administration, industry, public supply, and health—and were felt to be great achievements by the Spanish masses. It is not widely known that under the administration of the workers industrial production grew markedly and that the functioning of restaurants, theatres, education, health, and justice in Barcelona, stimulated by—among others—our ex-comrade Andres Nin, was a remarkable example of broad mass participation in the carrying out of appointed tasks. A considerable body of literature exists on this extremely advanced experience of proletarian democracy (and not just in the semi-mythological writings of anarchist authors).

Furthermore, to conclude from the lack of contemporary examples that a particular orientation is difficult if not impossible amounts in effect to rejecting the possibility of all revolutionary *innovation*—someone after all does have to be first, in order to begin something new! What precedent could the Russian workers have had before their eyes in 1917? What was the precedent for the Paris Commune? Every revolution is always an eminently innovative experience, and there is no reason to be frightened of that. The continuity that really counts and makes our aim a realistic one is the continuity between the day-to-day class struggle, in the maturity of capitalism as in its decline, and the revolutionary situation. The masses prepare for revolution much less by studying previous historical experiences or by comparing events in other countries than by their experience of struggle today before the outbreak of a revolutionary crisis—by the development of higher forms of self-organization and of anti-capitalist demands, by strikes and factory occupations. The direct democracy of workers' councils will develop more out of that than out of historical comparisons of a theoretical nature.

More serious is the argument that direct soviet democracy itself bears certain elements of indirect democracy, in that it is based on the delegation of power and on a pyramidal structure. I think that we need to utilize the historical experience and progress in political theory of the last half-century in order to develop the answers of Lenin in *State and Revolution*. There are three basic safeguards that *reduce* the force of the argument, although without eliminating it.

It should not be forgotten that, in the last analysis, the argument points up a *real contradiction* in the role of the workers' state as the last historical form of the state. It is a state form that begins at once to wither away, but it is no less a state form, that is to say, 'special bodies of men exercising repressive functions'. If we thought that the anarchist project was not utopian and that it was possible to leap straight from bourgeois society to a stateless society, then we would be the most convinced of anarchists. We are not anarchists because we think that it is impossible, for objective and subjective reasons, to bypass the stage of the workers' state, of the dictatorship of the proletariat. Moreover, the Spanish experience shows that an artificial attempt to avoid the centralization of *workers' power* does not lead to a situation of no power, but to the maintenance or reconstruction of *bourgeois power*, which is ten times more bureaucratic, repressive, and authoritarian.

Now, we are not blind to the limits of proletarian democracy, any more than was Lenin. In so far as the state does not wither away all at once, in so far as it survives, so too do bourgeois right and elements of bureaucracy survive. The experience of the Russian revolution, the nightmare of Stalinism, and the deepening of our understanding of the phenomenon of bureaucracy should alert us to the need for safeguards additional to those foreseen by Marx and Lenin: the eligibility of all to hold state posts, the possibility of recalling all delegates, the reduction of their earnings to the level of the average wage, and a more or less speedy rotation of delegates.

The first and perhaps most important of these three further safeguards is that the state of proletarian dictatorship must from the outset be a state that is beginning to break up. This is the concrete form of its withering away. What I mean by this is that the centralization of power is justifiable only for a certain narrowly demarcated range of problems. It should be the Congress of Workers' Councils that takes decisions concerning the allocation of national resources. For it is the working class that bears the sacrifice of not consuming a share of what it produces, so it is up to the working class to decide the extent of the sacrifice it is prepared to accept. But once it has been decided to devote 7, 10, or 12 per cent of national production to education or health, there is absolutely no need for state management of the education or health budgets. It is pointless for the Congress of Workers' Councils to take on this task of management, which can be much better assumed at the more democratic level of school or higher educational councils, and councils of medical staff and patients. The people who sit on these bodies will be different from those who are delegated to the Congress of Workers' Councils. This breaking up of the functions of the central state means that dozens of councils will be meeting at the same time and involving tens of thousands of people on a national and continental scale. And as the same kind of process will be occurring at the regional and municipal level, this 'breaking up' will allow hundreds of thousands or even millions of people to participate in the direct exercise of power.

The second important safeguard is a much closer attention to the problem of the rotation of posts than was possible for the Bolsheviks, who were faced with a working class that was culturally underdeveloped and a minority of the population. In the industrially advanced countries, a much more radical application of the principle of rotation of posts will be possible than obtains, for example, in Yugoslavia. If this principle is strictly applied (for example, by prohibiting the election of the same delegate more than twice), then after a number of years a very large number of people indeed will have been involved in the exercise of power in the various congresses and other assemblies. The idea of the participation of all workers in the direct exercise of power will thus take on a concrete form.

Third, I have always had great reservations about the formulation: the social division of labour remains inevitable. I think that there is a lack of conceptual clarity involved here in the frequent conflation of the term 'social division of labour' with what I would call the 'occupational division of labour', or 'professionalization', or 'diversity of occupational activity'. The social division of labour refers to *qualitatively different social functions*, ultimately reducible to the functions of production and administration (or accumulation). Now, although the occupational division of labour cannot be overcome in the first phase of socialism, our aim is to begin immediately the overcoming of the *social* division of labour—that is the whole meaning of the term 'self-management'. And for that it is necessary to secure the adequate *material conditions*, rather than to speculate on the level of maturity, preparedness or unpreparedness of the working class, etc.

It is clear what these material conditions are. First, there must be a sweeping reduction in working time that will allow workers to enter the soviets and attend congresses. If they work eight or nine hours a day, plus two or three hours travelling time, they will not be able to be involved in management or administration. A long working day means the division of society into those who produce and those who manage; it inevitably means the survival of 'professional politicians' in the soviets. Only the reduction of the working day by half will create the conditions for a genuine democratic management, that is to say, the involvement of hundreds of thousands or millions of workers in the management of the economy and the state.

Another material condition is the breaking of the monopoly of information, which is itself only one facet of the monopoly of culture. Thanks to data processing, electronic computers, and television, it is today much easier than in Lenin's time to make information of all kinds available to everybody, and thus to make possible workers' management of the economy, the state, and society. This participation of workers will be made materially easier by the smashing of a whole series of cultural obstacles to it, through the lengthening of the period of school education, the revolutionizing of education, the elimination of the division between a youth spent at school and 'adulthood', etc.

A further condition will require considerable innovation: the socialist constitution must allocate the majority of posts (at least in bodies exercising central state power) to persons engaged in productive activity—not only to male workers, but also to women. This is an indispensable safeguard, because ultimately bureaucratization is based on the professionalization of management functions. The only way to check this is for a majority of those exercising central political power to continue working in production, which is possible, of course, only if it is accompanied by the breaking up of management functions that I mentioned earlier. Once all these measures are put into practice, the basis of bureaucratization will be considerably reduced.

An additional problem that should be touched upon is whether a socialist revolution can go together with a rise rather than a decline of the productive forces. This question was already prominent in the debates between Bolsheviks and Mensheviks and has continued to occupy revolutionaries, centrists, and ultra-lefts over the past fifty-five years. Many dogmatic theorizations of the Russian experience of 1917-19, especially by Bukharin but also by Bordiga and other revolutionary leaders of the period, rested on the assertion that a decline in the productive forces was inevitable during a socialist revolution. I will leave it to others to pronounce on 'the inevitable laws of history', but in the present, exceptionally favourable conditions for socialist revolution in Western Europe, such a hypothesis is not very credible. Unless there were an outbreak of nuclear war or a military intervention with large-scale bombing, there is no reason to suppose that a socialist revolution in Spain, Italy, or France would be accompanied by a decline in material production. On the contrary, the post-war development of the productive forces has confirmed that the industrial system constructed by the bourgeoisie conceals vast reserves for the expansion of production.

In fact, one of the main reasons for the decline of the productive forces after the October Revolution was the generalized withdrawal from and sabotage of production by the technical intelligentsia and managerial staff. Engels, by the way, had expressed great fear that this would be a more or less universal feature of socialist revolutions, even in industrialized countries. But as many have been pointing out ever since May 1968, this is most unlikely in the West today, for there has been a radical change in the nature of the labour performed by the technical intelligentsia, which has been increasingly integrated into the production process itself as a result of the third technological revolution. As the intelligentsia is increasingly proletarianized, technical workers become more and more subject to the laws of the labour market and therefore tend to identify, first in practical behaviour and then in consciousness, with other sellers of labour-power. The highly unionized intelligentsia has participated in great strike actions and even radical anti-capitalist movements in several imperialist countries, May '68 in France being a prime example. It follows that the proletariat today, which encompasses a significant portion of the intelligentsia—much more than the Russian proletariat in 1917 or even the German proletariat in 1918 or 1923—will be immeasurably more capable of maintaining and even expanding production and productivity regardless of the behaviour of the former owners and factory managers.

Thus it is not at all utopian to anticipate a sweeping reduction in the length of the working day simultaneously with an increase in material production. I am convinced that the accomplishment of these tasks will be greatly facilitated by the introduction of workers' management, the development of workers' initiative, and the flowering of the spirit of self-organization and creativity amongst the broad masses in the field of technology and the organization of labour. In the bourgeois theory of the firm and the industrial unit, there is an optimum level of performance which is never identical to the maximum level (and the capitalists have themselves learnt this to their cost!). Once this optimum level is reached, once industrial units become excessively large, the *faux frais* of production grow faster than the unit cost of production falls. There is a sudden flood of bad decisions as the ability to form a global view is lost. Planned self-management, based on the self-activity of the workers, will absorb and overcome these experiences of bourgeois management in a way that is impossible for the capitalists themselves.

Under the leadership of Lenin, the Bolsheviks did not always counterpose soviet institutions to representative democratic institutions (the National Assembly elected by universal suffrage in geographical areas). Despite the capacity of the Constituent Assembly for exclusive political centralization, Lenin fought after the April Theses right up to October, against the equivocations of the bourgeois government, for a political system articulating soviets at the base to Constituent Assembly at the top. (Collected Works, Vol. 24, p. 99; Vol. 26, p. 200.) Zinoviev and Kamenev held a similar position, stressing moreover that such a system would provide a national body with a legitimacy that the Central Executive Committee of the Soviets did not possess. That was also the position of Rosa Luxemburg after the overthrow.

Your question strikes me as exceedingly abstract, pitched at the level of general principles. I know of no Marxist study that approaches the problem in such an abstract form, not even Luxemburg's to which you refer. For us, as for Luxemburg, the real problem is *the coupling of democratic freedoms with the soviet form of organization*. Here historical experience shows not only that the two are compatible, but that they must be combined with one another. A soviet form of state, involving the direct exercise of power by the workers—and not by the party substituting itself for them—is inconceivable without the maintenance and broadening of democratic freedoms beyond the level existing under a capitalist regime. Similarly, such freedoms are indispensable for proletarian democracy within a single revolutionary party and *a fortiori* in a multi-party system such as the Fourth International has envisaged since its adoption of the Transitional Programme in 1938.

In this connection, we should be aware that there are two aspects to the evolution of the Communist Parties in recent years, and that one of these is positive. This evolution is in fact taking place under a dual, contradictory pressure. On the one hand, these parties are bending to the pressure of the bourgeoisie and Social Democracy—

for example, in their abandonment of the concept of 'dictatorship of the proletariat'. We completely disagree with such concessions and continue to uphold the entire classical Marxist-Leninist polemic against the inadequacies, the formalism, the class character, and the indirect, oppressive, and severely truncated nature of bourgeois parliamentary democracy. *But the second dimension of this evolution represents a concession to the working class of Western Europe —a class which has developed a profoundly anti-bureaucratic consciousness in reaction to the Stalinist experience and does not want a repetition of Stalinism.* There we can only say 'bravo'!

When Marchais says that he is abandoning the word 'dictatorship' because it recalls Hitler and Pétain, the hypocrisy is quite transparent. No one in France or any other European country identifies the Communist Party with Hitler or Pétain. What he really means, but does not dare say out of sympathy for his former friends in the Soviet bureaucracy, is that when the masses of Western Europe hear the word 'communist dictatorship' they think not of Hitler or Pétain, but of Stalin, Hungary, and Czechoslovakia—in other words, of a bureaucratic dictatorship which they do not want.

In the tradition of Marx's writings on the Paris Commune and of Lenin's *State and Revolution*, the dictatorship of the proletariat is for us a dictatorship that consolidates and deepens all democratic freedoms—the freedom of the press, the right to demonstrate, the freedom of association and of political parties, the right to strike, and trade-union independence from the state. Naturally, such a way of posing things is also an advance on the model of the Soviet Union under Lenin and Trotsky. In any case, those comrades never made a model or norm out of their pioneering achievements, which were the first attempt at proletarian dictatorship under very unfavourable circumstances. On the contrary, Lenin repeated dozens of times that one must not construct dogmas. It is this realistic and lucid, flesh-and-blood Lenin who should serve as our inspiration, not those formulas also to be found in his writings which justify the temporary defensive measures taken by the Russian revolution by raising them to the level of theorems, or even axioms.

Let me take the concrete example of political parties, which is both important and relevant today. What does Lenin say on this question in *The Proletarian Revolution and the Renegade Kautsky?* He says that it is no accident that neither the Bolshevik programme nor *State and Revolution* advocates suppressing the right to vote of the bourgeoisie, for this is not a matter of principle under the proletarian dictatorship. He even adds ironically that the Cadets left the soviets of their own volition. The meaning of this is clear: the Cadets had a place in the soviets, and as long as they remained in them no one tried to drive them out. When they left in order to launch the civil war, of course that was quite another matter. When someone starts firing at you, you have to use all means to defend yourself including rifles. Give up shooting, Cadet gentlemen, and no one will drive you anywhere—that is the conclusion which can be drawn from this passage from Lenin.

We should be quite clear about the dynamic that would be unleashed if one were to insert into the soviet constitution of tomorrow the clause: 'Only workers' parties will be legally tolerated or recognized; bourgeois parties will be banned'. Not only the Stalinists and Mao-Stalinists—which is bad enough—but even certain pseudo-Trotskyists, who go around *very* light-mindedly dishing out labels of 'petty-bourgeois' and 'bourgeois', will start saying that the Social Democrats are a bourgeois party. The Communist Party, the party of 'social-imperialism', will also be defined as a bourgeois party. As for the Trotskyist organizations, they too will find plenty of people, including some donning 'Trotskyist' masks, who will accuse them of being 'petty-bourgeois' or even 'counter-revolutionary traitors'. The result will be that only the self-proclaimed 'revolutionary' organization, or only the one that is in agreement with the thoughts of Chairman Mao, will be 'genuinely' proletarian, even if it represents only a tiny minority.

Such a dynamic can assume terrifying proportions. Any real constitutional or institutional defence of the multi-party principle is impossible once you start introducing criteria that are subjective and subjectivist. The only *objective* criterion is that of *soviet legality*. Any party will be recognized that respects the socialist constitution *in practice*: it may have an anti-socialist programme and carry out anti-socialist propaganda, but it will not be permitted to throw bombs or organize civil war. Once it starts that, it will be outlawed. If the bourgeois parties content themselves with discussing and persuading people, we are quite confident that the working class of Western Europe is sufficiently strong and clear-thinking not to hand back the factories that it has seized from the bosses, simply as a result of skilful bourgeois propaganda. For us, ideas are the most effective means of waging the struggle against bourgeois ideology, which is merely strengthened by bans and other administrative measures. Our chosen weapons are the weapons of propaganda and education of the working class, and for us there is only one limit to the defence and extension of democratic freedoms under the proletarian dictatorship: the limit imposed by the need to prevent any attempted restoration *by force* of the exploitative regime of private property and bourgeois power. The dictatorship of the proletariat is a dictatorship to the extent that, as the *Communist Manifesto* puts it, it takes 'despotic measures' against private property and the bourgeois state, crushing the violence and power of the bourgeoisie. But it does not take despotic measures against bourgeois ideas or bourgeois parties which confine themselves to propaganda and 'counter-education'. On that level, the political superiority of Marxism, of the armed people in possession of economic power, seems to me quite adequate to prevent a return to capitalism.

If I have not answered the question about whether parliamentary organs are necessary, it is because I think that it is an *essentially tactical* matter. We should not treat it as a question of absolute principle, and it will not necessarily be answered in the same way in every country. If a parliamentary organ is used in an attempt to repress and 'roll back' the self-organization of the masses, then it is a clear instrument of counter-revolution and we have to take a position accordingly (such was the case in Portugal in 1975, as it was in Germany 1918 and in Russia after October 1917). It should not be forgotten that Rosa Luxemburg took a quite unambiguous position against the transfer of power to the Constituent Assembly in Germany. She—and the Spartacist delegates at the First Congress of Workers' and Soldiers' Councils—opposed the convocation of the Constituent Assembly, arguing instead for the maintenance of the sovereignty of the Congress of Councils as the only representative organ of power of the German working class. *But once that sovereignty is established, then it is not a question of principle whether there should be a parliamentary organ to deal with secondary matters*. Its usefulness is not all that clear to me, but the answer will depend on the national political tradition of various countries and on the role such an organ might play as an arena of struggle between the major cultural and ideological currents. What is essential is that political and economic power should be firmly and genuinely in the hands of the armed workers organized in soviets.

Trotsky's own thinking on this question underwent an unquestionable evolution, which we have to continue. Like Lenin, Trotsky combined two elements in the period of 1920-21. On the one hand, in order to defend soviet power in extremely difficult and dangerous conditions, they took decisions—with an iron determination that we can only approve of—which led them to introduce measures that broke in practice with soviet democracy, and they assumed full responsibility for this. Going further than Trotsky, Lenin declared in 1920 that the Soviet state was no longer a healthy workers' state, but a workers' state with bureaucratic deformations. He was absolutely lucid about this and did not aim to deceive anyone. Of course, one can discuss whether one particular measure or another was justified in the given conjuncture, but that is not the essential point. More important is that these measures were recognized, at least implicitly, as representing deformations, and not general rules. For example, neither the theses of the Third International on the dictatorship of the proletariat nor *State and Revolution* contain any mention of a one-party state. Or take another example: the interdiction of factions at the Tenth Congress of the Bolshevik Party. Manifestly, this measure was an exceptional one taken under the pressure of no less exceptional conditions. That it was in contradiction with the tradition of Bolshevism and the practice of the Communist International is shown by the fact that the Bolsheviks themselves never attempted to establish it as a norm within the International.

However, there was also a second, infinitely more dangerous aspect to their actions in this period. This was their attempt to give some of these measures a general theoretical foundation that is quite unacceptable. For example, Trotsky wrote in 1921 that soviet democracy is not a fetish, and that the party can exercise power not only in the name of the working class, but even in exceptional circumstances *against* the will of the majority of the class. We should be incomparably more cautious before adopting formulations of that kind, because we know from experience that in such a situation it is a bureaucracy rather than a revolutionary minority that will come to exercise power against the majority of workers—a fact that Lenin and Trotsky were themselves to recognize a year later. As far as theory is concerned, the year 1921 was the nadir of the Bolsheviks' history and Lenin and Trotsky made a whole number of errors.

Trotsky always displayed a pronounced reticence to make self-criticisms of actions he had taken when he was in power. But there is evidence that he did become aware of the errors of 1920-21. Near the end of his life, he wrote in a letter to Marceau Pivert that whatever view one takes of the correctness of the ban on factions in the party, it was clear that it assisted the establishment of the Stalinist regime and the bureaucratic dictatorship in the USSR. What is that if not a *de facto* self-criticism? Moreover, when Trotsky said in the *Transitional Programme* of 1938 that he was in favour of freedom for all soviet parties, he had undoubtedly drawn the conclusion that the lack of such a constitutional right opens the door to the use of the argument 'You are a potential party' against any faction, and of 'You are a potential faction' against any current or tendency. In that direction, it is not only socialist democracy that is stifled, but also inner-party democracy. In the period 1936-8, Trotsky had become fully aware of the inner logic of such positions, and was implicitly undertaking a serious self-criticism. In our own thinking on the question, we should not let ourselves be restricted by an uncritical defence of all the decisions taken under the leadership of Lenin and Trotsky.

I think that the Bolsheviks were wrong in 1921. They should not have banned the Menshevik Party; they should not have banned the anarchist organizations; and they should not have suppressed multiple slates in elections to the soviets after the end of the Civil War. The paradox is quite striking: during the Civil War the Bolsheviks allowed themselves the luxury of an opposition in the press and in the soviets, but once the war was over they made an error of judgement. They thought that the main danger following the introduction of the NEP was a political resurgence of the petty and medium bourgeoisie, which would threaten the restoration of capitalism in the short term. That was an error of conjunctural analysis, but it was no less an error. The peasantry was much too dispersed and demoralized to pose an immediate threat to soviet power. (Of course, in the long term, as the Left Opposition pointed out, this analysis was correct, and six years later, in 1927, the danger became acute.) But in 1921 the main danger was not bourgeois counter-revolution; it was the depoliticization of the working class and the rapid process of bureaucratization. The measures taken at that time assisted and developed that process. We should have the courage to recognize that this was an error and that the Opposition slogan of 1923 'Extend rather than reduce soviet democracy' was valid from 1921 onwards.

Dual Power and Workers' Governments

Unlike the Russian working class, the working class of the advanced capitalist countries of today has a tradition of mass trade-union and political organization and institutions with which it identifies. Moreover, the reformists, both Social Democratic and Stalinist, will fight against the development of soviets. Do you think that in spite of everything dual power will take on the soviet form, or that it may be expressed in other ways—through a bloc of left forces, or even through the trade unions?

Here we can base ourselves on lengthy historical experience, the lessons of which are absolutely clear and unambiguous. Whenever a revolutionary crisis has broken out in an industrially advanced country, where there is a working class at the height of its social, political, and economic maturity, we have witnessed the emergence of soviet-type organs. However different they may have been in name or origin, there is not the slightest doubt about the nature of these organs. It is true that in the Spanish revolution of 1936-7 an organizational bloc was imposed at the level of the towns and the organs of political power, but there was nothing of the kind at the level of the workplace: there the masses organized themselves. In most West European countries, the workers' movement is divided between different fragmented mass organizations, which are themselves not free from internal contradiction, and which furthermore rarely encompass a majority (or more than a slight majority) of the masses. Given this situation, a powerful and impetuous revolutionary movement of the proletariat will have to find a form of self-representation which involves the class in its entirety. History has produced nothing better than the soviet form, which is not an 'invention' of the Bolsheviks or the Trotskyists, but the result of real historical experience.

Of quite a different order is the question of the precise origin of these organs in each country, and the way in which the existing political and trade-union mass organizations will be combined with and represented in them. History has already given a wide range of answers to this, and there are even considerable differences between the two experiences in Russia. The first soviets arose in 1905 out of strike committees, whereas in 1917 the opposite happened: the Executive Committee of the Petrograd Soviets was constituted before the appearance of soviets throughout the country. In Spain 1936 it was quite different again: rank-and-file committees sprang up, which were then topped off by a bloc of organizations.

The most important thing for revolutionaries is to do away with all schematic and *a priori* thinking—something which is relevant to many lively debates within the Fourth International and in the European revolutionary Left in general. We should not think that there is only one possible slogan, or only one form in which workers' councils can appear in the present situation. Under certain circumstances, for example of defensive struggle of the working class against the rise of fascism, it is quite possible and even likely that organs of workers' power will only emerge from bodies of the united-front bloc of parties and trade unions. That was what Trotsky plausibly envisaged in Germany until 1933. But in other circumstances, for example in France between 1934 and 1936, Trotsky was quite correct in rejecting this idea. He accused the centrists and even some pseudo-Trotskyists of thinking that Blum and Thorez had first to come to an agreement before there could be action committees. He rejected the argument that the development of organs of dual power had to be subordinated to the signing of an agreement at the top between the apparatuses. He thought it quite likely that the opposite would happen: that the rank-and-file would first build these committees, and that only afterwards would the bureaucrats at the top agree to accept them. The Portuguese experience has given us sufficient warning of the dangers of any kind of schematism. In all their writings on revolutionary situations, Lenin and Trotsky insisted that the main task is to keep one's eyes and ears open for developments in the working class and for signs of the real organizational direction it is taking—and not impose some theoretical schema on this real tendency of the workers to find their own forms of self-organization.

Will the reformists always and everywhere combat this spontaneous growth of workers' councils? The sectarian answer would be 'unfortunately not'! But as I am not a sectarian, I will simply say 'no'. The rational kernel of the sectarian response is the obvious fact that the task of revolutionaries would be much easier if the bureaucrats were 'bravely' to swim against the tide. It would be so simple to isolate the bureaucratic apparatuses if they set themselves against millions of workers identifying with their councils. Unfortunately that is not how things happen; the bureaucrats are much too shrewd. What they generally do when the workers' councils are mushrooming is to enter and identify with them, keeping close to the real movement. You only have to re-read what Ebert, Noske, and Scheidemann wrote in the Germany of 1918 to understand that. The real problem will be the political confrontation with the reformists inside the councils.

We should also avoid a schematic view of relations between the workers' councils and the mass organizations and be prepared for all the possible variants that can arise. The basic determinant will clearly be the historical traditions and peculiarities of the Western working class, especially the much greater weight of the trade-union movement in these countries than was the case in Russia. There are two dangers to be avoided. The first is that of being dragged into the swamp of centrism, which devotes its energies to preparing a soup with no nutritive value at all. The ingredients of that soup are well known to us: the preservation of the institution of parliament, combined with affirmations of the sovereignty of the workers' councils, the sovereignty and independence of the trade unions; multiplicity of parties, combined with acceptance only of a 'limited' right of tendencies; and so on and so forth. In short, an attempt to reconcile the irreconcilable. The line that separates revolutionaries from reformism is clear enough: we are for the destruction of the bourgeois state apparatus; we say that it is impossible to make a socialist revolution whilst respecting, tolerating, or appeasing that apparatus; we are for the transfer of power to organs of self-representation of the working masses, and for a sovereign Congress of Workers' Councils to exercise that power. The centrists would like to avoid such a clear choice, but every time a revolutionary crisis breaks out, history gives fresh proof that room for equivocation does not exist.

The second danger to be avoided is that of sectarianism. There is a real function for the trade unions. Life itself will determine the exact sphere of their authority and the exact form of their fusion with the soviets. Although blocs of organizations are for us less democratic than directly elected organs, we will obviously not reject such blocs where they exist in the name of something that has not yet appeared. That would be a stupid sectarian attitude. We should remember that although Trotsky correctly criticized the bloc character of the Central Committee of Militias in Barcelona 1936, he nevertheless considered its dissolution to be the main crime of the reformists and centrists, including Andres Nin, and the beginning of the decline of the revolutionary upsurge in Spain. Moreover, there were also representatives of a bourgeois party, the *Esquerra Catalan*, in that committee, and Trotsky never suggested as a watchword: 'Let us first expel the bourgeois parties before recognizing this Central Committee of Militias as the organ of workers' power'.

Is it not highly likely that in countries in which the structure of bourgeois democracy is well established, it will be necessary to go through a period of what was termed in the early Communist International a workers' government, either in the strong or weak sense of the term; in other words, a government composed of workers' parties, possibly even including some petty-bourgeois parties, but having a programme that calls for a break with capitalism? Is it not likely that the workers' movement will have to pass through a phase of such governments before the creation of institutions of dual power? Further, is it not also likely that there will be pro-soviet representatives in parliament before the generalization of dual power? Is it conceivable that there could be a revolutionary situation without the election of a single advocate of a revolutionary solution to the general crisis of society?

It seems to me that you are introducing too many speculative elements into what is actually a rather clear-cut problematic. I would prefer to approach the question this way. First, in countries with strong bourgeois-democratic traditions—and even more so in imperialist countries emerging from dictatorships, in which case bourgeois-democratic illusions tend to be greater than in countries where those traditions run deep—it is inconceivable for the power of workers' councils to develop unless the working class undergoes concrete experiences with higher forms of democracy than bourgeois democracy. The workers must be able to compare the merits of both in practice.

Second, I would agree that it is unlikely that a real struggle for soviet power could occur without a revolutionary Marxist current gaining enough strength in the working class to win representation in parliament. And third, it is inconceivable for a situation of dual power to arise in a country with a long-standing traditional labour movement without that situation disrupting the present total control of the reformist, class collaborationist bureaucracies over these parties.

These three statements seem to me nearly self-evident. But to draw further implications from them would be to raise a series of speculative hypotheses so detailed that it would be quite difficult to answer simply yes or no. Just to give you one example. I said that in general a dual-power situation would imply a revolutionary-socialist current strong enough to win representation in parliament, *if parliamentary elections were held at that time.* But since many parliaments are elected for terms of four or five years, it is quite possible for there to be great upheavals between elections which alter the relationship of forces within the working class drastically. In that event, if no new parliamentary elections were held during that period, there would be a very serious cleavage between the composition of parliament and the real relationship of forces, especially within the trade unions, workers' councils (if a situation of dual power exists), and other forms of representation of the working class.

As for the question of a workers' government, the Comintern resolution on this question describes several possible variants. One of these entailed not merely an upheaval in the traditional, class collaborationist leaderships of the mass parties of the working class, but also a take-over of the official leadership by a left wing, or else a massive split and the emergence of a party like the USPD in Germany. Now, this is not necessarily the only form in which such an upheaval could occur. It is the most favourable, of course, but not the only one. In fact, if we look at what has happened since 1920-21— and we have seen some formidable upheavals since then—we must conclude that in the light of historical experience the case of the USPD seems quite exceptional. There was, for example, no such split in the Spanish Socialist Party between 1934 and 1936, except in the youth league, and this went rather badly, since it was the Stalinists who won over the split group. In the 1940s many people, including Trotskyists, hoped or expected that the British Labour Party would be taken over by a Bevanite left wing, but it did not happen. Nor was there any split of a left wing. Other examples could be given as well. In fact, wherever more radical developments have taken place, they have been marginal—like the PSIUP in Italy or the PSU in France—and not at all comparable to the USPD development.

Personally, I am now convinced that the established leaderships of the Socialist and Communist Parties in Western Europe will not form a workers' government of the type to which you are alluding. The most they can do is to found a bourgeois workers' government, the second category dealt with in the Communist International resolution. But that is something else entirely; it is not a government beginning to break with the bourgeoisie.

But such a government could proclaim *that it will break with the capitalists, even though it does not really do so.*

That is quite different. The difference is pointed out in the analysis of the Comintern and is especially confirmed by historical experience. We have now gone through six or seven Labour governments.

But none of these had a programme proclaiming the need to break with capitalism.

True. But my point is that in the foreseeable future there will not be any alliance of a Communist and Socialist Party in Western Europe going beyond the programme of, for example, the Union of the Left in France. And that did not proclaim any break with capitalism. In the best of cases—and even this is quite hypothetical—we will see programmes of the sort raised by the British Labour Party in 1945, which was a radical reformist programme, or of the Austrian Socialist Party, which called for the nationalization of not unimportant sectors of the economy.

None of these programmes is in any way anti-capitalist. None can even be compared to the programme of Unidad Popular in Chile. Even there, the anti-capitalist character of the programme was dubious, but the dynamic was more radical. In Western Europe, however, with the traditional working-class parties that exist today, it is difficult to visualize any development going beyond the Union of the Left or the Labour Party programme of 1945.

Would it then be correct to conclude that you do not consider it very important to develop programmatic demands and slogans directed at this sort of bourgeois workers' government—demands pointing to how a real break with capitalism could be brought about? Are you saying that it will be impossible to impose anti-capitalist measures on such governments?

You are speculating again. No one can foresee the exact forms in which revolutionary situations will erupt in Western Europe. It is impossible to devise any particular pattern that can be applied to all cases. What you are describing is but one variant. I do not rule it out completely, and I entirely agree that wherever there is a government composed exclusively of representatives of the labour movement, revolutionaries have to formulate demands insisting that this government break with capitalism. But it is quite another thing to say that this will be the primary channel through which working-class consciousness will rise to a qualitatively higher level. This may occur as the result of direct struggle, a general strike, a confrontation with reaction or the state apparatus—there are simply too many variants to subsume them all in one schema.

Again, this is clear from what has actually happened in Europe over the past forty years. In France in 1936 the crisis emerged from the combination of a Popular Front election victory and a general strike; in Spain it came out of a direct confrontation with the fascists; in Portugal it came out of the downfall of a senile Bonapartist, semi-fascist government through a military conspiracy; more recently, in Spain again, it came out of the bourgeoisie's delay in removing a dictatorship that by the seventies no longer corresponded to the real relationship of class forces. That makes four variants already.

The more general problem—raised in a cursory manner by Trotsky but insufficiently developed by revolutionary Marxists for a long period—is this: in an advanced capitalist country with a highly sophisticated political structure and a complex social system, where there is a long conservative tradition in the labour movement, it is inconceivable for the workers to opt directly for soviet forms of organization and later for soviet forms of power without tremendous new experiences of struggle and new advances in consciousness. This is not merely a matter of building the revolutionary party independent of what is going on in the working class; you cannot make a revolutionary turn within a predominantly reformist working class. That is simply impossible; it would be a bureaucratic, adventurist, and idealist schema.

The question of what sort of tactics to adopt towards a bourgeois workers' government must be approached in this spirit. One thing is clear. The essential tactical weapon for winning the majority of the masses under such a government is the united front, subject to certain crucial political stipulations. But in the highly complex and delicate situation of a left government—one identified by the masses as a government of the workers' organizations—this tactic would have to be based on a carefully balanced attitude towards the government. (I am not talking here of a 'historic compromise' government—which is just the 'classical' coalition government of large bourgeois and reformist parties.) The attitude of revolutionary Marxists should not be a schematic one, or consist of constant calls for the overthrow of the government—which would sound to the masses strangely like the calls of the Right and the far Right. I am not saying that our attitude should be one of support: we are naturally not for such a government, but for its replacement by a genuine workers' government. Nevertheless, it will be a bourgeois *workers'* government and seen by the masses as such. It would be sectarian and completely unproductive to adopt the same attitude towards it as we do towards a straightforward bourgeois or Popular Front government.

We would fundamentally change our position only if the government began to repress the mass movement. That was the position of Lenin in April 1917, as can be clearly seen by reading all his writings from March to June 1917. For example: 'We are not yet for the overthrow of this government, in that it is supported by the majority of the workers'. He changed his attitude only after the repression following the July Days. So long as such a government does not engage in repression, we should adopt an attitude of 'critical toleration', of pedagogic propaganda opposition, in order to allow the masses to learn from the experience. Concretely, this means raising a series of demands that correspond to two basic criteria.

First, it is necessary to intensify the break with the bourgeoisie and thus to demand the removal of the one or two wretched bourgeois ministers in the government. Of course, that will not change much in itself—it will remain a bourgeois workers' government even without those ministers. The experiences of Spain 1936 and of Chile have similarly made clear the need for a thoroughgoing purge and elimination of the whole repressive apparatus of the bourgeoisie, the disbanding of repressive bodies and an end to full-time judges. In addition, there are all the economic demands of the masses related to nationalization under workers' control, which express the logic of dual power.

The second basic category of demands addressed to the government concerns the riposte to the inevitable bourgeois acts of sabotage and economic disruption. Here the guiding policy should be one of tit-for-tat: the occupation and take-over of factories followed by their co-ordination; working-out of a workers' plan of economic reconversion and revival; the extension and generalization of workers' control in the direction of self-management; the running of a whole number of areas of social life by those directly concerned (public transport, street markets, crêches, universities, agricultural land, etc.). Numerous layers will move from reformism towards left-centrism and revolutionary Marxism through discussing these questions in the framework of proletarian democracy and through their own practical experience, *protected by the intransigent defence of the freedom of mass action and mobilization*, even when it 'embarrasses' the plans of the government or cuts across those of the reformists. This break from reformism will be assisted by the illustration, consolidation, and centralization of varied experiences of self-organization; it will not be helped, however, by sectarian excesses, by insults of the 'social-fascists' type, or by ignoring the special sensitivity of those who still place their trust in the reformists. The policy of winning the masses by the united front is thus inextricably bound up with the affirmation, extension, and generalization of dual power, up to and including the consolidation of workers' power by insurrection.

The objective results of the policies of the reformists are the following: growing impotence of the left government; inability to meet its promises; rising disillusionment amongst the masses and the creation, thereby, of a fertile ground for demobilization and demoralization and the return in force of reaction, whether through violence or even by legal and electoral means. This confirms that we have no choice in the matter: either we extend the mass outflanking towards victory or else decline and defeat are inevitable. In such a period there is a race between two movements, one leading to an outflanking of the reformist apparatuses and the other to a retreat of the masses as a result of the reformists' bankruptcy. The first will win the day only if the social and political relationship of forces has at least some favourable elements: if the mass movement is not broken but grows broader and broader; if self-organization is strengthened and generalized, rather than rapidly broken up; and if the revolutionaries succeed in overcoming their weakness and isolation, and forge thousands of new bonds with the masses on the basis of an extension and generalization of genuine, lived experiences of the united front (rather than that propagandistic caricature which consists of demanding that the reformist leaderships give an answer in order to expose them in words). This road does not provide a guarantee of victory; but it is the only chance there is.

Results and Prospects in Southern Europe

Let us continue with a related point. Isn't there an inherent danger in the prospect of the outbreak of pre-revolutionary situations, particularly in southern Europe, despite the enormous positive potential? As you say, the reformists show no sign of wanting to go forward to a successful revolution, even if they assume control of the government. The bourgeoisie, of course, will strive to resolve the pre-revolutionary situation through a victorious counter-revolution. And as you have just pointed out, even if the masses throw up soviet organs, revolutionaries can hardly expect to win over the majority in the short run. What aims should revolutionary Marxists pursue under such conditions?

Your question rests on a basic premise that I dispute. It is not true that the revolutionary vanguard is incapable of winning over the majority of workers in the revolutionary period opening up in southern Europe. The essential historical function of the period from 1968 to the present day has been to allow the far Left to accumulate sufficient forces to enter this revolutionary period with the realistic possibility of winning over the majority of the working class.

Of course, we need to be a lot more specific: I would make four basic points. In the first place, every revolutionary experience shows that we have to start from the uneven development of class consciousness—an idea that the reformists and centrists find hard to grasp. We have already mentioned the examples of June 1936 and the Liberation. There is not the slightest contradiction in saying that *the overwhelming majority of the masses can at the same time vote for the reformist parties and partially break with them in practice.* In a revolutionary situation, class consciousness develops by leaps and bounds, although not on all fronts at once. The masses may think that the only useful way of voting in the parliamentary elections is for the Socialist Party or the Communist Party. At the same time, they may think that in the struggle against reaction at the workplaces and in the colleges the only useful way of acting is independently of those parties. A meticulous analysis of the attitude of the Portuguese proletariat throughout 1975 would provide fresh confirmation of the uneven growth of class consciousness. I think that we shall see the same thing in France, Spain, and Italy. But I will go even further: it is not impossible for the majority of the class to vote in the workers' councils for the seizure of power by the councils, while still being prepared to vote for the reformist parties in parliamentary elections. Even the result of consultative polls, expressing a concrete political choice, varies according to whether they are held in isolated booths or in mass assemblies, in an atomized or a collective way. The trade-union bureaucrats and the bosses know very well that a mass meeting and a referendum or postal vote will produce different results on a proposal to declare or call off a strike.

This leads us on to the second question: the outflanking of the reformist leaderships. It is quite possible, and even likely that a *dual process* will occur in Western Europe. The masses will accord the parliamentary majority or left government a relative, guarded, and mistrustful trust—the contradictory formulation expresses the reality well. At the same time, they will show a tendency to break out of the limits to action laid down in advance by the reformist, class-collaborationist programme, with its avoidance of a break with the bourgeois system. It is the inexorable logic of the unfolding class struggle, rather than the theoretical clarity of the masses, that will determine the dynamic of this process.

The greatest analytical weakness of the reformists and centrists lies in their failure to understand this logic, despite its clear demonstration in the revolutionary experiences of the industrialized countries, including at the outer limit Chile. The world today is one in which a proletariat of greatly increased social, economic, and political weight is faced with a crisis of capitalist relations of production and of all other bourgeois social relations; it is unthinkable that a qualitative deepening of the activity, combativity, and demands of the masses should not lead to a veritable explosion of class conflict that paralyses the capitalist economy and the bourgeois state. Any socialist or communist who thinks this proletariat, representing at least 60 or 70 per cent of the population, can be told: 'You are in power. The factory belongs to you. Now it is possible to raise the standard of living, reduce the length of the working day, extend nationalizations and put through progressive social legislation', and who also thinks that it is simultaneously possible to achieve an increase in capitalist investment, an increase in the mass or even rate of profit to finance this capitalist growth, such a person is an utterly ridiculous utopian dreamer. No one believes that, either in the workers' camp or in the bourgeois camp. Only dishonest or completely naive conciliators can spread around such fairy-tales. In the present climate in southern Europe, therefore, we can rule out the possibility of the masses' remaining passive if a left government takes office. This will inevitably be accompanied by an intensification of the class struggle, a flight of capital, an investment strike by the capitalists, sabotage of production, constant plotting against the government by reactionaries and the extreme right supported by the state apparatus, right-wing terrorism, and so on.

Now, the workers will not fail to react. They will place no trust in the bourgeois police to fight against the plotters, or in the minister of finance to halt the flight of capital. *Outflanking is not brought about by a state of mind, trust or mistrust, nor by 'leftist agitators' stirring things up. It is a result of the inevitable head-on collision between the major social classes.* Moreover, although the programme of the Union of the Left in France is perfectly compatible with the capitalist system, it is no accident that it is more radical than the programme of the Popular Front. It reflects the changed relationship of forces since the thirties and the deepened structural crisis of capitalism. Today, reforms that are 'broad' enough to be of significance to the popular masses of Western Europe require considerably more sweeping changes in the functioning of the economy and society than those that could be envisaged in the twenties or thirties.

This intensification of class conflict has a twin dynamic: on the one hand, in the direction of an ever wider outflanking of the bureaucratic apparatuses by the masses; on the other, towards a creeping paralysis of the 'classical' mechanisms of a Social Democratic or reformist government. Once again, the experience of the first stage of the Allende government is highly illustrative. The flight of capital in Italy and Spain in 1975 and 1976, under the mere *threat* that a left government could come to power, gives us some idea of what would happen if such a government actually did take over. In such circumstances, it is utterly utopian to hope to govern by traditional, routine methods and to remain within the framework of bourgeois parliamentarianism and a Common Market which allows the free circulation of capital.

It is the reformists and centrists, not we revolutionaries, who are thus the real utopians. We are convinced that the reformist apparatuses will inevitably and rapidly be outflanked, in the context of what I have called the uneven development of class consciousness. I am not talking necessarily of a spectacular electoral break with the traditional parties; the outflanking could take intermediate forms, including the radicalization of a section of those parties themselves and a tendency struggle or even split within them. That is almost inevitable in such a situation, especially as the far Left is no longer marginalized and without importance, but an already recognized political force.

The third point concerns the duration of the process. Here the conclusion could only be pessimistic if we thought that everything would be over within three months. Nowhere could the forces of the far Left win over the majority of the working class in such a short period. However, to think that things will be settled in three months is to underestimate the deep crisis of the bourgeois order and bourgeois leadership, as well as the degree of working-class combativity. The only recent points of reference we have are those of Chile and

Portugal: the process lasted three years in Chile, where the working class was infinitely weaker than in Western Europe, and where there was a much greater danger of direct intervention by US imperialism; in Portugal, the crisis lasted nearly three years and did not conclude with a bloody defeat for the proletariat. I mentioned earlier Germany 1918-23 and Spain 1931-7 as examples of a process stretching over a number of years; it is over such a long period that revolutionary organizations could expect to win the support of the majority of the workers in the councils. These organizations already have thousands of members and tens of thousands of sympathizers, and in a protracted period of crisis they could gain tens of thousands of new members and hundreds of thousands of sympathizers. None of this will happen, however, unless these organizations carry out correct policies, especially in relation to the united front.

The fourth point that has to be made is in answer to the following objection, which is perhaps the most powerful one of all. 'Practically everything to which you refer has already been seen in Chile. There was a left government in a state of paralysis; there were leftist sections of the masses storming marginal fortresses of the bourgeoisie; there were internal squabbles in the workers' movement, following clashes between the reformist majority and the revolutionary minority. And in the end what that led to was the triumph of reaction through a bloody coup d'état and a crushing defeat of the workers' movement'. In answering this, I must first repeat what I said earlier: no one can give an absolute assurance of victory. The correct revolutionary strategy has never been based on the certainty of a working-class victory. All we can say is that it is only our strategical and tactical line of march that can make that victory *possible*; but it cannot guarantee it. Additional factors are necessary for victory, in particular a favourable balance of forces which cannot be precisely calculated in advance.

The much less favourable objective and subjective situation in Chile was obviously the final determinant of the balance of forces between the classes and between the reformist apparatuses and the far Left. In Western Europe the situation is much more promising from both points of view: the degree of self-sufficiency is incomparably higher than in a country like Chile, and the proletariat has a much greater capacity for fighting back and winning support at an international level. Moreover, we have a formidable 'secret weapon' of which we make no secret: namely, the growing identity between the programme and aims of a proletarian revolution in Western Europe and the existing programme of a section of the workers' movement in the most 'stable' countries: Britain, Holland, Austria, West Germany. Socialist diplomacy will be able to stage its own 'Brest-Litovsk' if an economic blockade is organized against Portugal, Italy, Spain, or France to 'punish' the working class for establishing workers' control or self-management, whilst the trade unions of northern Europe are moving towards the same positions. That will obviously not be so easy if the revolution wears the hideous mask of Stalinist dictatorship. But if it presents instead the smiling Communist face of sovereign workers' councils, then I do not think that it will be easy to mount such a blockade against European socialist countries.

Even the Chilean army, which was of a quite particular kind, was not automatically immune to the virus of socialism and revolution. In fact, one of the catalysts of the coup d'état was the fear of the counter-revolutionary officers that the virus was spreading amongst the ranks, especially in the navy. Of course, the military plotters were aided by the treacherous ineptitude of the Popular Unity leaders faced with these first signs of rank-and-file insubordination against the army and navy officers, and by the remarkable political weakness of the centrist far Left, which had a completely wrong position on work in the army. Here too, I think that we will be able to avoid these mistakes and obtain better results. The recent experience of the soldiers' movement—especially in Portugal, but also in France and Italy—shows that we are already in a better starting-position than were the Chileans. In highly industrialized countries—where even the composition of the army reflects the social structure of the country—it is extremely unlikely that a gigantic revolutionary upsurge will not find expression in opposition movements within the army. All these are trump cards that were not available in Chile.

In any case the essential point is that we have no choice in the matter. When there is an impetuous rise of an anti-capitalist and anti-bureaucratic mass movement, faced by the counter-revolutionary hardening of nearly the entire bourgeois apparatus, anything that demobilizes the working class and puts a brake on the workers' offensive, and anyone who tries to dampen down their enthusiasm, can only serve the counter-revolution. The proletariat has never profited from demobilization and division in its camp during the course of class battles. When there is an extreme polarization of social forces, the only measures that serve the workers' cause are the widening and generalization of the mobilizations and of the tendency of the class to united self-expansion. We must put the centrists and vacillating forces on their guard against the grave danger of measures that repress, fragment, divide, or demobilize the mass movement on the pretext of 'not alarming reaction'. Anything that has a demobilizing effect immediately shifts the balance of forces in favour of the bourgeoisie.

Conversely, anything that mobilizes and unifies the working class and the toiling masses shifts the balance of forces in favour of the working class. That is the whole basis of our orientation. It is what gives real coherence to our goal of winning over the majority of the working class; it is one of our political trump cards. *In a revolutionary situation, the revolutionary Marxists must be the force most committed to the strengthening of class unity and organization.* They must constantly advocate the unity of the class apparatus of the workers, and this is made easier by the fact that the organs of workers' unity are precisely the organs of its self-representation: the workers' councils. We defend workers' unity in as much as we defend the organs of workers' power in a situation of dual power.

So far, your whole discussion has been framed by the assumption that the emergence of pre-revolutionary situations in southern Europe will be marked by the advent of left governments, or bourgeois workers' governments. But hasn't that scenario been called into question by the whole period since the events in Portugal in November 1975? Over the past three and a half years there seems to have been a generalized and cumulative recession in the strength of the Left in the labour movement throughout Europe. We have seen not only the major setback in Portugal, but also the debacle of the Communist Party's policy of 'historic compromise' and austerity in Italy; the wreck of the Labour government's policies of the 'social contract' and austerity in Britain, destroyed by militant trade-union action and followed by the electoral victory of the Conservative Party; the crisis within the Union of the Left in France and its electoral defeat in 1978. Finally, even in Spain the bourgeoisie has achieved a partial success: the transition from the Francoist dictatorship to a bourgeois-democratic monarchy without an experience of dual power or of mass struggles challenging the state apparatus inherited from the dictatorship itself. Here, of course, the reformist leaders—Felipe Gonzales of the Socialist Party and Santiago Carrillo of the Communist Party—were successful in maintaining their hegemony over the proletariat and in limiting the instances of outflanking.

This is one of the central questions under discussion by the militants and sympathizers of the Fourth International in preparation for our next World Congress. We are debating this question publicly. The leadership of the Fourth International has drafted a very long document dealing with this matter, and it is difficult to summarize such a complicated question in a few paragraphs, but I will try.

To start with—and this is probably the most controversial aspect of my answer—we would deny that the character of the period has changed. We do not deny that a serious defeat has been suffered in Portugal. A revolutionary process had been under way up to November 1975, and that process has now ended temporarily. That much is clear.

Outside Portugal, however, the situation is different. Nowhere in southern Europe—where the situation has been highly unstable, on the verge of a pre-revolutionary situation almost continuously—has a qualitative change occurred. In Italy, Spain, and France the bourgeoisie has been unable to stabilize its regime to a point anywhere near what happened in the late forties and early fifties, after the end of the post-war revolutionary crisis.

It is our opinion, however, that this condition of basic, underlying instability has indeed been altered by the combination of two essentially new ingredients. First, economic circumstances have changed, with the sudden reappearance of massive unemployment and the threat of even greater joblessness. The international austerity offensive of the employers caught the working class unawares and unprepared. Here I am not referring to the reformist misleaders, whose role is obvious. Rather, I mean the bulwark of the working class, the vanguard, the organizing cadres, the shop stewards—all those comrades who have been in the forefront of proletarian struggle in the past period. These comrades were well seasoned and experienced in mounting struggles to defend real wages against inflation, but they were not at all prepared for a fight against massive unemployment. This lack of experience was compounded by the total capitulation of the bureaucracy—the Communist Party in Italy and Spain, Social Democracy in most other countries—to the ideological and political aspects of the bourgeois offensive on this front. Indeed, the bureaucrats became the greatest transmission belt for these bourgeois ideas, injecting them into the labour movement. This combination of bureaucratic treachery and a spirit of disorientation among the workers created a certain space for some initial success for the employers' offensive. Thus, we can say that the proletariat, having been on the offensive for a long period, has now been thrown onto the defensive temporarily. That is one new ingredient.

The other—which *apparently* acts in the same direction but could potentially have quite opposite effects—results from the change in the economic situation and the maturation of the various anti-capitalist mobilizations of the previous period. Initially, these mobilizations were sectoral, divided, and spontaneous. But their very momentum carried them in another direction, as central political tasks and government alternatives became the key issue. This was primarily the result of the shift in the economic cycle itself, because it is one thing to fight militant struggles and strikes against inflation—that can be done on a factory by factory, branch by branch, or city by city level. But it is quite another to deal with a million and a half unemployed. That battle cannot be fought city by city; the problem can be solved only on a national (some would even say European) basis.

The same is true for many of the sectoral struggles and issues. For example, limited mass demonstrations and even national campaigns can be held to demand free abortion, a halt to the construction of nuclear power plants, the right of soldiers to vote, the general right to vote at 16, and so on. But once these movements gain momentum, and especially when they start merging with one another, then what is posed is the question of a government alternative, which means a central political solution. And here, of course, spontaneous or semi-spontaneous mass movements of the type we have seen over the past decade reach an impasse, because they cannot generate alternative political solutions spontaneously. This must come out of the political field, as the result of changes in the relationship of forces within the organized labour movement, through the growth of the revolutionary organizations, their rising credibility in the eyes of broader masses. And here, of course, there is an obvious time lag, from which the movement has suffered. Great potential for militant struggles in the factories and the unions has arisen, and great potential for sectoral social mass movements too, but there has been no credible overall political alternative to the reformists. Since the reformists were at an impasse and a left alternative was lacking, the bourgeoisie took the offensive.

We must, however, look more carefully at these two new ingredients, which up to now have been mutually reinforcing. The first—the lack of reaction, or better, delay of reaction, by the working class to the offensive of the employers against jobs—was obviously mainly a question of time. Why? Here we start from one of our key notions in judging the present situation in the imperialist countries—especially in Western Europe, but not only there. We are deeply convinced that the basic shift in the relationship of social forces that occurred in the fifties and sixties as the result of the development of late capitalism has not been turned around by the capitalist class. And we note—and this is especially striking in Britain—that despite massive unemployment and the temporary successes of the anti-working-class offensive of the employers and the government, the organized strength and self-confidence of the working class have not at all declined. The same is true in every country in Western Europe, without a single exception.

The 1979 steelworkers' strike in West Germany was a striking confirmation of this. This strike—the first industry-wide steel strike in Germany since the end of the war—came as a big surprise to many who had completely misjudged events in Germany during the past few years. True, there has been serious repression, ominous restriction of democratic rights, many negative developments. But all this did not alter the basic relationship of forces between the workers and the capitalist class produced by all the economic progress of the past twenty years. You simply cannot strengthen capitalist industry, develop the productive forces, and stimulate a twenty-year boom without also strengthening the working class. This basic thesis of Marxism has been confirmed throughout capitalist Europe.

A similar point applies to Spain. I doubt very much that the Spanish situation can be judged a political success for the bourgeoisie.

One can, of course, point out that they have succeeded in making the transition without too great an upheaval. In fact, you did not mention their greatest success: they made this transition without having to sacrifice the fascist-originated army and repressive apparatus. But a high price has been paid. Previously, there were 200,000 workers in illegal trade unions; now there are as many as four or five million members of legal unions—three times as many as during the Second Republic. There have been two or three demonstrations in Madrid larger than any during the civil war. Of course, this does not mean that the level of consciousness of the Spanish working class is as high today as it was in 1936 or 1937. Nevertheless, there has been a tremendous build-up of proletarian strength in Spain. The capitalists are not at all happy about that. They have done the best they could in a difficult situation, but this cannot be called a victory for them, for they have had to make wide concessions to the working class. I do not consider that the transition from a Bonapartist, semi-fascist regime to bourgeois democracy in a country like Spain constitutes a concession by the workers to the capitalists. I rather consider it a concession by the capitalists to the workers. The bourgeoisie has been compelled to grant the workers democratic freedoms, and it is probable that the temporary success of the austerity policy was partly due to the fact that the working class considers that success tremendously important.

This, by the way, has been the argument of the Communist Party: we exchange some economic concessions for the conquest of democratic rights that will enable us to recoup in the long run. You could call this an opportunist, counter-revolutionary manoeuvre to prevent an immediate explosion in Spain. I would agree. But it is not a totally incredible argument. Workers who were thrown into prison for every strike they organized for twenty-five or thirty years can suddenly turn 500,000 people into the streets for the official funeral of Largo Caballero, the first, left Socialist prime minister in Spain during the upsurge of the revolution. The workers, who can now go on strike legally by the millions, regard this as revenge for the defeat of 1939. They do not see it as a victory for the bourgeoisie, but as a big step forward, a victory for themselves. Granted, the reformists have gained some credibility from all this, but I personally am pleasantly surprised by the limits of this phenomenon. The prestige of the reformists in the eyes of the workers is nothing like what it was just after 1945. There has been a breathing space during which the pace of the class struggle has slowed somewhat. But no more than that. The pace is now picking up again rapidly. And it cannot be said that the basic relationship of class forces, which had swung against capital during the previous period, has been turned around.

On balance, we can say that over the past three years the bourgeoisie has made very meagre gains out of the initial disorientation of the working class in face of massive unemployment. But there is every sign that this disorientation is now being overcome.

Something similar is occurring in regard to the second new ingredient as well. Granted, there is still disarray. Ideological crisis and soul-searching are the order of the day amongst both Euro-communists and Social Democrats in France as a result of the 1978 electoral defeat of the Union of the Left. A similar process may be discerned in Italy, and it is on the cards in Spain too. Even here, though, there is a significant new element to which particular attention must be paid. Because of a series of factors—the strength of the working class, the weakness of the bourgeoisie, the crisis of the bourgeois order, the general social crisis, the failure of the reformists to present a real anti-capitalist alternative, the lack of credibility of the far Left—the groping for an alternative solution is taking a detour through the trade unions. The unions are being forced to fill the political vacuum by raising questions of economic and even overall social policy affecting a multitude of issues (like nuclear power, for example). The reason is obvious: no other credible force within the labour movement and the general public is raising these issues, but the need to do so is felt by millions of people.

In my opinion this can only be a temporary expedient, because it is not the function of the trade unions, which are not equipped to play such a role. They can do all these things on a propaganda, even agitational, level, and they can mount mass struggles around some of these demands, but they cannot offer a concrete political solution. The next stage, I am quite convinced, will be that this pressure will be expressed within the mass parties of the working class, after it mounts within the unions.

We can therefore sum up as follows: there has been no change in the character of the period; there has been a phase of some disorientation, of adaptation to new conditions, but the capitalists have not succeeded in stabilizing the situation.

The points you make about Spain are undoubtedly well taken. No one could reasonably maintain that the working class in Spain has suffered any sort of defeat over the past few years. But isn't there a sense in which the analysis of the Fourth International has been faulty? Before the death of Franco, the FI argued that because of the weakness of the Spanish bourgeoisie—its lack of an organized political leadership, for example—and the strength of the working class, Francoism could be liquidated only through a revolutionary general strike. In fact, that was the axis of all the FI's political statements on Spain. It was further argued that this strike would trigger a revolutionary crisis that would place a social transformation on the agenda. Now, isn't it true that one form of bourgeois rule— Francoism—has been replaced by another—parliamentary democracy—through an evolutionary process without the outbreak of a revolutionary crisis? Isn't that in contradiction to the predictions and analysis of the FI?

Your balance-sheet of the 1974-1977 process in Spain is oversimplified. There *was* a tremendous rise in mass struggles in 1974 and 1975. In fact, if my information is correct, during the first half of 1975 the Spanish workers surpassed the world record for strike days per thousand wage-earners. There *were* a series of regional general strikes, which were clearly political, openly advancing political demands. The objective trend *was* towards a revolutionary general strike throughout Spain. The Fourth International and its Spanish comrades were correct a thousand times over to concentrate all their efforts on driving that objective trend to its ultimate logic, for that would have transformed the situation not only in Spain, but also in Portugal and possibly in France and Italy too.

What then occurred was a sensational turn in the political situation, a turn that involved both the bourgeoisie and the mass reformist parties of the working class, Social Democracy and the Communist Party. Fearful of the prospect of an explosive revolutionary situation that could have become completely uncontrollable, big business, the king, and the leaders of the army suddenly decided that the lesser evil was to abandon the 'liberal' dictatorship for a *de facto* parliamentary regime with legal trade unions and workers' parties (including revolutionary parties). They knew that this would entail considerable risk, given the political, social, and economic contradictions in Spain, which are deeper than in any other major imperialist country. I am quite sure that history will confirm the amplitude of those risks. But given the alternative of an immediate revolutionary explosion or the buildup towards a medium-term explosion (which could turn out to be even more violent), the bourgeoisie decided that the latter option was, for the moment, the lesser risk. The necessary conclusions were then drawn.

The leaders of the reformist mass parties, on the other hand, changed their attitude on one key question. They made their peace with the monarchy, the Franco-monarchist army, and the Francoist repressive apparatus. They accepted the transference of these institutions—unpurged, unbroken, and with full powers—into a constitutional regime which thereby becomes a parliamentary democracy with all the trappings of a bonapartist strong state. This in turn reduced the risks for the bourgeoisie, especially when the reformists combined this historic capitulation with the so-called Moncloa Pact, which stipulated a wage freeze and dealt a demoralizing blow to the process of mass unionization throughout Spain.

Once this completely new situation took hold, political mass militancy reached a ceiling through which it could not burst spontaneously. As far as the broad masses were concerned, the exchange of all these concessions for free trade unions, free elections, free political parties, and a free press appeared positive by and large. *Political* mass mobilizations therefore subsided, especially those independent of the Socialist and Communist Parties. The price paid for this exchange—wage freeze, mass unemployment, persistent repressive potential of the army, bonapartist power of the monarchy—was not immediately obvious to the masses and will be assimilated only gradually. When it is assimilated, there will undoubtedly be mass reaction.

It is true that we underestimated the possibility of this sort of manoeuvre, for which, by the way, there is scarcely a precedent in the twentieth century, but I do not think this reflects an incorrect estimate of the relationship of class forces in Spain at that period. It is true that we overestimated the potential for spontaneous mass mobilizations on political issues on the part of a working class which, while extremely militant, does not now benefit from the sort of cumulative political experience it had amassed from 1930 to 1936, which experience was a key factor in the events of July 1936.

The Crisis of Eurocommunism

The Communist Party of Spain, of course, has been in the forefront of the development that has come to be called Eurocommunism. But the Eurocommunist programme has suffered some very serious set-backs in Western Europe in past years—to some extent in Spain itself, but more so in France and Italy. Do you think that the hopes and illusions it aroused will now be more difficult to rekindle and that in this sense we are likely to see what might be termed a crisis of the Eurocommunist perspective?

To some degree, yes. In the short run I would say yes without any qualification. But we must be cautious and distinguish between what is conjunctural and what is inherent in the nature of the period. Any new upsurge of working-class struggles will immediately make the Eurocommunist project more useful and credible even in the eyes of the liberal bourgeoisie.

In France, for example, we are now seeing a return to direct action by the workers. This, especially in the absence of any electoral prospects in the short term, conflicts with the basic tenets of the Eurocommunist design. Ever since the formation of the Union of the Left, the workers have been told: don't strike, prepare for election victories. Well, the electoral plans failed, and now there is an upswing in strikes. Of course, piecemeal actions against the government's austerity offensive are ultimately ineffective. The workers understand that, and the propaganda of our comrades for a general strike has been getting a good response among the workers. Even if that is not a sufficient answer, it would at least be a step in the right direction. The vanguard of the French workers, Communist workers included, are increasingly fed up—*ras-le-bol*, they call it.

What will come out of this is not clear. I am not predicting a new May '68, or even a general strike, for that matter. But if the new wave of strikes and direct action continues to mount, the Union of the Left, or some similar formation, may well begin to look like the lesser evil to many people: the less radical sectors of the labour movement, a portion of the petty bourgeoisie, and perhaps even a sector of the bourgeoisie itself.

The fundamental problem we face in all the European countries remains this: so long as the revolutionary left is not strong enough to be considered a credible political alternative to the existing mass parties of the working class, and so long as the workers are sufficiently experienced and conscious to believe that these parties, as they now exist, are unable to implement the anti-capitalist policies required to overcome the capitalist crisis, there is an objective stalemate that is very difficult to overcome by any particular manoeuvre, line of propaganda, or agreement. If all the leaders of the Communist and Socialist Parties could patch up their differences, perhaps they could win the elections by a hundred thousand votes. The difference in France was so slight that unaccountable factors could have decided the outcome. But in itself this would not make that great a difference. On both sides of the barricades there is great scepticism about the feasibility of any broad reformist policy in conditions of economic crisis. Nobody really believes it can work. The capitalists don't believe it, the workers don't believe it, and even the bureaucrats themselves don't really believe it. This, and not the squabbling between bureaucrats, is the deeper root of the present impasse. The workers see the failure of the reformists, but they do not yet believe that revolution is possible. Hence the deadlock.

It is no simple matter to find the way out. United-front proposals are, of course, one important element. But we must not foster illusions, even unwittingly, that have already been abandoned by a good part of the working class. One must be quite careful in the way one presents these united-front and 'workers' government' proposals. On the one hand, there is no doubt that if the Union of the Left in France, for example, had won a majority in the elections of March 1978, a very powerful dynamic of radicalization would have been touched off, leading to a general confrontation—if not immediately, then in six months or a year or so. That is why we hold that the defeat of the Communist and Socialist Parties in those elections was a real defeat for the working class.

On the other hand, this is a far cry from saying that under certain conditions Marchais and Mitterrand could begin implementing anti-capitalist policies. We do not believe this is possible under the present circumstances. It is therefore important not to emphasize solely the positive results of unity of the reformist working-class parties. Great expectations that prove to be unfounded can lead to great disappointment and demoralization. This is exactly why the existence of a credible left alternative is so critical. The reaction of the working class to the ineffectiveness and betrayal of a reformist government is as different as day and night depending on whether or not such an alternative exists within the labour movement.

In that sense, there is a race against time in Western Europe today—or rather, a race between the strengthening of the revolutionary movement and the successive phases of hope and despair of the masses with the official, traditional mass organizations. I am optimistic in one respect: we have more time than I myself thought a few years ago, because of the depth of the social crisis of the capitalists. That gives us more time than we thought, but not unlimited time. The Italian and French working class, for example, have shown astonishing militancy over the past decade. I think there have been six general strikes in Italy since 1969. But this cannot go on forever.

What, then, would be the shape of a bourgeois reactionary offensive against the proletariat, if the working class does not seize the initiative?

In the short term, such an offensive would have no chance of success. In the long run, of course, it does. But before there could be a strategic defeat of the working class, there would have to be many new phases of struggle, perhaps some defeats in preliminary skirmishes, which would not preclude important victories in the subsequent period. But if there were a strategic defeat, a decisive shift in the relationship of class forces at the expense of the proletariat, then there would be an onslaught not only against some of the fundamental conquests of the working class over the past twenty-five years, but also against basic democratic rights. The bourgeoisie is well aware that a conscious and well-organized working class with the right to strike and with very broad possibilities of organization and demonstration is well placed to block any decisive shift in the economic situation.

Thus, if there is a strategic defeat of the working class, I think you will see a radical curtailment of the right to strike and of trade-union freedom in general. And this will have deep implications for the political structure of the countries concerned. In other words, there would be authoritarian political regimes—not necessarily fascist-type states, although I would not exclude that either, but authoritarian regimes qualitatively different from those that exist today. I do not take it lightly when I say that a strategic victory of the capitalist class over the working class in any *key* country of Western Europe would be a disastrous turn of events. As I say, this is extremely unlikely in the short and even medium term, but it cannot be excluded for all time. That is the worst aspect of the policies of Social Democracy and Eurocommunism, and to a large extent also of the 'orthodox Stalinist' parties, if we may call them that. For all their lauding of bourgeois-democratic institutions, for all their ideological genuflections before bourgeois-democratic values, they completely underplay the potential dangers of the European situation. They sow the same sort of illusions that were peddled by their Chilean counterparts between 1970 and 1973: it can't happen here; we have democratic armies; we have democratic traditions; and so on. This is a perilous illusion, for it *can* happen here.

I once criticized Santiago Carrillo for his incredible statement that a Social Democratic prime minister in Spain today would mean a military coup tomorrow. That is a ridiculous and disastrous thing to say. What he really wants is for Suárez to remain in power. He does not even want the replacement of Suárez by a mild Social Democrat, so far to the right has he swung. But that said, there is absolutely no doubt that the counterparts of Mola, Quiepo De Llano, and Franco already exist in the Spanish army—and everyone knows their names. That is the other side of the coin, where Carrillo is as guilty as he is on the first side: he doesn't name these people, does not ask that they be purged from the military, does not call upon the workers to oust them themselves. He pretends that the danger can be eliminated by some clever manoeuvre: just keep the workers calm enough and the bourgeoisie will behave itself. He fails to understand that the dynamic of class contradiction and the conflicts inherent in bourgeois society will inevitably give these people ever greater weight in bourgeois politics in the long run, as the only *ultimate* alternative to a powerful, combative working class and an uncontrollable economic and social crisis.

The Hegemony of Reformism and the United Front

Earlier in the discussion you made the point that nobody really believes in the effectiveness of reformist solutions in Western

Europe any more. Here you have pointed out that the reformist leaders have failed to understand the dangers inherent in a situation in which the rising conflicts of capitalist society tend to strengthen the hand of those bourgeois forces that favour mass repression against the workers. Taken together, these statements would seem to imply that in the long run the reformist parties will be incapable even of defending the immediate interests of the working class. Yet when all is said and done reformism has successfully dominated the workers' movement for decades now. How do you explain the longevity of this hegemony? How can it be overcome through revolutionary activity within the working class?

I am currently working on a book devoted to examining just that question. In it, I will try to formulate a general theory of the working class, the workers' movement, the socialist revolution, and social-ism. For the moment, let me try to summarize some of the lines along which investigation should be conducted.

To start with, let us note that the reality of the class struggle in the advanced capitalist countries since the First World War—or since 1905, for that matter—cannot be reduced purely to the formula 'reformism dominates' or to the opposite claim that 'the workers tend spontaneously to be revolutionary but the reformist traitors prevent them from making the revolution'. Indeed, both these propositions are analytically absurd.

The first would imply simply that socialism is impossible, the second a demonological conception of history. Neither is capable of accounting for historical reality. The fact is that during periods of the normal functioning of bourgeois society, the working class is indeed dominated by reformism. This is actually little more than a truism, for how could capitalism function normally if the working class contested its very existence through direct action on a daily basis? But capitalism has not functioned normally throughout the past sixty or seventy years. Periods of normality have been inter-rupted by the outbreak of crises, of pre-revolutionary and revolu-tionary situations. It is impossible—economically, socially, and psychologically—for the working class to live in a constant state of revolutionary ebullition. This alternation of conditions therefore poses the same old question of the temporal limits of revolutionary and pre-revolutionary crises.

And that brings us back to the fundamental Trotskyist problematic: that of revolutionary leadership; of the concordance between the elevation of the class consciousness of the proletariat and its capacity for self-organization; of the construction of a revolutionary leadership. The coincidence of all these factors *can* lead the crisis to an outcome other than 'business as usual', which itself breeds reformist domination. For the benefit of those who may seek to label this analysis 'revisionist', let us recall that this sort of revisionism has deep roots, since even Lenin said that the working class is 'naturally trade-unionist' during periods of the normal functioning of capitalism and 'naturally anti-capitalist' in revolutionary or pre-revolutionary situations.

The reformists will probably continue to hold the majority within the working class during 'normal' periods, if indeed the expression has any meaning during the phase of capitalist decay. In any event, it is clear that there is a fundamental difference between a situation in which there is dissension between small, isolated revolutionary groupings on the one hand and the apparatuses of mass parties that are virtually all-powerful in the working class on the other hand, and situations in which the revolutionaries have already crossed the threshold of primitive accumulation of forces, even though they still represent only a small minority of the class. In the latter case, the struggle to wrest hegemony over the masses from the reformists becomes infinitely easier, once the revolutionary crisis erupts.

The weakness of the revolutionary organizations during and immediately after the Second World War, for example, was such that any real political challenge to the reformists was impossible. In the eyes of the masses, the revolutionaries did not represent a genuine alternative to the reformists and Stalinists; the relationship of forces would have had to be shifted first. But revolutionary organizations with not several hundred but ten thousand or so members *can* realistically hope to join battle with the reformist apparatuses once more favourable conditions arise. The social composition of the organizations and their ability to recruit a sufficient number of working-class cadres who are recognized as genuine, or at least potential, leaders of the class in the factory, are also decisive elements that can be studied in detail in a number of specific cases: the Bolshevik Party between 1912 and 1914, the left wing of the Independent Social Democratic Party (USPD) in

Germany between 1917 and 1920, the revolutionary Left in Spain between 1931 and 1936.

To this we may add that the disappearance of an anti-capitalist tradition is a relatively recent phenomenon, one which accompanied the definitive turn of the Communist Parties in the industrially advanced countries at the end of the Second World War, and especially at the end of the Cold War. This sort of anti-capitalist education had continued even during the Popular Front, the Stalinist policy being implemented on two levels, so to speak. Today, Social Democratic and Stalinist reformism are joining forces to keep the working class a prisoner of bourgeois and petty-bourgeois ideology. But any vision of the class struggle that focused exclusively on this aspect of reality would underestimate the almost structurally anti-capitalist mainsprings inherent in the class struggle during any phase of pronounced instability.

That the working class is spontaneously anti-capitalist during pre-revolutionary times has been confirmed on a sweeping scale in country after country: Germany 1918-1923, Italy 1917-20, France 1934-36, Spain 1931-36, France again in May '68, Italy again in 1969-70 and 1975-76, Spain again in 1975-76, Portugal in 1975, and so on.

On the other hand, these explosions of spontaneously anti-capitalist activity (and consciousness) have less lasting effects on class consciousness and allow the reformists to regain control relatively rapidly unless they are taken up by powerful anti-capitalist mass organizations like the Communist Parties of the early twenties or by a significant-sized workers' vanguard that is constantly wary of the bureaucratic apparatuses.

Another phenomenon—often confused with this one—is the stratification of the working class and the connection between this stratification and the various levels of consciousness within the proletariat. What may appear as a swelling of the numerical strength of the reformists at the beginning of revolutionary or pre-revolutionary situations is above all a consequence of the extension of politicization to sectors that had previously been politically passive. This sort of expansion of the reformist forces therefore does not contradict the concomitant radicalization of the more seasoned layers who have long experience in political activity.

Take the example of March and April 1917 in Russia. The

enormous surge of support for the Mensheviks and Social Revolutionaries during those months was not at all the product of any decline in support for the Bolsheviks among the conscious workers. On the contrary, the Bolshevik grip on the vanguard of the class was growing. But the reformists were growing even faster, since hundreds of thousands of workers who had never before been politically active were turning to the movement for the first time. And they, of course, initially gravitated to the more moderate forces.

Does this analysis of the class consciousness of the proletariat imply that the policy of the workers' united front must be the fundamental strategic line of revolutionaries?

Here we must distinguish two political, or rather socio-political, objectives. The working class cannot overthrow capitalism, exercise power, and begin to construct a classless society unless it attains a degree of unification of its social forces and a level of politicization and consciousness qualitatively higher than what exists under the capitalist system in normal times. Indeed, it is only through such unification and politicization that the entire class constitutes itself as a class for itself, beyond any distinctions of occupation, level of skills, regional or national origin, race, sex, age, and so on.

The majority of workers acquire class consciousness in the highest sense of the word only through the experience of this sort of unification in struggle. The revolutionary party plays a crucial mediating role in all this. But through its own activity it cannot replace this experience in united struggle by the majority of the workers. The party alone cannot be the source of acquisition of this class consciousness for millions of wage-earners.

Now, the organizational framework most suitable for this unification of the proletarian front is a system of *workers' councils* that can assemble, federate, and centralize all working men and women, both organized and unorganized, without regard to political affiliation or philosophical creed. No trade union, no united front of parties, has ever been able to achieve such unification by itself. Nor will it ever be able to do so.

For this reason, revolutionary Marxists always press for the unification of the demands and struggles of all working men and women—not only economically, but also politically, culturally, and so on. They strive to combat any manoeuvres that would tend to divide the class. They act as the most resolute and effective advocates of the most united mobilizations and struggles. And this, by the way, requires that special attention be paid to the super-exploited and doubly oppressed sectors of the class; otherwise this unification cannot be achieved in practice.

Without any doubt, then, the policy of unification of the proletarian front is a constant, a *permanent strategic objective* for revolutionary Marxists.

This problematic of the unification and politicization of the entire proletariat, however, is distinct from the question of particular proposals for united fronts addressed to different organizations and political currents within the working class. I will not go into the objective and historic origins or particular role of these various parties and organizations. But I would like to examine the precise articulation between the policy of the united front as it concerns the two traditional mass parties of the workers' movement—the Communist and Socialist Parties—and the strategy of unification and Marxist politicization of the entire proletariat.

There are a number of reasons why these two sets of problems are not identical. First, the Socialist and Communist Parties do not at all include—or even influence—all working men and women. Second, within the proletariat there are vanguard layers, some organized but many not, who have drawn conclusions from the past betrayals of Social Democracy and Stalinism and who already deeply distrust the bureaucratic apparatuses of these currents. Third, within the working class the bureaucratic leaderships of the Socialist and Communist Parties uphold political orientations that often conflict with the immediate interests, and always conflict with the historic interests, of the proletariat. It is therefore perfectly possible for them to conclude united agreements designed to disorient, curb, and fragment workers' mobilizations. This is particularly the case during revolutionary and pre-revolutionary situations, when these apparatuses typically strive to prevent the seizure of power by the proletariat.

But although these two sets of problems are not identical, they cannot be completely separated either. For in all countries in which the organized workers' movement has a long tradition, a significant section of the class continues to manifest some degree of confidence in the Socialist and Communist Parties, not only in elections, but also politically and organizationally. It is therefore impossible to make any real progress towards the unity of the proletarian front while disregarding this relative confidence or by assuming that the Socialist or Communist workers will join this front regardless of the attitudes and reactions of their own leaderships.

It follows that a policy of united front directed towards the Socialist and Communist Parties is a *tactical component of the general strategic orientation. But that is all it is—a component of, and not a substitute for, this orientation.* This is particularly true since the maximum unification and politicization of the entire proletariat requires *both* the commitment of the Socialist and Communist workers *and* a break by the great majority of these workers with the options of class collaboration upheld by the bureaucratic apparatuses.

It is interesting to note, by the way, that the simplistic reduction of the strategy of unification of the proletarian forces and maximum elevation of class consciousness to the policy of the united front of the Socialist and Communist Parties is frequently paralleled by the spontaneist illusion that the actual formation of such united fronts is alone sufficient for the workers to break with the reformists, by virtue of the breadth of united struggles that would result. Even more illusory and spontaneist is the notion that the experience of a 'government without capitalist ministers' would suffice to open the road to a break by the toiling masses from reformism and to the formation of a genuine, anti-capitalist 'workers' government'.

The experience of history shows that these notions are false. It is enough to recall, for example, that after no less than *six* 'pure' Labour governments in Britain—and by that I mean governments containing no bourgeois ministers—the reformist apparatus continues to maintain its grip on the majority of the working class, even though this apparatus is integrated into the bourgeois state and bourgeois society more tightly than ever and even though it advocates and practises a policy of ever closer class collaboration with big capital.

The tactic of the united front serves the strategy of unification of the proletariat and elevation of its consciousness only if various conditions are adequately fulfilled.

First, united-front proposals addressed to the Communist and

Socialist Parties must centre on the most burning issues of the class struggle and must call upon the leaderships of these parties to unite in order to fight for specific objectives that *articulate the interests of the workers* on these issues. They must therefore contain a programmatic facet—otherwise they could even (under revolutionary conditions) facilitate operations against the working class.

Second, these proposals must be formulated in a manner that is credible to broad masses, at times when it appears possible to implement them and in forms that take due account of the level of consciousness of the workers who still follow these parties. In other words, one of the essential functions of these proposals is *actually to bring common action about*, or at least to exert such pressure from the ranks that the apparatuses would have to pay a high price for their refusal to opt for the road of united action.

Third, either through the actual achievement of the united front (which is, of course, by far the most favourable variant) or through mounting pressure from the ranks in favour of the front, these proposals must unleash a process of mobilization, struggle, and, at a certain point, self-organization of the masses either through the broadening of the front itself or through the struggle for it. This process, which is related to the growing role of the revolutionary party, accentuates the objective strength of the proletariat, increases its self-confidence, raises its level of consciousness, leads massive sectors of the working class to break with reformist ideology and strategy, and cultivates the capacity of the workers to go beyond the bureaucratic apparatuses in action.

Fourth, in order to facilitate this entire process, the revolutionary party has to link these united-front proposals with warnings to the workers about the real nature and objectives of the leaderships of the Socialist and Communist Parties; there must be no illusion that the character of these parties can be changed through the united front; there must be no reliance on these leaderships (or on a government composed of them) to implement the objectives of the united front and to defend the interests of the proletariat. The call for the united front must therefore be accompanied by the preparation of and call for initiatives by the workers themselves to solve their problems through their own mobilization, their own struggles, and their own self-organization on the broadest possible scale. The united front must facilitate and stimulate these various processes and cannot at all substitute for them.

I would close by adding one final point, which is that in my view Trotsky's efforts to formulate a correct solution to these problems—which run through nearly all his writings, from 1905-6 to his intervention in the discussion in the Communist International about the united front, to his impassioned warnings in Germany in 1923 and again in 1930-33, to his battles on France in 1934-36—constitute one of his most important contributions to Marxism. Moreover, it would be a mistake to believe that this problematic is relevant only in the imperialist countries. On the contrary, the socio-political unification of the proletariat is at least as important in the underdeveloped countries and is a central element of the strategy of permanent revolution for that very reason—and in not a few of these countries, particularly in Latin America and the Indian sub-continent, the question of organizational united fronts with reformist workers' parties is a burning one as well.

2

Permanent Revolution in the Third World

One of Leon Trotsky's major contributions to Marxism was his formulation of the theory of permanent revolution. Indeed, this theory is probably more closely associated with his name than any other. He first developed it to analyse and predict the course of the Russian revolution, arguing that there would be no intermediary bourgeois stage in that revolution, that the 'classical' tasks of the bourgeois revolution would be solved by the working class under the dictatorship of the proletariat. He later generalized the theory, applying it to the entire colonial world, where the Chinese, Vietnamese, and Cuban revolutions have confirmed its correctness, as did the Russian.

In the post-war period, however, there has been a great wave of de-colonization, most often led by bourgeois-nationalist political forces. This has led to the establishment of states with at least juridical independence, as the European colonial empires have collapsed. Is it not the case that revolutionary Marxists have tended to underestimate the capacity of the indigenous bourgeoisie of the colonial and semi-colonial world to win political independence and even to preside over rather thorough-going bourgeois revolutions? Hasn't the Fourth International underestimated the capacity for struggle of these bourgeois-nationalist parties and social forces?

I will answer your question at two levels. First, what has actually occurred, and is still occurring to some extent, although the process is now nearly finished, since there are very few colonies left in the real sense of the word, countries directly administered by the imperialist powers. Second, what are the implications of this process for the theory of permanent revolution?

To begin with, I would not deny that many Marxists, including Trotsky and the Trotskyist movement, have made imprudent generalizations from time to time about the impossibility of this or that. Indeed, one of the great lessons that must be drawn from 150 years of the international class struggle is that the utmost hesitation is required before saying that this or that development can never occur. What is impossible today, under the given relationship of forces, might turn out to be not so impossible tomorrow. I would remind you, for instance, that Trotsky also said that the nationalization of the coal industry in Britain was impossible under capitalism. As it happens, nationalization did occur, under a different relationship of forces, when the Labour government came to power in 1945. But I think it is rather foolish to take Trotsky, Lenin, or Marx (or other great figures in the history of human thought) to task for these sorts of statements, because in general they are not characteristic either of the function of their theories in the advance of human knowledge or of their political function. Everybody can make this sort of mistake, and does.

In fact, on balance I would say that this is one of the aspects of the changes in the world situation that the Fourth International grasped most rapidly. As early as 1947 it was stated very clearly in the resolution adopted at the Second World Congress, which met early in 1948, that we were in the midst of a process of general transition from direct to indirect rule of imperialism over colonial countries. We predicted a general trend towards the granting of national independence to former colonies; the colonial bourgeoisie, we said, would be transformed into junior partners with a certain degree of autonomy of their imperialist overlords.

It is important to note that this transformation was not the result of some clever manoeuvre by imperialism; rather, it was brought about by a radical change in the worldwide relationship of forces. If imperialism had not yielded political independence, capitalism could have been overthrown in a large part of the world. Just imagine what would have happened if British imperialism had tried to stick it out in India, had refused to withdraw—at a time when the Chinese civil war was flaring up, the Vietnamese war had already begun, and bourgeois society was far from stabilized even in Western Europe. It would have been a clear disaster for world imperialism. They could have 'lost' India as they did China; in fact, they could very well have

lost part of Western Europe too. Consider the price the British working class would have had to pay for a full-scale colonial war under a
Labour government in 1947. It is unthinkable that such a war would
have been accepted passively.

The imperialists were therefore forced to effect that retreat
because of a change in the relationship of forces. Some imperialist
powers did it cleverly and rapidly, some foolishly, after holding on
for a long time. Those that opted for this latter course paid a heavy
price; the Fourth Republic in France, for example, was overthrown
largely as a consequence of its short-sighted colonial policy. But by
and large, the retreat was made. And I think we predicted this
correctly at a time when the process had barely begun.

Now, does this contradict the theory of permanent revolution? I
do not think so, but again we have to discard simplistic, one-sided
interpretations of what this theory says. Since there has been a great
deal of attention paid to it (the British Communist Party has
published one of its most traditionally Stalinist pamphlets on just
this subject, and not by chance), I would like to take the opportunity
to recapitulate what the theory argues, its real framework and its
essential premises, which have often been badly misunderstood.

The initial premise of the theory is that Marx's famous dictum that
the advanced countries mirror the future of the less developed ones
ceases to be accurate with the rise of imperialism. France and
Belgium did generally follow the pattern of English development;
Germany and Italy by and large repeated French development,
although without a radical bourgeois revolution. Japan, Austria,
and Tsarist Russia started on that road, but were unable to traverse it
completely. This, however, was the end of the matter. Once the
general imperialist nature of the world economy was established, it
became impossible for less developed countries to repeat *completely*
the process of industrialization and modernization undergone by the
imperialist countries.

There are three essential reasons for this, which were summarized
by the young Trotsky, more intuitively than through deep historical
study, when he first formulated his theory in 1905. First, the weight
of imperialist capital on the world market (and therefore in every
country, including the backward ones) was such that any organic
process of industrialization in competition with imperialist capital
was ruled out so long as imperialism dominated. Second, the native

bourgeoisie in these countries was trapped between its desire to industrialize and modernize on the one hand and its close relations with agrarian property on the other hand. Because of this close relationship, the bourgeoisie had no interest in effecting a radical agrarian revolution, for to do so would have been to destroy a significant part of its own capital. Such an agrarian revolution, however, is the precondition for the creation of the extensive internal market required for a thorough, organic process of industrialization. Here there was also a political consideration: the working class was relatively stronger than the bourgeoisie in many of these countries, so the bourgeoisie feared any radical upheaval in the system of property relations, since any such upheaval threatened to run out of control. Third, the peasantry—which would have provided most of the potential participants in the bourgeois revolutionary process (and whose revolutionary potential Trotsky never denied, by the way)—was unable to offer central political leadership for that process. It was historically condemned to follow either a bourgeois or a proletarian leadership. If the peasants were led by bourgeois forces, the counter-revolution would be victorious, because the bourgeoisie, for the reasons I have just outlined, would inevitably go over to the counter-revolution in the course of the revolutionary process. Hence, only if the peasants were won over by a proletarian leadership, or at least participated in a revolutionary process over which the proletariat had established hegemony, would there be full realization of their revolutionary potential to destroy all forms of landed property that were impediments to a full-fledged process of modernization.

Now, these observations provide the foundation of the first law of permanent revolution: the proletariat can take power in an underdeveloped country before it takes power in more developed ones; indeed, without the conquest of power by the proletariat in the underdeveloped countries, there will be no complete and genuine realization of *all* the historic tasks of the bourgeois-democratic revolution. Obviously, this in no way implies either that *no* task of the bourgeois-democratic revolution can be accomplished without proletarian leadership or that no revolutionary process can even *begin* in an underdeveloped country unless the proletariat has established political hegemony over the peasantry. Trotsky, of course, never said anything like that, which would have meant that no revolution could have even begun unless a Bolshevik leadership was already established.

If we examine what has happened since 1945, we ought to conclude that these predictions have not been belied. National political independence has been won in most former colonies, which have now become semi-colonies, or dependent capitalist countries. Industrialization has started in many of them and has developed to a certain point. Greater or lesser agrarian reforms of many varieties have been introduced in some of these countries. But I think it would be hard to disagree with the statement that a complete, organic process of industrialization and modernization has not occurred in any of them—without a single exception. And it would be hard to deny that this is linked to the absence of a radical agrarian revolution to clear the way for the creation of an extensive internal market. Conversely, it would be equally hard to deny that precisely in those countries in which a socialist revolution occurred—China, Vietnam, and Cuba, for example—these conditions were realized; and under these conditions a process of industrialization and modernization could begin—and has—in a manner totally different from countries like India, Egypt, or any other country in which that radical agrarian revolution has not taken place.

I would like, however, to add a supplementary point—a new element in the situation—which Trotsky did not foresee and which we have taken note of rather belatedly, although not as belatedly as one might think. I am referring to the change in the structure of imperialist capital in the metropolis itself, all the aspects of what I call 'late capitalism'. This change of structure led to a new attitude by imperialist capital towards the partial industrialization—or perhaps it would be better to say intermediary industrialization—of a certain number of underdeveloped countries. I think I can safely say that I was one of the first people to take note of this—in the fourteenth chapter of my book *Marxist Economic Theory*, which was written in 1960. In essence, this phenomenon can be summarized as follows: once the sector producing and exporting equipment goods gains dominance in the metropolis over the sector producing and exporting consumer goods (including even durable consumer goods), imperialism acquires an interest in a certain degree of industrialization in the dependent countries. The reason is evident: if you export machinery, you need customers, and you seek them throughout the world. This leads to a change in the relationship between the various fractions of the international bourgeois class, and this in turn leads to a change in the ruling bloc in some of the key countries of the underdeveloped world. The classical ruling bloc was that of the big landowners, 'comprador' bourgeoisie, and imperialist capital dominating the production of raw materials and primary products. That dominant bloc had no interest in large-scale or rapid industrialization—quite the opposite.

Now there is a new dominant bloc in some of these countries: a bloc of native capitalist monopolies, technocrats of the state and military apparatus, and multinationals interested especially in the export of industrial equipment. This bloc, unlike the previous one, has an interest in industrializing these intermediary economies up to a point. This shift in the composition of the ruling bloc in some countries is therefore linked both to structural changes in the metropolis of the imperialist bourgeoisie itself and to important changes in the social composition of the intermediary countries, for there have been major upheavals there.

Is there not a danger in the way you have presented this problem? In a sense, you seem to be setting excessively high standards for what would be considered genuine bourgeois revolutionary developments in the 'third world'. After all, in the advanced metropolitan countries the solution of the various tasks of the bourgeois revolution required a prolonged period. The process was highly uneven; accounts with the feudal landowning class were settled in very different ways in France, Britain, Germany, Japan, and so on. Furthermore, the classical Marxist conception of the essential tasks of the bourgeois revolution does not centre on full-scale modernization or industrialization. The French Revolution of 1789, for example, scarcely produced full industrialization in France, not in the short term anyway. Rather, the bourgeois revolution essentially involved the ouster of those power-holding classes based on pre-capitalist social relations, or in the case of the American War of Independence, the elimination of the colonial state apparatus and the creation of an independent state. And of course, generally associated with that was an agrarian revolution as the basis, or an essential component, of the creation of this new state apparatus. Could we not say that in the nearly three-quarters of a century

since Trotsky first enunciated the theory of permanent revolution—
a period marked by tremendous revolutionary struggles, wars and
civil wars, dramatic political transformations and conflicts of every
type—the tasks of the bourgeois revolution have actually been
accomplished, albeit in a partial, lengthy, and uneven fashion, in a
number of intermediary countries of the 'third world'? Many of
these states now possess independent, capitalist state apparatuses
capable of propelling modernization and industrialization forward.
After all, even in the countries in which there have been socialist
revolutions, industrialization is far from 'organic' and complete.
But if we look at countries like Mexico, Brazil, Algeria, Egypt, and
even India, we see states that are now politically independent and do
not rest on pre-capitalist social strata; and surely many of these
countries have seen agrarian reforms as far-reaching as those in
some of the metropolitan countries.

If all this is true, one of the basic postulates of the theory of
permanent revolution must now be qualified and corrected: that the
tasks of the bourgeois revolution can be fully accomplished only
through the dictatorship of the proletariat. Would you agree with
that?

No. In fact, I would strongly disagree. To start with, Trotsky uses
exactly the same words as I used before: the *complete and genuine*
solution (not the *beginning* of a solution) of the tasks of the
bourgeois-democratic revolution. The way you formulate your
characterization of the bourgeois revolutions of the past, on which
basis you evaluate what has been going on in the so-called intermediary countries, is faulty, in my view. (In passing, by the way, I
would not consider Egypt one of these intermediary countries.
Brazil, Mexico, yes; India, dubious but perhaps. Others are South
Korea, the city states of Hong Kong and Singapore, which are
special cases, and Argentina.)

You put too much emphasis on the bourgeois character of the
state and the elimination of pre-capitalist social relations or relations
of production. Why do I say that? Because the law of uneven and
combined development obviously continues to operate in the epoch
of imperialism—more than ever, in fact. The backwardness of a
country like Brazil or even India in 1950 cannot be compared to the
'backwardness' of France in 1789. I do not want to repeat the debate

which has been going on for several decades now about the nature of Latin American agriculture, or more generally about agriculture in many of the colonial countries in the nineteenth century. My good friend André Gunder Frank has pushed the debate even to the nature of agriculture in the sixteenth century.

Let us leave that aside. But my own feeling is that even when Trotsky was writing, semi-feudal social relations in the literal sense of the word—not to mention semi-feudal state apparatuses like the absolute monarchy in Russia or the monarchy in France before the revolution of 1789—were very little prevalent in the colonial countries. One can cite the special case of the Indian princes and the portion of India over which they ruled, but that was an exception. In most of the colonial world, the general weight of this sort of absolutism was much reduced, not through revolutionary processes but by the simple logic of imperialism. As imperialism consolidated its control, there was an integration of big landowners, the comprador bourgeoisie, and imperialist capital, which progressively changed the nature of the landowners themselves. The transition from semi-feudal to semi-capitalist land ownership is nearly inevitable under these circumstances, except under the most extreme conditions of congealed social relations. For example, as early as the 1940s, the *traditional* landowning oligarchy remained predominant in Latin America only in the most backward countries. Even a family like the Somozas in Nicaragua, generally cited as an example of classical oligarchic rule, operates in practice as modern entrepreneurs in many ways, gangsters that they are. (A feudal overlord is not a gangster.)

I would therefore place more emphasis on the property relations, particularly as they relate to the conditions of the peasantry and to the possibility of minimum economic development and progress. As an interesting aside, I would remind you that as late as 1916 Lenin, who at that time still excluded the possibility of the inauguration of the dictatorship of the proletariat in Russia, set out the alternative of Russian development as follows: either the Russian (i.e. Tsarist) form of agriculture or the American (referring, of course, to American farming of the nineteenth century). Well, Lenin was of course wrong about the alternative for Russia, and he was soon to realize this. But if we look around the 'third world', we find no country in which the American form of agriculture (capitalist in its purest form) took hold. No one can seriously maintain that this is the predominant form of agricultural development in Brazil, let alone India.

Now, what is the consequence of this? It is formidable: the failure of any of these countries to bring about this form of agricultural development has prevented the genuine modernization of these countries. What I mean by modernization is very simply this: the opportunity for more than one thousand million people—because that is the scope of the problem on a world scale—to escape from extreme forms of degradation, misery, semi-famine, obscurantism, and complete lack of possibility of development, capitalist or otherwise. If we draw a balance-sheet of even the most successful of these intermediary bourgeois states—South Korea, Brazil, or Mexico—we will see that this has not happened. It is generally estimated that about 20 per cent of the population has been integrated into the internal market in some form in these countries. It should be noted that this does not mean that their standard of living has risen significantly, but only that they are now capable of purchasing some modern consumer goods. Now, in some countries this is indeed a formidable achievement if measured in absolute figures. In India it would mean that the system has generated sufficient industrialization to involve more than a hundred million people, in Brazil about 20 million. But this statistic can be expressed in an opposite form: 400 million people in India and 80 million in Brazil have been totally excluded from this process. Hence the formula: genuine and complete resolution of the democratic tasks of the bourgeois revolution is impossible under a bourgeois state. The process can only be begun, and there are sharp objective limits to its development.

Here I would like to add another point, more controversial amongst both revolutionary Marxists and the workers' movement in general. This is the second aspect of the question we are discussing, namely the exact relationship of these states to imperialism. Now, I would be inclined to say that the degree of political autonomy of imperialist capital that has been achieved by these states is greater than Marxists expected thirty or forty years ago. In fact, I think it is now wrong to call countries like Brazil or India semi-colonial in the sense that their governments should be considered stooges of some imperialist power. They are not. Earlier I referred to the power bloc now ruling in these countries; obviously, the component that comprises the native ruling classes is much larger and more autonomous today than in the past.

But I would immediately add that I think it would be a disastrous analytical mistake with fatal political consequences to fail to recognize the other side of the coin: these remain *dependent* countries, with *dependent* bourgeoisies. This, of course, has implications for the degree of resistance these state apparatuses can muster against imperialism. The hold of the international imperialist economy, of imperialist capital, on the economies of these countries remains such that the formula of dependence is wholly justified. This hold is reflected in many ways: financial and technological dependence, subjection to international institutions like the International Monetary Fund, monetary subordination to international money markets, the ability of imperialism to continue to manipulate and dominate the terms of trade, the degree to which the industrialization process in these countries is integrated with the needs of imperialist capital, the weight of imperialist corporations in the industrialization process, and so on.

The Limits of Dependent Accumulation

One of the developments to which you have pointed in recent years has been the rise of what you have called a new, autonomous finance capital in a number of dependent capitalist countries, including, among others, Iran, the Arab countries of the Gulf, Brazil, and South Korea. It is now several years since you first made this observation. Have the latest trends of development confirmed it? If so, doesn't this sort of phenomenon raise problems for the theory of permanent revolution?

I believe that developments of recent years have completely confirmed that observation. The most striking cases are Brazil, Mexico, South Korea, and Iran. For all these countries, the evidence that has been amassed from various sources has been overwhelming. In the case of Kuwait, Saudi Arabia, and the Gulf countries, much additional evidence has been provided by Mohammed Jafar, in his articles published in *Inprecor/Intercontinental Press*. In India the phenomenon is older. In my book *The Second Slump* I made mention of the Birla group, which is Indian-owned and operates in twenty different countries, with a total staff of 200,000. Here we have a bloc of capital with greater extension than some of the biggest British firms. Many other instances could be added, too: the Mexican financial groups structured around the big banks (Banco Nacional de Mexico, Banco de Comercio, Banco Mexicano), which control more than a hundred companies; the Khashoggi group in Saudi Arabia, with holdings of more than a thousand million dollars; the Ghaith Pharaon group in Saudi Arabia; the Matarazzo group in Brazil; the Rezai, Barkhordar, and Khosrowshahi groups in Iran; a number of major blocs in South Korea and Hong Kong. It is true that in some of these cases, the degree of independence from imperialist capital is not clear; it must be determined on a case-by-case basis. But when the Hong Kong financier Wong Chong-po buys out Bulova, Switzerland's second-largest watch-maker, it is evident that he is not acting as the agent of some imperialist multinational.

Most of these cases involve typical instances of finance capital; there is simply no other way to describe them. Indeed, if we want to present a more precise picture of the structure of the capitalist world today, we must introduce some rather new terminology. It is quite clear to me that countries like Brazil, Mexico, South Korea, and Argentina must be considered 'semi-industrialized'. Brazil's industrial exports, for example, are cornering a mounting share of the Latin American market. The industrialization in these countries is not a product purely of the rise of an autonomous finance capital. More and more multinationals are transferring some of their production centres to less developed countries where real wages are lower and raw materials prices less inflated. Also in *The Second Slump* I pointed out that the Volkswagen 'beetle', largest-selling automobile in the industry's history, is no longer produced in West Germany, but imported there from new VW facilities in Mexico and Brazil. Today there are more industrial workers in the greater metropolitan area of São Paulo than in most industrialized concentrations in the advanced capitalist countries. It is reasonable to say, then, that the countries we call 'semi-industrialized' stand somewhere between Italy or Spain on the one hand and Chad, Mali, or Paraguay on the other.

The consequences of this development are, of course, weighty.

One of them is that the objective weight of the proletariat in the revolution in these countries will be greater than in any of the previous socialist revolutions, including even the Russian, since in some of these countries, the urban population already constitutes the majority of the population and the wage-earners already constitute the majority of the active population. This was not the case in Russia in 1905 or 1917. Another important consequence is that these countries are—and will be—more and more directly involved in classical over-production crises than they were in the past. In other words, they will increasingly *combine* the effects of backwardness with those of large-scale capitalist development. Indeed, this is one of the factors now undermining the Brazilian dictatorship, and it played a role in precipitating the Iranian revolution.

At the same time, this phenomenon must not be looked at in a one-sided way. For one thing, it is quite clear that for the most part these groups of autonomous finance capital in the semi-industrialized countries operate in the interstices left to them by the dominant multinational imperialist corporations. This is one reflection of their continuing dependent status in the world capitalist economy. Furthermore, the use of the term 'semi-industrialized' in no way implies that these countries have become 'imperialist', or even 'sub-imperialist'. Such formulas are highly confusing, because they obfuscate the *fundamental* differences between imperialist and dependent countries. In some ways, stepped-up industrialization has made these countries—the most developed of the underdeveloped countries—more and not less dependent on imperialism than before. They are more dependent on imperialist technology, more closely integrated into and therefore subjected to the imperialist world market. Extensive sectors of the national bourgeoisie are more strongly tied to multinational firms. In fact, their relative economic successes have enhanced their dependence on the international credit system. Furthermore, in cases in which there is a conflict of interest over markets between imperialist corporations and newly developed industries in the dependent countries, the latter are particularly vulnerable to protectionist measures taken by imperialist governments, especially in a context of relative stagnation, or even contraction, of world trade. In 1976, for example, the Hong Kong textile industry was seriously hurt by an embargo imposed by Canada and by import restrictions ordered by Australia. In 1977 the Common Market countries moved to reduce their imports of six of Hong Kong's leading industrial products. Even the United States, Hong Kong's prime customer, has been threatening to take similar measures. Because of the relationship of forces between the imperialist countries and the countries of the 'third world', the underdeveloped countries are usually unable to retaliate effectively against these sorts of measures. In general, then, they can develop industries only to the extent that they 'fill holes' left by imperialist capital. Only in the case of relatively marginal products will they be able really to challenge imperialist domination of the market.

Even more important, however, is the fact that the *social structure* of these countries still reflects their dependency. The unresolved agrarian question, the huge mass of rural and urban unemployed, the cultural backwardness (high rates of illiteracy, for example), the extent of persistent imperialist economic domination, and other such factors mean that the coming revolution in these countries will be a permanent revolution and not a purely socialist one, even though it is not certain that the struggle for the unresolved national-democratic tasks will play the role of triggering the revolutionary process in all cases. Because of the weight of the working class in these countries, it is possible that demands of a 'purely proletarian' nature could launch the revolutionary process. Even in that case, however, these unresolved bourgeois-democratic tasks would have to be brought rapidly to the forefront of the struggle.

The contention of some of our critics on this point that we have brought the theory of the permanent revolution into question by placing 'undue emphasis' on the autonomy of these new sectors of finance capital is absurd. Those who make this allegation seem to have forgotten that the theory of permanent revolution was first formulated by Trotsky to apply to a country that Lenin considered one of the major *imperialist* countries of the time, namely Russia. True, it was far the most backward of the imperialist countries, and one could probably make a case that Tsarist Russia in the early part of the twentieth century was actually a country that *combined* aspects of an imperialist country and aspects of a semi-colonial one. The fact remains that Russia was one of the central participants in the imperialist war. Moreover, we have never sought to claim that Brazil, Argentina, or Mexico today exhibits even this kind of combination, which is why we have always rejected the formula of 'sub-imperialism'. In any event, an autonomous finance capital surely existed in Russia in 1917, so if the theory of permanent revolution was valid then, there is certainly no reason to assume that the rise of an autonomous finance capital of lesser power in some semi-industrialized countries today suddenly renders the theory invalid. What is especially peculiar about this point made by some of our critics is that the more usual charge hurled against the theory of permanent revolution is not at all that it is inapplicable to countries in which there is an urban proletariat of significant size as the result of a process of industrialization, but rather the opposite: that Trotsky made a mistake in generalizing the theory to countries that were so backward that the weight of the working class was negligible.

This point seems valid enough. Implicit in what you say, however, is the notion that there are objective limits to this process of industrialization in the 'semi-industrialized' countries and therefore also objective limits to their ability to qualitatively alter their social structure. If there were no such limits, then at least some of these countries could theoretically continue their development to the point that they would become fully modernized capitalist societies in which the tasks of the bourgeois revolution had been solved (at least as much as those tasks have been fully solved even in the most advanced countries). A 'purely proletarian' revolution would then be on the agenda. That, certainly, would mean that the theory of permanent revolution had turned out to be invalid after all. What, then, are these objective limitations? What is it that prevents a country like Brazil, or some of the OPEC countries, from becoming a full-fledged modern capitalist nation?

Let me begin by dealing with the OPEC countries. Here there are a number of factors that severely limit their ability to undergo a genuine process of industrialization in the long run. To start with, as we in the Fourth International have pointed out on a number of occasions, there has been a tendency to strongly exaggerate the actual accumulation of exchange reserves by the oil-exporting countries. Indeed, there was a good deal of deliberate falsification by imperialist circles on this point, the ideological aim of which was evident: they were (and still are) trying to convince the workers of the imperialist countries that the 1974-75 recession was in large part, if not primarily, the fault of the 'oil sheikhs' and that since the cause of the crisis was external to the economies of the advanced capitalist countries, the only solution was 'austerity' of one variety or another. The World Bank, for example, had initially made the fantastic claim that the OPEC members would soon accumulate $650 thousand million in exchange reserves. Similar sources alleged that the balance of payments surpluses of the oil-exporting countries would total $80 thousand million in 1975. All these figures have had to be constantly revised downward. The real figure on the 1975 balance of payments surpluses, for example, turned out to be only $57 thousand million, and by 1977 it had fallen to about $21 thousand million.

Now, one reason for this consistent overestimation of the supposed treasure of the OPEC members, apart from the deliberate falsification, is that even the resources generated by the huge increases in oil prices have not sufficed to finance long-term industrialization in most of these countries. The result is that those oil-exporting countries with significant-sized populations actually faced balance of payments *deficits* because of the massive expense of the imports they needed for their industrialization plans. Nigeria, Algeria, Iran, Iraq, and Venezuela, for example, all ran deficits, despite their oil income.

In the final analysis, this simple statistical fact is a reflection of the socio-economic backwardness of these countries. Nearly all of them lack an infrastructure capable of supporting genuine industrial development. The result is that huge outlays are required to establish the sorts of transportation and communications networks (to take only one example) that were developed in the advanced capitalist countries over a period of many decades. In other words, the retrograde social structure of these countries has a twofold negative effect on their industrialization plans: first, much greater infrastructural investments are required; second, vast imports of technology, machinery, and so on are also needed, since these societies are unable to generate these supplies themselves. This means that even the limited industrialization that is now occurring in these countries cannot be sustained, let alone significantly expanded, unless the vast oil income continues to flow in, not just for the next few years, but for decades.

Now, there are various reasons why this is unlikely to happen. For one thing, the exact relationship of oil sales and prices is not as straightforward as many people think. A good portion of the income of the OPEC members will be wiped out by the combination of rising prices for their imported goods and technology and the continuing devaluation of the dollar and the pound sterling. The ruling classes in the OPEC countries are, of course, well aware of this, which is why they constantly threaten to index oil prices to the prices of manufactured goods or to take other measures to counteract these downward pressures on their incomes.

Any success they have in this, however, would simply intensify the second factor that will tend to lower the surpluses available to them for economic development: the gradual substitution, over a long period, of alternative energy sources (and the related phenomenon of the discovery and exploitation of oil deposits elsewhere in the world). In the long run, the combination of these two processes will lead to a relative decline in oil prices consequent to over-production. It is therefore highly unlikely that the OPEC countries will enjoy a sufficient income over a long enough period to finance a really thorough-going process of industrialization and modernization. And again, in the final analysis, all these problems reflect their continuing dependence on and subordination to imperialism.

Finally, there is another factor that must be taken into account, and that is the evolution of the international capitalist economy as a whole. In *The Second Slump* I argued that this economy has now entered a 'long wave' of extremely sluggish growth or even stagnation. All available evidence confirms this, and indeed this is one of the factors that accounts for the gravity of the 1974-75 recession and the slow and hesitant recovery that followed. Under these conditions, any real progress in the overall industrial capacity of the OPEC countries implies an aggravation of the crisis afflicting the competing sectors of industry in the imperialist countries. This, in turn, aggravates the general economic crisis and ultimately has negative consequences for industrial development in the OPEC countries themselves. The international capitalist economy is, in important ways, a unitary whole. It is therefore impossible to examine the prospects for economic development in one section of it in isolation either from the whole or from the other component parts. It has been our analysis—and again, all the available evidence confirms this—that the world capitalist economy is not at all heading into a period of vigorous expansion. Quite the contrary, coming recessions will be deeper, booms and recoveries even more hesitant and uneven. Now, under those conditions, with the imperialist countries themselves having difficulty maintaining significant growth rates, it is hard to conceive of a protracted spurt of industrial construction in the *less developed* and *less vigorous* economies. There may be, of course, an individual exception during this or that brief period, but by and large we can rule out the sort of growth that would be required to transform the socio-economic structure of the countries of the 'third world' to the point that a 'purely proletarian' revolution would be on the agenda.

The ultimate truth of this assertion may be seen if we take a quick look at the position of these countries in the world market. That position is, to say the least, marginal. Take one example. The total exports of the EEC countries to Brazil, India, and Pakistan stagnated or declined throughout 1975, 1976, and 1977. I pointed this out in *The Second Slump* as well, but the point bears repeating. These three countries, with their total population of something like 800 million, buy fewer commodities from the nine Common Market countries than does Austria alone, whose population is less than 8 million! What is the reason for this striking disparity? It is obvious. The Brazilian 'model of development' was based on the super-exploitation of the proletariat and the impoverishment of the peasantry. The result, as I mentioned earlier, is that only about a fifth of the population is included in the domestic market. And this establishes a limit not only to Brazil's ability to absorb commodities from the imperialist countries, but also to its own industrialization programme. It all comes down to the same point in the end: imperialism has been unable to lift the populations of the dependent countries out of poverty and misery; these countries therefore cannot serve as adequate markets either for massive new imports from imperialist countries or for extensive industrialization of their own economies.

All these various points can be summarized as follows. There has been—and it is still continuing—a restructuration of the world market. One of the features of that process is that some of the most developed of the underdeveloped countries are experiencing a not insignificant degree of industrialization, which is, at bottom, a result of the combination of two tendencies: first, the transference by imperialist capital of some production centres to the dependent countries; second, the rise of an autonomous finance capital in these countries which does have an interest in pursuing these industrialization plans. But the system as a whole continues to be dominated by imperialism, and there is no sign that this is changing in any important way. There are therefore absolute limits to the industrialization programmes of these countries, and none of them—or at least no country with a significant-sized population—will succeed in making the transition from 'semi-industrialized' to fully industrialized, with all the socio-economic consequences this entails. Within that framework, however, the ruling classes in these countries now command a much larger slice of autonomous capital than they did previously; this means that they appropriate a significantly larger share of globally-produced surplus-value than before. To deny that would be to deny an evident fact of life. But at the same time, to interpret that fact to mean that any significant-sized dependent capitalist country will succeed in undergoing a process of industrial development such that the socio-economic structure of that country comes to mirror the structure of the advanced capitalist countries so that the tasks of the bourgeois revolution are resolved and the country in question faces a socialist revolution of the same type as countries like France, Germany, or even Spain, would be to fall into an abusive generalization whose political consequences would be disastrous.

Permanent Revolution: Theory or Strategy?

What you are essentially saying is that the theory of permanent revolution is less an analytical tool than a political strategy for revolution applicable to countries at a certain stage of development. It is not so much a matter of making predictions as of determining the strategic goals and tasks of the proletariat and its allies.

I do indeed prefer the expression 'strategy' of permanent revolution, although the distinction between 'analytical tool' and 'strategy' is artificial to some extent, since the strategy, if it is to be scientific (in other words, not utopian, but realizable), must be based on a lucid objective analysis. In that sense, what we are really discussing when we talk about whether or not permanent revolution is applicable to this or that country is the *set of tasks* faced by the exploited classes of that country. It is here that the distinction between permanent revolution in the dependent countries and 'pure proletarian' revolution in the advanced capitalist countries becomes truly meaningful.

Perhaps one way to grasp this more clearly is to look at the actual historical development of the theory/strategy of permanent revolution. As we know, the original formulation of the theory in 1905 was basically an attempt to uncover the motive forces of the coming Russian revolution in the light of the lessons of the 1905 experience. What would the class dynamics of that revolution be, and what would be the role of the working class within it? Those were the questions Trotsky was dealing with in *Results and Prospects*. In the years prior to the October Revolution, the expression 'permanent revolution', associated almost exclusively with the name of Trotsky, meant simply that the coming revolution in Russia would place the working class in power and that once in power, the workers would be compelled to take radical measures against bourgeois property relations if they were to resolve the problems posed by Russia's lack of a bourgeois revolution. During those years, permanent revolution was counterposed on the one hand to the position of the Mensheviks, who held that the coming revolution would inevitably be bourgeois and that the leadership of it would therefore logically devolve to the liberals, and on the other hand to the position of the Bolsheviks, a more nuanced one which maintained that although the tasks of the revolution were bourgeois, they would be accomplished by an alliance of the proletariat and peasantry. Once that alliance had seized power, according to this view, it would inaugurate a 'democratic dictatorship of the workers and peasants'. Trotsky characterized this formula as 'algebraic', in the sense that the relative weight of the two classes in the alliance was left unspecified, as was the class character of the state dominated by that alliance.

Now, in practice the Bolsheviks, under the impetus of Lenin, came to adopt the strategy of permanent revolution in the course of the upheavals of 1917 itself. I know of no evidence, however, to indicate that Lenin ever reconsidered permanent revolution from the theoretical standpoint. In effect, during the spring of 1917 he came to assign the peasant component of his algebraic formula the value of zero. This is what the April Theses represented, and they were so interpreted by the Bolshevik Old Guard, which initially received them as a 'Trotskyist' deviation. If the peasant component of the 'algebraic' formula of the 'democratic dictatorship of the workers and peasants' were assigned the value zero, then the formula would simply equal 'dictatorship of the proletariat'.

The entire question was then shunted to the sidelines by the pressure of events. During the desperate years of the civil war, discussion of the theoretical implications of October for the under-developed countries was not high on the agenda, especially since the wave of revolutionary struggle that followed the First World War was centred mainly in developed Europe. The central priority for the leaders of the Bolshevik Party and the Third International at that time was to extend the revolution to the advanced capitalist countries. It was only later, during the twenties, and especially after the experience of the Chinese revolution of 1926-27, that the debate around permanent revolution became current again and the theory was further developed by Trotsky. By that time, however, the terms of the discussion had changed dramatically. The process of Stalini-zation of the Communist International was well under way and the 'theory' of socialism in one country had become the prime dogma of the crystallizing bureaucracy. In that context, the old Bolshevik theory of the 'democratic dictatorship of the workers and peasants' was revived, this time not as an algebraic formula to be applied in a particular country, but as a strategic prescription designed to subordinate the proletarian parties in the colonial countries to their own bourgeoisies (the Kuomintang in China, for example).

In that sense, the revival of the formula 'democratic dictatorship of the workers and peasants' in the middle and late twenties was an adjunct of the theory of socialism in one country; as such it was an instrument of the increasingly conservative bureaucracy. The heart of this Stalinist version of the 'democratic dictatorship' was its division of the world into countries that were 'ripe' for socialism and those that were not. All the countries of the colonial world (eventu-ally all countries in the entire world, but that came later) were placed in the second category. In terms of political strategy, this meant that the revolutionary workers' parties in those countries should not attempt to win hegemony over the peasants, seize power, and establish the dictatorship of the proletariat, as was done in Russia in 1917. That was dubbed utopian, since these countries were allegedly not 'mature' enough for socialism. Instead the parties of the Comintern were urged to support the bourgeoisie in an effort to make a 'democratic' (that is, bourgeois) revolution. Only in the indefinite future would these countries then become 'ripe' for a socialist transformation. The Menshevik theory of 'two-stage revolution' was thus resuscitated and generalized—but in a form even further to the right than before, since the Mensheviks had at least upheld the organizational independence of the proletarian party from the party of the liberal democrats.

Now, it was in that context that Trotsky wrote the book entitled *Permanent Revolution* and completed the theory that had hitherto remained largely implicit in his writings on the Russian revolution. In other words, the theory/strategy of permanent revolution was developed in direct opposition to the theory/strategy of socialism in one country and the Stalinist version of the 'democratic dictatorship'. Apart from the 'first law' of permanent revolution which I mentioned earlier—namely that the complete and genuine solution of the tasks of the democratic revolution is possible only through the dictatorship of the proletariat—what else did the theory assert in its 1929 form?

First, that because of the great weight of the peasantry in underdeveloped countries there can be no solution to the problems of the revolution without an alliance of the proletariat and peasantry. Second, that this alliance can be forged in practice only under the political leadership of the proletariat and its vanguard, organized in the revolutionary party, which in turn means that the victory of the democratic revolution can occur only through the establishment of the dictatorship of the proletariat. Third, that historical experience had demonstrated that the peasantry, for a variety of reasons, was incapable of organizing itself into an *independent* party playing an independent role. No matter how great the revolutionary role of the peasants, the peasantry would politically follow either the bourgeoisie or the proletariat, but in no case could it conquer state power itself and establish a regime expressing its own class interests. In other words, the 'peasant component' of the 'democratic dictatorship of the workers and peasants' would *always be zero*, and the 'democratic dictatorship' could therefore be realized only in the form of the dictatorship of the proletariat supported by the peasantry. Fourth, that this dictatorship of the proletariat, having risen to power at the head of the democratic revolution, would, if it was to accomplish the tasks of that revolution, be compelled to infringe deeply upon bourgeois property rights. The seizure of power, then, would mark not the completion but the *initiation* of the revolutionary process of transformation of the social relations of the country in question. The democratic revolution, in Trotsky's famous phrase, 'grows over directly' into the socialist revolution, which in turn cannot be completed except on an international scale. The revolution is therefore 'permanent' in the twofold sense that the transformation from 'democratic' to 'socialist' revolution occurs without any discontinuity and that this process of revolution on a national scale must also merge continuously with the extension of the process internationally.

Conceptually, then, the theory/strategy of permanent revolution challenged the division of the world into countries 'ripe' for socialism and countries that were too 'immature' for socialism. Rather, it maintained that a country in which the proletariat was too weak to win hegemony over the peasantry and seize power itself was 'too immature' not only for socialism, *but also for a successful democratic revolution*, which, by virtue of the socio-economic and/ or political weakness of the working class, could not be completed. Implicitly, then, we have not two categories of countries—ripe for socialism, unripe for socialism—but three: those countries in which the bourgeois revolution has already occurred and which are therefore 'ripe' for the proletarian revolution in the 'pure' sense; those countries in which the tasks of the bourgeois revolution have yet to be completed, and in which the working class therefore faces the task of winning hegemony over the peasantry, seizing power, accomplishing these bourgeois tasks in a 'permanent' process that 'grows over directly' into a socialist transformation of society; those countries in which the proletariat is so weak that the tasks of the bourgeois-democratic revolution cannot be completed. This does not mean that the bourgeoisie cannot *hold power* in countries of the second category, even for a protracted period. But it does mean that *so long as bourgeois rule has not been overthrown, the tasks of the democratic revolution will not be completely and genuinely resolved.*

Now, what we must ask ourselves in judging whether this theory has been confirmed by events is whether any country of category two has elevated itself to category one through a process of capitalist development under the rule of the bourgeoisie. Is there a dependent capitalist country, or an ex-colony, that has undergone sufficient socio-economic transformation that the tasks now facing the proletariat in that country are substantially identical to the tasks facing the proletariat of countries such as Germany, France, Britain, or the United States? Once we pose the question in this manner, the answer becomes evident. There is no such country, and there is no reason to expect that there will be one. To be sure, in some dependent countries, there has been significant industrialization. But that only places the permanent revolution on the agenda in a more pressing manner than previously. The class contradictions of these countries are that much sharper; the proletariat has that much greater possibilities of actually maintaining its political and organizational independence and of establishing its hegemony over the peasant masses. But the basic tasks have not changed. We could put it, somewhat metaphorically, like this: It has now become politically crucial to distinguish between Argentina and Mexico on the one hand and Chad and Paraguay on the other; but not to the point that we submerge the qualitative difference between Argentina and Mexico on the one hand and Germany and France on the other.

Let us follow up on this question of 'stages'. Some interpretations of the permanent revolution seem to emphasize that any and all popular struggles in the 'third world' necessarily acquire a socialist character very rapidly. Might it not be the case, however, that there could be an entire period, a phase of the unfolding permanent revolutionary dynamic, if you will, during which the fight for democratic demands is predominant. This would not be a 'stage', since these struggles would not occur strictly within the framework of the bourgeois state; but on the other hand, the various popular struggles during this period would be directed primarily at the highly repressive state apparatuses of the local bourgeoisie which exist in many dependent countries. There have been various cases—Cuba under Batista, for example, or more recently, Nicaragua—in which we have seen upheavals in which the entire people, even including sections of the bourgeoisie, seem to be united in opposition to a tiny bourgeois clique that controls the state apparatus and is often supported by imperialism.

Failure to appreciate this can sometimes lead to a tendency to denigrate the importance of democratic demands. One remembers, for example, a whole series of condemnations of the Chinese Communist Party in 1949 in which many Trotskyists interpreted the emphasis on democratic tasks as a kind of refusal to begin the construction of socialism. In retrospect, these condemnations seem misguided, and perhaps reflected a failure to theorize properly the relationship between the democratic tasks and the revolutionary process as a whole.

It may well be that some comrades claiming to be Trotskyist have never really understood the theory of permanent revolution and are under the illusion that it maintains that the tasks of the revolution are at bottom identical in the underdeveloped and advanced capitalist countries. But this has nothing to do with what the mainstream of the Fourth International has upheld since its very inception. There is nothing in the strategy of permanent revolution that suggests that popular struggles in the dependent countries must start around proletarian demands. On the contrary, it is highly unlikely, although as I mentioned before, it could happen in some of the semi-industrialized countries. Even there, however, it is not at all certain that purely proletarian and socialist demands will come to the forefront at the first moments of the revolutionary process.

The very socio-economic structure of these countries is such that democratic demands are likely to be predominant in the first period of the revolution, provided that by democratic demands we also mean those demands relating to the agrarian question. This was, after all, the essence of the revolutionary process in Russia, which began as a battle against the tyranny and absolutism of the Tsar and for the emancipation of the peasantry, and not as a fight for socialism. These were typically democratic demands, and Trotsky never denied it. On the contrary, that was the whole basis for the strategy of permanent revolution in its original form: these central demands would win the support of the overwhelming majority of the population but could be won only if the proletariat itself took power. But the proletariat represented only about 10 per cent of the population; it therefore would have been the purest adventurism to assume that the workers could have taken power without becoming the champions of those demands which were at the centre of the concerns of the overwhelming majority of the population, most of which consisted of the petty bourgeoisie, the peasantry. Far from being a surprise for Trotskyists, the predominance of the democratic demands in the opening period of the revolutionary process is a confirmation of the analysis of Trotsky. If any correction has to be introduced today, it is that in semi-industrialized countries, where the working class is numerically larger and the peasantry smaller than in Russia, questions of political democracy are likely to be more prominent than demands around the agrarian question. But even this depends on the social and political structure of each country. It would not be true, for example, in India, where the overwhelming importance of the agrarian question is evident. It would probably not even be true in large parts of Brazil.

What we must be wary of is the danger of falling into tactical and political traps as the result of an excessively schematized view of the dynamics of the struggle. That is why I do not like the word 'phase'. Granted, it is not as bad as 'stage', for the reasons you mention. But it still introduces some notion of time sequences, which is a wrong approach, in my view. What is important is to see the revolutionary process not as a series of time intervals during which one or another variety of demand is more or less prominent, but to see it as a continuous struggle for a mix of slogans and demands in which there is no clear separation between 'democratic' and 'proletarian' or 'socialist'.

The dangerous political trap that awaits anyone who opts for the time-sequence approach is this: the democratic demands of the 'first phase' of the revolution become identified, even if only by default, with demands for institutions of a bourgeois-democratic character, for bourgeois parliamentary democracy. As we have seen in Spain and Portugal in recent years, this trap is a danger even in advanced capitalist countries. The fact is, however, that there is nothing automatic in the link between democratic demands and bourgeois-democratic state institutions. And if one has this identification in mind, one will tend to try to impose it on the actual historical process itself, as Social Democrats, Stalinists, and people coming out of the Stalinist tradition have been doing consistently for the past fifty years or so. (I am speaking here about rank-and-file cadres; in the case of the leaderships of these currents, we are obviously dealing with a different problem.) One of the consequences of this attitude is that those who hold it become blind to the possibilities of the emergence of forms of direct democracy, proletarian democracy, and working-class self-organization in the course of mobilizations for democratic demands. As we saw in Russia and in many other countries as well, such forms of proletarian self-organization tend to arise spontaneously out of revolutionary struggles. The problem is that although they arise spontaneously, they do not spontaneously strive to replace the existing state apparatus; they do not coordinate and centralize themselves spontaneously and do not automatically challenge the legitimacy of the bourgeois state directly. This requires revolutionary leadership. And any political current that is blinded by the schema that a 'phase' of democracy is required and that this 'phase' therefore necessitates bourgeois-democratic state institutions will logically attempt to repress these embryos of self-organization as premature, as not in conformity with the character of the stage—or phase, or whatever term is used—of democracy. A party with this line will play an objectively counter-revolutionary role—regardless of the intentions of its membership or even leadership. That is the trap that must be avoided.

What must be emphasized is that workers' councils, peasant councils or communes, and other forms of self-organization of the toiling masses can arise at the earliest stages of an apparently 'democratic' revolutionary process. I am not saying that they always will arise, but they *can*. Whether they do or not depends on many factors: the historical background of the country and the tradition of its labour movement, the relationship of forces within the mass movement between those who favour such forms and those who oppose them, the degree of autonomy of the mass movement, the degree of class consciousness, or fifty other factors. The important thing is to keep an open mind, to pay close attention to what the workers and peasants are actually doing, and not to rule out any possibilities on the basis of preconceived schemas.

There is an organizational and political logic to the strategy of permanent revolution as well as a socio-economic one. When we say that the democratic tasks can be solved only through the dictatorship of the proletariat, we are also saying that proletarian leadership of the struggle is impossible unless the working class has its own, independent organizational and political structures: trade unions, parties, soviets, and of course, a revolutionary party that can grasp the potentialities of the situation and seize all available opportunities to unfold the proletarian content of the democratic struggles in the dependent countries. This is one of the gravest accusations we Trotskyists make against both the classical Stalinists of pro-Moscow inclination and the Maoists: they uphold a schema that fails to emphasize the independent organization of the working class in such a revolutionary process. Worse, they have frequently favoured the dissolution of any such independent organization into the parties of the 'progressive' national bourgeoisie.

In reality, however, this line is adventurist, because from a Marxist point of view it is pure folly to nurture grandiose schemes of insurrection, armed struggle, the seizure of power, without building the elementary tools of a proletarian party to impel the independent organization of the working class forward. Moreover, their adventurism is compounded by a thoroughly idealist conception of class consciousness and organization. Trotsky made the point that it is not at all materialist to expect that any social class will sacrifice its own class interest—provided, of course, that it is conscious of that interest. Is it conceivable that the proletariat, in alliance with the peasantry, could lead the revolution, destroy the absolutist state, dissolve the absolutist army, arm itself, exercise state power—and then return to the factories to allow itself to be exploited by private owners? The question answers itself. Workers who acquire such self-confidence in the revolutionary struggle will never submit passively to capitalist exploitation. To make them do so would require not merely ideological convincing, but also repression. That is why there is no interruption in the revolutionary process, why there are no 'stages'—unless the workers are prevented, either through treacherous leadership or through armed repression or through a combination of the two, from organizing themselves independently.

It is interesting to note that even the Bolsheviks were overtaken by events when they tried to apply 'time sequences' to the mobilization of the proletariat, albeit in a revolutionary form. They, including Trotsky, had a very clever time scheme between November 1917 and the summer of 1918: first we have workers' control, then the nationalization of the big monopolies, then wider nationalizations, and so on. From a purely theoretical point of view, it is probable that this would have been the most effective way to begin the construction of socialism in Russia. But it was totally abstract; it ignored the actual dynamics of the upheaval in class relations triggered by the conquest of power by the working class. What happened was that the workers, full of self-confidence and emboldened by their historic victory, were simply not prepared to suffer the existence of private owners, even private tradesmen, for any length of time. They therefore began carrying out the socialist revolution at their own rhythm.

There is a great lesson in this. The imposition of time schemas on the real mobilization of the proletariat leads to bureaucratization in the best of cases, to severe bureaucratic deformations of the revolution from the very outset, deformations that later have nefarious effects even on the system of economic planning, as we have seen quite graphically in China. In the worst of cases, it leads to the bloody defeat of the revolution. Such is the danger of any conception that attempts to impose any sort of preconceived 'time schemes' on the revolution in the underdeveloped countries.

The Pattern of Anti-Imperialist Struggle

One of the observations Trotskyists have made about the semi-colonial world is that the pattern of class struggle there differs from the pattern prevalent in the advanced capitalist countries. In particular, the masses seem able to recover from defeats more quickly in the underdeveloped countries, but gains have been correspondingly less durable. This observation seems confirmed by the sharp ups and downs of the anti-colonial and anti-imperialist revolution. There was the de-colonization of the fifties, then the radicalization of nationalist regimes in the early and mid-sixties, followed by a series of victories for imperialism: the Congo, the coup and slaughter in Indonesia, the 1967 war in the Middle East, and so on. Now, with the events in southern Africa, Angola, Ethiopia, and elsewhere, the tide seems to be turning again. Can we establish a sort of periodization of the colonial revolution? And if so, what are the underlying reasons for the various swings of the pendulum back and forth? Are we likely to see a new upsurge of anti-imperialist struggle in the eighties?

There has been a general trend of nearly continuous crisis of the imperialist order in the colonial and semi-colonial countries ever since the victory of the Chinese revolution, if not since the latter stages of the Second World War. The chain of explosions and revolutions in the 'third world' has been almost constant, with outbreaks occurring in one or another part of the colonial and semicolonial world. But this does not mean that there is a continuous upsurge of struggle in all of them, nor does it mean that there is a universal cycle of ups and downs. The strict periodization you propose seems to me a bit forced.

Just to give one example: there was clearly a downward trend in the Latin American revolution beginning with the defeats suffered in Bolivia and Chile and lasting through the victory of the military coup in Argentina and even beyond. Only since 1978 have there been indications that the downswing of revolutionary struggle throughout the continent is being reversed. Concurrent with these setbacks in Latin America, however, we saw a big upsurge of struggle in Africa, first in the then Portuguese colonies, then in Zimbabwe, Namibia, and Ethiopia. Then, perhaps most important of all in the long run, came the thunderbolt of Soweto and the new period of struggle by blacks in South Africa. On the other hand, the picture in Africa was not wholly positive, for the Mobutu regime managed to survive its most serious test since it came to power. And we should not forget that from the mid-sixties to the mid-seventies, the most crucial struggle in the semi-colonial world was the war in Vietnam, the conclusion of which represented the greatest defeat for imperialism since the Chinese revolution. So it would not be correct to say that the period inaugurated by the Brazilian coup of 1964 was exclusively one of imperialist advance in the dependent countries. Rather than look for universal cycles, then, we should limit ourselves to more regionally limited ones, whose patterns are easier to discover and analyse.

To explain these cycles, we must concentrate primarily on the question of leadership and on the closely related question of the scope and social composition of mobilizations. Both these points are in turn closely related to the *relative* degree of development and underdevelopment—in other words, the class relations at the outset of and during the revolutionary upheavals.

While we should be wary of laying down any universal laws, the historical evidence so far does suggest that the less developed a country is, the easier it is for a non-proletarian or non-revolutionary leadership of an anti-imperialist movement to make significant gains against imperialism and to mobilize broader forces against it without at the same time breaking with imperialism completely. There are two basic reasons for this. First, the conquest of national independence or the nationalization of some imperialist property is generally of less concern to international capital in the less developed than in the more developed countries. Second, both international capital and the native ruling classes have less to fear from a process of permanent revolution in the less developed countries.

It seems to follow from this that important victories against imperialism are, *at present*, more difficult to obtain in the key, semi-industrialized countries of Latin America, or in India, or in southern Africa, than in the more backward parts of Asia and Africa. Of course, peculiar circumstances, such as the relative importance of particular raw materials to be found in one or another under-developed country, could make imperialism more hesitant to switch from direct to indirect rule in that country, or to switch from indirect rule through outright stooges to indirect rule through more sophisticated political forces (including petty-bourgeois nationalists). Key strategic or political considerations can also play a role in such matters.

By and large, however, I would defend this thesis: increasingly, the conquest of political independence by the working class and the labour movement, the severing of organizational and political ties with bourgeois and petty-bourgeois nationalism, is an *absolute precondition* for new advances of the revolution in countries like Brazil, Argentina, Mexico, Colombia, Peru, India, and so on. In the political document *Dynamics of World Revolution Today*, on the basis of which the major forces of the Fourth International were re-united in 1963 after a ten-year split, the point was made that for a variety of reasons, which were detailed in that document, the working class had found it possible to conquer power in some countries of the semi-colonial world with a 'blunted instrument', in other words, a party and leadership that did not fully measure up to the programmatic and organizational standards of the Bolshevik Party. It is my opinion that this can no longer be repeated in the semi-industrialized countries—that is, in the most developed of the underdeveloped countries.

In the cases of the more backward countries, some initial and partial successes in the struggle against imperialism can still be registered under petty-bourgeois or class collaborationist leadership, although a complete solution to all the tasks of the bourgeois-democratic revolution is, of course, not possible under such a leadership.

In a certain sense, this means that some of the conditions of struggle in the semi-industrialized countries now more closely approximate those of the advanced capitalist countries. In this respect there is a particular phenomenon to which insufficient attention has been paid. In many of the imperialist countries in the late sixties and early seventies we noted the rise of what we call a new mass vanguard—a layer of activists (of increasingly proletarian social composition in recent years) prepared to mobilize independent of and even against the traditional reformist leaderships. It is my opinion that this phenomenon, central in explaining many of the most important events of world politics in the past ten years, is not limited to the imperialist countries alone, but also affects a number of the semi-industrialized dependent countries—not all of them, but some. One of the most striking cases is Argentina. The people who led and participated in the *cordobazos*, the insurrectionary general strikes of the late sixties, were the same sort of people who played the driving role in the May '68 explosion in France and in the turmoil of the Prague spring in Czechoslovakia. The fact that this is true despite the very different economies and even social structures of these three countries is linked in part to the common transformations in technology, industry, and the composition of the working class which are now occurring in the most advanced imperialist countries, the most developed of the underdeveloped countries, and the most highly industrialized of the bureaucratized workers' states.

It is true, of course, that this point should not be overemphasized, but the change in the cultural and political background of the working class on a world scale is nonetheless an increasingly important element in the international class struggle. In the semi-illegal trade-union movement of São Paulo we are now seeing developments strikingly similar to what was happening in the union movement in Spain just before the death of Franco. This is no accident. Ultimately, it is related to the sort of industry and urban culture that is now growing apace in countries like Brazil—and this produces a certain type of radicalized working-class youth, militant and distrustful of the traditional bureaucracy.

This will be an increasingly decisive factor in the future—and it is cause for great optimism, especially when one considers that the two countries I mentioned, Brazil and Spain, were both ruled by dictatorships in which there was no political freedom whatever and in which the slightest participation in organized political activity entailed enormous personal and physical risks (and still does, although less so, in Brazil). We should not exaggerate the number of people who were actively involved in the workers commissions in Spain under the dictatorship. It was not a large number, but it was sufficient to provide a new backbone, a new vanguard, for a working class that had grown from 3 to 9 million as the result of economic development. That process itself played no small role in altering the political conditions fundamentally, and once those conditions changed, the relatively small vanguard led a process of class organization affecting millions of proletarians. Something of a similar kind is now going on in Brazil and in several other semi-industrialized countries, and the results will be crucial in the 1980s.

The Lesson of Iran

The most massive upheaval in the underdeveloped countries in recent years has occurred in one of the countries in which a certain degree of industrialization has occurred—Iran. What are the main lessons that can be drawn from the overthrow of the Shah?

The main lesson of the Iranian upheaval as it has unfolded so far is that mass mobilizations become invincible once they cross a certain threshold of amplitude and resolution. The Teheran insurrection that overthrew the Shah's regime—and the parallel insurrections in other major Iranian cities—was the largest urban mass insurrection to occur in contemporary history, involving literally millions of people. This is a striking confirmation of a key thesis of revolutionary Marxists in their debate with Social Democrats, Eurocommunists, and 'third worldists'. The basic argument of all these tendencies—supported even by centrists like Régis Debray—is that urban mass insurrections are powerless against a well-equipped modern army and can lead only to senseless slaughter.

Now, the Iranian army was probably the fourth most powerful army of the capitalist world. It had modern equipment certainly equivalent if not superior to that of the British army. Its members had been nursed and coddled by the ruling classes, given great material advantages. Nevertheless, it began to disintegrate under the impact of the huge mass mobilizations, which returned to the streets again and again in larger and larger numbers despite the murderous repression. Could one really maintain that the proletarian masses of Argentina or Brazil, or Spain or Italy for that matter, are so inferior to the Iranian masses in political consciousness, moral resolution, militancy, and organizational capacity that they would be unable to repeat what the Teheran masses have been able to achieve? Could it be seriously argued that the armies of these countries would be less sensitive to millions fighting in the streets than the Iranian army was? We contend that the opposite is true, if only because of the much greater weight of the proletariat in the active population and the larger number of soldiers of proletarian social origin in these countries.   *2/3/18*

It is true that democratic slogans and issues like those at the origin of the mass mobilizations in Iran traditionally appear to have a wider and more electrifying appeal than 'purely' proletarian-socialist slogans, especially in countries ruled by corrupt dictatorial regimes. But we must not unduly generalize such observations; there is no reason to draw the false conclusion that regardless of the socio-economic and political structure of a country, mass mobilizations of the scope of those in Iran can be achieved *only* through the struggle for democratic rights. If the workers' movement succeeds in systematically mobilizing and organizing the wage-earning masses around anti-capitalist demands under conditions of social and political crisis, mass actions as big as those in Teheran—or even larger—are perfectly possible. That is the basis of our alternative strategy in both the imperialist and the more developed of the under-developed countries. What has happened in Iran tends to confirm that this strategy is eminently realistic.

The great unanswered question about the Iranian events is, of course, the role of Islam. The reasons why the Shiite clergy estab-lished hegemony over the mass mobilizations against the Shah's dictatorship must be analysed by Iranian comrades better versed in the history of both Islam and Iran than I am. But this analysis cannot substitute for a clear political stand on certain issues. We correctly supported the uprising against the Shah even though it was led by the clergy. We would support the new Iranian regime in any real conflict with imperialism. But in all conflicts between the new regime and sectors of the masses struggling for their just demands, we stand 100 per cent on the side of the masses and against the regime. This applies not only to proletarian or semi-proletarian sectors of the masses struggling for their elementary right to organize and for higher living standards (here any other attitude would be class betrayal), but also to national minorities fighting against oppression, to women fighting against discrimination and reactionary religious codes, to all those fighting against state repression for sexual 'crimes', and so on. The attempt to impose religious codes by force is no more 'progressive' in Iran today than it has ever been anywhere since the dawn of modern bourgeois society. To identify revolution with religious obscurantism is an act of ideological treason no less detrimental to the cause of Iranian and world socialism than the more classical forms of capitulation to oppressor classes.

Cuba 1959-1979

One of the most striking instances of an actual process of permanent revolution occurred in Cuba. The Cuban revolution celebrated the twentieth anniversary of its victory this year. How would you assess the importance of this victory twenty years on?

The Cuban revolution occupies quite an exceptional place in the history of post-war revolutions. It is the only victorious revolution that was not led by a force originating from the Stalinized Communist International and heavily influenced by Stalinism, at least in the basic theoretical education of its leading cadres. In fact, as was well known in the late fifties and early sixties (but increasingly forgotten in left-wing circles today), the Cuban Stalinists strenuously opposed the early July 26 Movement and the rural and urban guerrilla struggles of the Revolutionary Directorate. They even gave aid and comfort to the Batista dictatorship on more than one occasion, openly sabotaging Fidel's strike call in 1958 and participating in Batista's fake 'elections'. Even after the July 26 Movement seized power, the leadership of the Cuban Communist Party (known as the Popular Socialist Party, PSP) opposed the course of the Castro government when the expropriation of the bourgeoisie was initiated and the evolution to a workers' state set in motion.

Several essential features of the Cuban revolution have been widely misunderstood and need fresh emphasis today. First, although it is true that the defeat of Batista's army by the Fidelista guerrillas was a necessary precondition for the victory of the revolution, it was by no means sufficient. There has been more than one instance in Latin American history of the overthrow of a reactionary dictatorship and even the destruction of much of its army without the expropriation of the ruling class and the demolition of its political power. It is relatively easy in a semi-colonial country to reconstitute a shattered bourgeois army, or at any rate easier than in an advanced capitalist country. Such an attempt was indeed made in Cuba after the July 26 Movement seized control of Havana; it was even directed by the newly appointed president of the republic. But tremendous mass mobilizations, triggered by the general strike of 1-2 January 1959 and by the decision to launch a radical agrarian revolution, destroyed these attempts, as they destroyed the bourgeois state apparatus. This process was accompanied by a split of the July 26 Movement into pro-bourgeois and pro-socialist (i.e. proletarian) wings. These momentous class struggles of 1959 and 1960, combined with the victory of the proletarian wing of the July 26 Movement, brought about the thorough destruction of the bourgeois state apparatus and the establishment of the Cuban workers' state, which was in no way the automatic or inevitable product of the victory of the guerrilla struggle itself.

Similarly, although it is true that US imperialism was taken by surprise by the political evolution of the Fidelista movement immediately after it entered Havana, Washington reacted brutally and rapidly once the anti-imperialist and anti-capitalist dynamic of the mass mobilizations and their leadership became evident. The decisive factor in preventing a massive intervention by American troops was the wave of solidarity with the Cuban revolution internationally, especially in Latin America itself. Any direct US invasion threatened to ignite the entire continent, and that was a risk Eisenhower and later Kennedy dared not take. It was for this reason, and not because of some misjudgement of the situation, that US imperialism opted for action through mercenaries, saboteurs, and commando operations, of which the 1961 invasion was the climax. But such operations, which were eventually successful in Guatemala in 1954, failed to roll back a revolution that had mobilized and armed literally hundreds of thousands of men and women. The historic reason for imperialism's defeat in Cuba lies in these mobilizations and the deliberate course of the Fidelista leadership, and not in the alleged miscalculations of Washington.

Finally, the Cuban revolution was characterized from the start by a degree of mass activity, organization, and revolutionary spontaneity far beyond anything that had been seen since the Spanish revolution of 1936-37. The creative aspect of mass action and freedom was visible in many fields, from the transformation of Havana's villas into dormitories for boys and girls from the countryside studying in the capital, to the veritable explosion of revolutionary art, the armed militias (including many women) organized to guard public buildings, the sweeping campaign to eradicate illiteracy, the radical abolition of rent and payment for public services, the massive redistribution of consumer goods for the benefit of the poorest sections of the peasantry and the rural proletariat.

But although this process involved great mass mobilizations and an effort at mass political education the like of which has rarely been seen, its basic weakness was the *lack of institutionalized workers' power*, in other words, the lack of soviets. The Committees to Defend the Revolution could have become the *nuclei* of genuine soviets, but they did not evolve in that direction. A tremendous gap arose between the mass mobilization and the popularity of Fidel and Che's revolutionary line on the one hand and the actual exercise of power on the other. Here the weaknesses of the Fidelista leadership were telling. The PSP apparatus was able to insert itself gradually into that gap, increasingly incorporating and integrating successive strata of the revolutionary movement in the absence of an alternative orientation (especially on how to construct a workers' state based on socialist democracy) and given the inability of the masses to manifest their mobilization through democratic organs of workers' power.

Meanwhile, the Soviet bureaucracy shrewdly assessed the situation as less dangerous for its interests than could have appeared earlier. Moscow backed revolutionary Cuba against US imperialism, thereby gaining both prestige in Latin America and influence in

Cuba itself. The Cuban revolutionary leadership continued to command some leeway in both internal experiments and international initiatives, but the Soviet grip grew ever tighter, especially given the subsidization of the Cuban economy against the imperialist blockade. In the meantime, increasing numbers of officials in the Cuban state apparatus, party apparatus, and armed forces were trained and politically educated in the USSR. This has greatly stimulated the process of the establishment of bureaucratic control and the stifling of revolutionary mass initiative. The trend in this direction has been especially clear since 1967.

The early years of the Castro government were marked by an intense proletarian internationalism: the Second Declaration of Havana, the Cuban campaign for solidarity with the Vietnamese revolution, and so on. Today the Cuban workers' state is playing a role in Africa that many would see as an extension of that early internationalism. How would you assess the Cuban role in world politics?

The Cuban revolution was much less bureaucratized, less tightly controlled, than the Yugoslav, Chinese, or Vietnamese revolutions; the weight of proletarian or semi-proletarian layers in the mass mobilizations leading up to and following the seizure of power was much greater; the Cuban leadership was, at the outset, relatively free of Stalinist education and dogma. For these reasons, and probably others as well, internationalism loomed much larger in the policies of the Cuban revolution and in the consciousness of the Cuban masses than it did in the other socialist revolutions that have occurred since the Second World War. This is an undeniable fact, and a myriad of empirical evidence can be marshalled to illustrate it.

To properly interpret the later development of the Cuban role in world politics, however, other factors have to be considered as well. In the first place, because of the growing isolation of the Cuban revolution in Latin America and the continuous pressure of US imperialism, both economically and militarily, the Cuban workers' state grew increasingly dependent on Soviet aid, especially after the missile crisis of 1962. This dependence took a qualitative leap forward after the failure of the *zafra*, the 10 million tonne sugar harvest. Dependence then came to be expressed in a growing alignment by the Cuban leaders behind the international policies of the

Kremlin, of which Castro's support to the invasion of Czechoslovakia in 1968, grudging as it may have been, was the concentrated expression. This alignment had important political, ideological, and organizational consequences within Cuba itself. There is now an entire generation of middle and leading cadres of the Cuban Communist Party whose education and convictions are clearly Stalinist, which was not the case for the July 26 Movement or the Revolutionary Directorate in the late fifties and early sixties.

Second, a process of bureaucratization of the isolated Cuban workers' state has undoubtedly been under way for about fifteen years now, related to but partially autonomous from this mounting dependence on the Soviet bureaucracy. Material privileges have arisen and grown, as has repression of political criticism, cultural pluralism, artistic freedom, and so on. Exactly how far that process of bureaucratization has gone remains to be determined. Our movement is discussing this question right now. For the moment, however, we have not drawn the conclusion that a hardened bureaucratic caste exists in Cuba that can be removed only through a political revolution. But this does not mean that instances of bureaucratization are not much more severe than they were in the early, or even late, sixties.

Now, both these processes have imposed great limitations on the extent and content of the internationalism of the leadership of the Cuban Communist Party and the government in Havana. (It is, by the way, very difficult to judge whether these limitations have generated similar regression in the consciousness of the Cuban masses.) One striking example of this is Havana's alignment, almost total, behind Kremlin policy in Latin America and behind the strategy of the Stalinist Communist Parties of that continent. To some extent this represents an abandonment of some of the main lessons of the Cuban revolution itself and the reversal of the major policies enunciated in the Second Declaration of Havana.

It could be argued, of course, that this alignment is only temporary, that it is a pragmatic adaptation of the Cuban leadership to the defeats that have been suffered by the Latin American revolution and to the consequent isolation of Cuba. The trend *may* be reversed if there is a major new upsurge of revolutionary struggle in one or several key Latin American countries, not to mention a victory, the establishment of a new workers' state in Latin America.

It remains to be seen, however, whether it *will* be reversed. That in itself will be a key indicator of the degree of bureaucratization of the Cuban workers' state.

As for our overall judgement of the present Cuban role in Africa, it should be positive. Cuban policy in Africa demonstrates that the Cuban masses and leadership are still marked by a deeper internationalism than any other existing workers' state. The Cuban role was decisive in assuring the conquest of national independence in Angola, which represented an important victory for the African revolution. Without that intervention, it is likely that forces supported by the alliance of troops of the apartheid South African regime, imperialist stooges, and tribalist formations would have taken power in Luanda, which would have transformed Angola into a bulwark of counter-revolution against the rising tide of insurgency in many surrounding countries. Up to now, Cuba's military presence in Africa has generally had a positive effect on the development of the African revolution. The only possible exception is Eritrea, but here there is controversy over the facts. Some sources—including some comrades—deny that the Cubans have been involved in the repression of the national liberation struggle of the Eritrean people, which is a just struggle in our view. If there is direct Cuban support to the attempts of the Mengistu regime to crush the freedom struggle of the Eritrean people, we shall of course condemn it, but there is as yet no compelling evidence that such support has been extended.

There is, however, one major reservation that must be expressed about the Cuban role in Africa, and that is the complete Cuban identification with the state and government leaders in whose support they intervene, and the further identification of these leaders as 'socialist', 'communist', or 'proletarian'. We believe that this is incorrect even in the case of Mozambique, where the most advanced of the petty-bourgeois nationalist leaderships in Africa is currently in power and where social inequality is least glaring. It is even more incorrect in the case of Angola, where the leadership is now engaging in a typical balancing act: increasing its collaboration with Mobutu and with US, Belgian, Portuguese, British, and French imperialist firms while continuing to receive aid from the Soviet Union, the other bureaucratized workers' states, and Cuba. In the case of Ethiopia, the justification for such an attitude is flimsiest of all.

It would, of course, be utterly irresponsible to dismiss out of hand the tremendous conquests of the unfolding revolutions in Mozambique, Angola, Guinea-Bissau, and Ethiopia against the rotten colonialist or semi-feudal order that reigned in these countries previously. And it is of crucial importance to defend them against imperialist attempts to roll back these conquests. But it is one thing to hail, support, and extend these conquests, and quite another to present the states now in power as workers' states or to support these governments, even in their conflicts with the masses.

Southern Africa

Southern Africa is, of course, a region of vital importance to world imperialism, and one of the areas of the 'third world' that has been most turbulent in recent years. The problems of permanent revolution are posed as sharply in South Africa as in any other country. Do you think revolutionary Marxists should support the formation of 'international brigades' drawn primarily from elsewhere in Africa to assault the bastion of apartheid? Can this regime be brought down solely from within?

It is probable that South Africa will be one of the last fortresses of imperialism to fall, because there are several million people who have a clear material interest in clinging to defence of that fortress even against tremendous odds. Since it is likely that this regime will be able to acquire nuclear weapons, if it has not already done so, the price that will have to be paid for the liberation of the South African masses threatens to be enormously high—unless the revolutionary upsurge successfully conducts a conscious effort to neutralize, if not win over, a section of the white population, on the basis of considerations of physical survival. Under a favourable relationship of forces, such considerations could neutralize the effects of white South African desires to defend their material privileges at all costs. The effort to develop a non-racist leadership of the South African liberation struggle is therefore important—primarily in saving the lives of thousands, perhaps millions, of people, black Africans first of all.

At the present stage, talk of international brigades seems

premature, to say the least. The black masses of South Africa have tremendous potential power. They constitute the overwhelming majority of the proletariat of Africa's richest and most developed country, a majority without whose labour-power that economy would collapse, with all the disastrous consequences such a collapse would have for world imperialism. (South Africa is the leading producer of gold and diamonds in the capitalist world, and one of the major producers of uranium.) They have a deeply-ingrained class hatred of the imperialist/bourgeois establishment, fueled by their total exclusion from any political rights, by their status as foreign 'immigrant' labourers in their own country. Their struggle is also stimulated by their awareness that they are defending a cause whose justice is evident to the great majority of the world's population.

That tremendous power, however, is still largely unorganized and untapped. Indeed, all the efforts of the apartheid regime—both its barbarous acts of repression and its various political and ideological manoeuvres—are aimed at maintaining the aspect of the status quo most vital to the exploiters and oppressors: the disunity and lack of organization of the exploited and oppressed. At this stage, to talk of international brigades is to put the cart before the horse. Revolutionary Marxists should concentrate their efforts on the organization, unification, and mass mobilization of the South African masses, the potential of which was so strikingly demonstrated by the Soweto uprising and its aftermath, and on the mobilization of worldwide political support for that struggle.

The apartheid regime is now particularly vulnerable to mass mobilization, action, and organization because of the international context—much more vulnerable than it would be to a heroic onslaught by small groups of armed liberation fighters. The question of armed self-defence against the murderers who currently govern South Africa will certainly arise as the struggle unfolds, as will the question of international solidarity with the struggle in the most variegated forms. At this stage, however, international efforts along these lines would be premature.

Quite another matter is the question of the collective response of the African revolution to the cynical aggression committed by the Pretoria (and Salisbury) regime against Zambia, Mozambique, Angola, and other African states. Here collective armed resistance by African liberation forces on an international scale would certainly be on the agenda. Whether this would involve exclusively the regular armies of existing states, or international brigades of volunteers, or both, will depend on the state and tempo of world revolution, the character of the political leadership in at least some of the 'front-line' states, and the relationship of political forces within the liberation movements, as well as other factors.

The Emergence of Workers' States

To conclude, let us pose an analytical question which is closely related to the theory of permanent revolution. In a number of countries in recent years, mass struggles of one form or another have led to regimes in which the bulk of the means of production are nationalized and in which the leadership even claims to be not merely socialist but Marxist. Examples are Angola, Afghanistan, Ethiopia, and Mozambique. A similar problem has been posed in other countries in the past, Algeria for example. Even in the cases of Egypt and Syria in the middle sixties, some comrades raised the possibility that these states could have evolved, more or less 'peacefully', into workers' states. Nevertheless, the Fourth International does not regard any of these countries as workers' states; they are considered to be qualitatively different in character from Cuba, for example. What are the objective grounds for this distinction? In other words, what are the criteria for judging whether or not a workers' state has been created?

What you are essentially asking is this: why is it that we maintain that a socialist revolution triumphed in Cuba, whereas no socialist revolution occurred in Egypt or Syria in the sixties or in Mozambique, Angola, or Ethiopia in the seventies?

It would be dangerous to reduce everything to a single criterion. Instead I will present a chain of arguments. To begin with, the question of the suppression of private property in the means of production must be looked at concretely, in the light of the particular economic structure of the country concerned. If you have a country, for example, in which 90 per cent of the population lives in the countryside as subsistence farmers and there is a single factory producing, say, flour, then statistically the nationalization of that factory would mean that 100 per cent of industry has been nationalized. But no reasonable person would maintain that such a country had been transformed into a workers' state. In a country with such a socio-economic structure, given the weight of the peasantry and of agriculture in the national economy, the structure of property relations in the countryside would be the decisive factor. Here already we have one element that was not unimportant in determining our position on Algeria and Syria. In these two countries—and I am speaking now about the 1960s—private property remained predominant in the national economy because of its overwhelming predominance in agriculture, despite the high rate of nationalization of industry and even despite the reduction of the area of land owned by large landlords.

The second point, which is closely related to the first, has been a source of great confusion in recent years, largely as a result of state capitalist theories of the type advanced by Bettelheim. It is this: there is an enormous difference between the nationalization of the greater portion of private property in a country and the *suppression of the right to private property in the constitution of that country*. Bettelheim claims that this is a purely formal, juridical question, but that is not true at all. It is a pre-eminently economic, and very practical, matter. That which is eliminated can be easily reconstituted if it is not forbidden—and by that I do not mean forbidden on paper in a purely formal sense; I mean forbidden de facto. This means in turn forbidden both by law and by the secular arm of the law—the state—and all the institutions of the state. That this is not a formal point is shown by the evolution of Egypt. Many companies were nationalized during the 'radical' period of the Nasser regime, but their owners were paid compensation, and with this compensation they were able to accumulate capital. They could not buy large factories, since that was forbidden, but they could buy land, properties in real estate, stocks, and other items. The result was that although much property was nationalized, the capitalist class was not expropriated. It was therefore relatively easy to de-nationalize what had previously been nationalized, without the slightest social upheaval and with no discontinuity of the state apparatus. It therefore makes a big difference whether private property is eliminated in just a few fields—even if this applies to a good deal of industry in the underdeveloped countries—or whether it is simply outlawed. In the latter case, of course, some accumulation of private property can continue, but only illegally, and that again makes a big difference.

The third factor to be considered, which I have already touched on, is the nature of the state. It could be objected that our reasoning here is circular: inasmuch as there is no complete suppression of private property, we say that the state is bourgeois; inasmuch as the state is bourgeois, there is no legal and constitutional suppression of private property. But behind what may seem to be circular reasoning lies a concrete analysis. Who are the people in power and what is their attitude towards private property? How do they actually act in this domain? Here there is a world of difference between the Nasserist bureaucrat in Egypt and the Russian, Chinese, or Yugoslav bureaucrat today. One can say that they are all corrupt. It is my opinion that the Yugoslav ones are significantly less corrupt than the Egyptians, but let us leave that aside. The fundamental question is this: what do they use their ill-gotten gains for? This question must be answered not in the realm of abstract speculation, but in the hard facts of real life. If the bureaucrats use their money simply to acquire more consumer goods and privileges, such as cars, television sets, trips abroad, and so on, that is one thing. But if they use that money to acquire property which generates an income based on the exploitation of the labour of others, that is something different. In that case they are using their positions in the state apparatus as a means by which to engage in primitive accumulation of capital.

The two cases result in two qualitatively different social dynamics. The direction of that dynamic in the latter case is shown by what has been happening in Egypt over the past several years, a process which is also occurring in Syria and Algeria and will, we believe, happen in Mozambique and Angola in the future unless there is a new victorious revolution of a socialist character. The new bourgeoisie in these countries is quite visible, everybody knows their names. They are the people contacted by the multinationals when they engage in operations in these countries. On the whole, the individuals who compose this new bourgeoisie are not recruited from the old pashas or merchant classes. Many of them are former cabinet ministers or high functionaries who used their offices to accumulate large amounts of money that was later turned into capital. This is not at all the same thing as acquiring a refrigerator and an Alfa Romeo. These fortunes are accumulated in the form of stocks and bonds, and the next logical step is to invest them and use them to build up private industrial empires. It is usually at that point—when there is a significant number of such people who have amassed sufficiently large amounts of money waiting to be 'productively' invested—that the state begins the process of de-nationalization, opening up outlets for potential investors.

This is why the formula 'state bourgeoisie' is ultimately meaningless. Either it refers to state functionaries transforming themselves into private capitalists through the sort of process I have been describing here, in which case the important point is that we are dealing with *private* capitalists; or it refers to state bureaucrats who do *not* become private owners, in which case it is senseless to talk about a *bourgeoisie* that does not accumulate capital through the economic exploitation of the labour-power of workers.

There are, of course, other factors involved in determining whether a workers' state has been created. One of these is the degree of symbiosis with the international capitalist economy. It is not accidental, for example, that the high point of Nasser's measures of 'socialization' came when the Egyptian economy was almost completely isolated from the international capitalist economy and was dependent almost exclusively on Soviet aid. Conversely, the full scale 'liberalization', which is simply another word for the reintroduction of private capital on a grand scale, came at a time when the country was being thrown open to Western investment, in other words to the international capitalist economy. A related matter is whether or not foreign trade is monopolized by the state. Do individual productive units have the right to establish direct economic ties to international capital?

The presence of Gulf Oil in Angola, for example, is not an insignificant fact. It is important, however, not to apply this criterion too schematically. Gulf Oil has operations in Angola today, but they could be nationalized in the future. Those who attempt to erect nationalization of foreign companies as a decisive criterion in and of itself can fall into great difficulties. I once heard this sort of argument in regard to Algeria: that it was not a workers' state since the French oil companies had not been nationalized. In the end, however, they were nationalized. One must therefore be cautious in using this argument. Alone it is not decisive, but in combination with the other factors I have mentioned, it can be significant.

Lastly, there is another factor which, although it is not at all decisive in determining the class character of the state from the analytical point of view, is often crucial in deciding in which direction a particular underdeveloped country will evolve once the structures of the old state apparatus have been seriously shaken. I am speaking of the combination of the degree of mass mobilization and its consciousness and leadership. The scope of the mobilizations in Cuba in 1961 and 1962, particularly at points of crisis such as the counter-revolutionary invasion and the missile crisis, was a key factor in preventing a return to capitalist patterns and in impelling the Castroist government to proclaim the revolution socialist and to move to the complete suppression of private property in the means of production—against the advice, by the way, of most of the leaders of the Cuban Communist Party. Mass mobilization in itself, however, is no guarantee that this sort of development will occur. There were not a few mass mobilizations in Egypt for example. Indeed, immediately after the June 1967 war, when Nasser resigned, there was one of the greatest popular outpourings ever seen, nearly a million people innundating the streets of Cairo. Objectively, this mobilization was positive, since it prevented what would have been in effect a right-wing coup under the circumstances. But in the absence of proletarian consciousness and a revolutionary leadership, this outpouring, massive as it was, did no more than preserve the existing capitalist government, and did not even have the effect of driving it to the left.

This was also one of the tragic aspects of the Algerian revolution. Here again, there was a significant level of mass mobilization, but the issues at stake were unclear, even to many revolutionaries, let alone the masses. In that context, a figure like Boumedienne played a major role in halting a revolutionary process that could have led to the establishment of a workers' state in Algeria. And despite the radicalization that has occurred among some sectors of the masses in recent years, he remained an ambiguous figure in their eyes right to the end. At his funeral, there were massive demonstrations of people chanting, 'We want to continue along the socialist road of Boumedienne'. That, of course, is a mystification of what has actually happened in Algeria, and it demonstrates once again the point I made earlier: the presence or absence of a conscious and organized revolutionary leadership will be increasingly decisive in determining the evolution of the states of the underdeveloped countries.

3

The Transitional Regimes in the East

The sixtieth anniversary of the Russian revolution was celebrated just a few years ago. It was also the fortieth anniversary of the publication of Trotsky's The Revolution Betrayed, *which analysed the Soviet Union as a degenerate workers' state. Many historic events have occurred during the past four decades. We have seen the maintenance and relative stabilization of the Soviet bureaucracy, and the emergence—in a variety of historical conditions—of other bureaucratic regimes. What, then, is the validity of Trotsky's analysis forty years on? How has the Trotskyist movement added to it, and how has the theory stood up to the test of events?*

Trotsky's point of departure—and this is where the strength of his position on the character of the USSR lies—was the view taken by the entire working-class Left at the beginning of the Russian revolution of 1917 (subsequently abandoned by one revisionist tendency after another), that it was impossible to examine the origins and development of the Russian revolution while isolating Russia from the rest of the world. The paradox that lies at the root of the theory of permanent revolution—that the proletariat could conquer power in the less developed capitalist countries before doing so in the most developed ones—has meaning only in the context of a particular analysis of imperialism and the class struggle on a world scale. It is only because of the phenomenon of imperialism, or more precisely the beginning of the capitalist mode of production's decline, that Marx's old dictum that the most advanced countries mirror the future of the least advanced is no longer generally applicable in the twentieth century.

Trotsky drew two conclusions from this initial position. First, that the victory of the Russian revolution was possible only through the establishment of a dictatorship of the proletariat, supported by the poor peasantry. Second, that the construction of a classless society, a complete socialist society, in this backward country was obviously impossible. The Mensheviks stuck to Marx's nineteenth-century position. They failed to understand the consequences of the advent of the imperialist era. They did not understand the weight and logic of underdevelopment, which have so strongly marked the consciousness of contemporary revolutionaries and demonstrate what Russia could have become had it not been for the victory of the October Revolution. Stalin, on the other hand—and this remains true of the Stalinists to this day, as of all tendencies that analyse the nature of the Soviet Union solely on the basis of the internal trends at work within it—committed the parallel error of disregarding Russia's insertion into the world, with all its economic, military, and social implications, and of assuming that it was possible, under certain conditions, to complete the construction of a classless society in a single country.

What underlay Trotsky's theoretical position, independent of conjunctural formulations and trends, was that for him the fate of the Soviet Union ultimately depended on the outcome of the world-wide class struggle. Stalinism thus appears as an unforeseen variant of history, a function of what could be called the unstable equilibrium between the fundamental antagonistic social forces on a world scale. Stalinism is the expression of a defeat and serious regression of the world revolution after 1923. But it also reflects the long-term structural weakness of world capitalism, which has been unable to restore the capitalist mode of production in the USSR despite repeated attempts, both economic and military. Behind the formulae 'transitional stage' and 'transitional society' lies the reality of this not yet definitively decided test of strength between capital and labour on a world scale. In this sense as well, the way Trotsky formulated the alternative in 1939-40 remains essentially correct, although he was wrong about the timing. A crushing defeat for the world proletariat for an entire historical period not only could but inevitably would lead to the restoration of capitalism in the USSR. A crushing defeat for capital, for the world bourgeoisie, in several of the key capitalist countries would set the USSR back on course towards the construction of a classless society.

The Concept of 'Transition'

You used Trotsky's terms 'transitional stage' and 'transitional society'. Now, as it turns out, Trotsky's expectation of a relatively rapid liquidation of Stalinism, either through a proletarian political revolution or through a capitalist restoration, was wrong. In addition, other states have been created in which bureaucracies have consolidated power, in particular forms depending on particular conjunctures. Do these facts not enable us to give the notion of 'transition' a character both broader and more precise than it had in Marxist tradition at the time Trotsky was writing?

First of all, there is no 'Marxist tradition' on this subject in the real sense of the word. Marx himself had no time to dwell on this problem. Nor did Engels. After their deaths, vulgarization and simplification took hold, culminating in Stalin's famous writings on the modes of production through which all societies are supposedly required to pass—primitive communism, slavery, feudalism, capitalism, socialism. In reality, it is only in the most recent period, with the renaissance of Marxist historical analysis and the penetration of methods inspired by Marxism into academic historical research, that the foundations of this exciting chapter of Marxist theory have begun to be laid. But these foundations are still fragmentary; a lot remains to be done.

Today, taking only Europe and leaving out of consideration other parts of the world and other civilizations, we can see that there were actually long periods of transition between all the great modes of production. In the light of this observation, the case of Soviet society, far from constituting an exceptional, unusually long process of transition, appears as a quite limited one. Let us take two examples.

If you define the slave mode of production as founded essentially on the productive labour of slaves in agriculture and crafts (the principal sources of the social product), and if you define the feudal mode of production as founded essentially on the labour of serfs in agricultural production, then you find that a centuries-long period of transition separated the predominance of slave labour from the predominance of serf labour, at least in western, central, and southern Europe (I leave aside the Byzantine empire). This period saw, in varying forms and combinations, the elevation of the lot of the slaves side by side with the deterioration of the lot of the free peasants, especially those of the so-called barbarian ethnic tribes that penetrated the Roman empire. It was only through the fusion of these two social forces, which was probably completed around the seventh or eighth century, that the feudal mode of production proper became dominant.

The second example is clearer, although of shorter duration. The decline of serfdom is quite evident by the fourteenth and fifteenth centuries in the most advanced parts of the European economy, especially in the Low Countries, England, a portion of France, a portion of northern and central Italy, and Germany. In some of these regions, serfdom virtually disappeared as the predominant relation of production in agriculture. Now, the disappearance of serfdom does not immediately lead to the generalization, or even the large-scale extension, of wage-labour. In other words, there is manifestly another transitional period between the decline of serfdom and the rise of wage-labour; between the decline of the feudal mode of production and the flowering of the capitalist mode of production. (I say deliberately 'capitalist mode of production' and not 'domination of market or banking capital', which is something else again; I am speaking of capitalist relations of production.) This transitional period may also be characterized as the economic organization founded on petty commodity production (a term which is open to discussion), under which the essential producer is neither the serf nor the wage labourer, but the small-scale producer having access to the means of production and subsistence. In fact, it is the transformation not of the serf into the wage labourer but of this independent producer into the wage labourer that gives rise to capitalism as the predominant mode of production in the real sense of the term, since one of the characteristics of the proletariat is precisely that it is free, not subject to personal servitude.

This transitional period is shorter than the one that separated the slave from the feudal mode of production. It involves much greater difficulties of socio-economic analysis, because of the very complexity of the situations. In general, what we are dealing with here is a manifestation of the law of uneven and combined development. If you wanted to give a really precise definition of the relations of production prevailing in Flanders, Brabant, Lombardy, Tuscany, the Rhineland, and even certain French and English regions at the end of the fifteenth century, you would face extreme difficulties. It would be difficult to reduce them all to a single common denominator. There was a blending of semi-feudal relations of production, relations of production that underlie petty commodity production, and semi-capitalist relations of production; there was also the beginning of capitalist manufacture already founded on wage labour. Nevertheless, it is impossible to reduce all this to one formula, either feudalism or capitalism. This is the point I want to stress. In spite of the particular features of the epoch, we are clearly dealing with a transitional phase.

But under the slave or the feudal mode of production elements of the new mode are already developing in the form of new social relations of production. Can one say that elements of socialism can develop as new relations of production within capitalist society itself?

Obviously not. You can say that the preconditions for the existence of a classless society are developing within the capitalist mode of production, but not socialized relations of production. And it is exactly for this reason that the advent of a transitional society between capitalism and socialism is impossible without the prior overthrow of the power of the bourgeoisie; without the overthrow of the bourgeois state; and, I would say, without despotic incursions into the right of property—to use the formula of Marx and Engels in the *Communist Manifesto*. This is not an argument against the notion that the Soviet Union is a transitional society, analogous to those of the past. It is simply an argument justifying a different articulation of the new relations of production with the state power. This is in fact one of the strongest elements of our analysis. Post-capitalist relations of production cannot be developed within a society ruled by the bourgeoisie, governed by a bourgeois state. This means that the emergence of such relations of production is possible only *after* a socialist revolution.

This brings me back to the point of departure. The notion of a transitional stage, a society in transition between two great 'successive' modes of production in the history of humanity, is not an isolated phenomenon limited to Soviet society and all the problems related to the transition from capitalism to socialism. It is a phenomenon that has been manifested much more generally throughout human history. For Marxists interested in Africa, for example, there is a particularly fascinating question related to this problematic: the exact definition of what African society was at the time of the colonial occupation, and even during the phase following this occupation, in so far as it did not lead to a complete, radical transformation of the indigenous relations of production, particularly in the villages but even partially outside them. In reality, it is impossible to understand Black Africa in the second half of the nineteenth and the first half of the twentieth century without using the eminently transitional notion of 'social classes in formation' or 'nascent social classes'. This, in fact, is the rational kernel contained in all the theses of a supposedly 'African' socialism, according to which Marxism is inapplicable in Africa. Such theses are obviously quite erroneous. They fail to understand the historical process; they fail to understand development, taking mere snapshots of one moment of evolution. But the snapshot, although sometimes blurred, is not always inaccurate. In dealing with the typical African village at the end of the nineteenth or the beginning of the twentieth century—when after all 80-90 per cent of the population lived in such villages—one cannot say that feudal lords or owners of capitalist property confronted a mass of proletarians or small 'peasants in the process of becoming landless peasants. (I am speaking here of the typical African village, not the Arab village, which is different; nor the village in South Africa or the colonies settled by whites, which are different again; nor the colonial towns, which are different once more.) Granted, there are cases of feudalism or semi-feudalism in some African countries, in certain regions of some countries; there are even cases of semi-capitalist agriculture or semi-capitalist relations; and remnants of slavery persist here and there. But, I repeat, it is a process in which a good part of the population finds itself precisely in a phase of transition from classless to class society.

The analysis of the Soviet Union and similar societies is obviously less awkward with this conceptual framework of transition than it is with an ultra-simple Marxism. If one believes that things are either black or white, that there is either capitalism or classless society, that there is either the democratic power of the workers or—by *a priori* definition—the power of a new owning class, then one will be confronted with one mystery after another. But if one rejects these oversimplifications and returns to an approach that integrates all the dimensions of the problem of what constitutes class society, what constitutes the withering away of social classes, and what constitutes a classless society, then the fact that the transitional period has turned out to be longer than initially expected becomes less astonishing. Just because a certain type of society lasts longer than had been foreseen is no reason to deny, by definition, that it can be a transitional society. Just because a transition is more complex and—to put it paradoxically—less 'dynamic', since it 'transits' less rapidly than expected, is no reason to say that it is not transitional. The fact that one halts on a bridge for a long time instead of walking across does not change the character of the bridge or the fact of the crossing. It simply means that historical or individual factors have modified the pace, orientation, and possibilities of the traveller's progress. The bridge remains defined essentially as a means of communication between two banks above a surface of water. By analogy, a transitional stage between capitalism and socialism is defined, at least structurally, by the fact that there is no longer generalized commodity production; that the means of production are no longer commodities; that they have therefore, by definition, lost their character as capital; that the class of capitalists that existed in the country before the social revolution no longer holds political, economic, and social power; but that there are not yet truly socialist, self-managed, and free relations of production of the associated producers; instead there is a hybrid combination of elements of the past and elements of the future.

But this hybrid combination gives rise to something specific—and it is perhaps from this standpoint that we have advanced somewhat over Trotsky's analysis. It gives rise to the specific relations of production of this transitional stage. Here I must raise a theoretical problem that is not easy to understand but is one of the theoretical keys to a grasp of the socio-economic reality of the Soviet Union. I refer to the distinction between the notion of *specific relations of production*, which characterize any given social formation (a given social formation without relations of production would be a social formation without production; in other words, a social formation that could not survive, lifeless and without existence), and the notion of *mode of production*. Although it is correct to say that there is no social formation without specific relations of production, it is false to say that any specific relation of production necessarily implies the existence of a specific or predominant mode of production. One of the essential distinctions between transitional periods and the great 'progressive stages' of history outlined by Marx in the preface to his *Contribution to the Critique of Political Economy* is precisely that the former do not have a specific mode of production, whereas the latter are by definition characterized by such modes. Let us first look at the theoretical explanation of this distinction, in the light of which we will then return to the socio-economic analysis of the Soviet Union.

What characterizes a mode of production is that it is a structure whose quantitative, gradual modification, which occurs through evolution, is possible only so long as it is compatible with the internal logic of the whole, which, although it may be torn and contradictory, nonetheless remains an organic whole. This whole, like anything organic, can reproduce itself more or less automatically. I do not say that it reproduces itself more or less automatically through the economic mechanism alone—this is a characteristic which in the final analysis is applicable only to the capitalist mode of production. In the pre-capitalist modes of production, the articulations between the various instruments of economic, political, and ideological reproduction can be markedly different from what they are in a bourgeois society. But the essence of the problem remains the same: once launched into orbit, the structure remains in this orbit and can be diverted from it only by social revolutions or counter-revolutions, by explosions, by very violent perturbations.

On the other hand, precisely because of their generally hybrid character, the relations of production of a society in transition between two modes of production can decompose of their own accord, evolve in various directions without necessarily experiencing revolutionary perturbations of the same type as the social revolutions necessary for the passage from one mode of production to another. The passage to petty commodity production was not preceded by the seizure of political power by petty commodity producers: there was no 'petty-commodity-production state'. There was a feudal state and then a bourgeois state. The advent of capitalism did not require a social and political revolution to decompose the relations of production founded on petty commodity production. The mere penetration/expansion of money-capital in the economy, in a context determined by the world capitalist market, by the domination of market capitalism, sufficed to bring about this phenomenon of decomposition. To sum up, one may say that the fundamental difference between the relations of production characteristic of transitional phases on the one hand and modes of production on the other is a qualitatively different degree of stability.

Examining the situation in the Soviet Union in the light of this distinction, we may draw a number of conclusions. First, it can easily be demonstrated that—contrary to claims that the relations of production in the USSR are essentially socialist—the term 'socialist' cannot be used to apply to that social formation unless it is emptied of all content. There is no genuine regime of the associated producers, and the mass of direct producers are in fact maintained in a position of impotence and of subordination to the managers of the means of production. This is not solely a 'normative', moral, subjective judgement, although there is no reason to dismiss this aspect of the Marxist analysis: a Marxist never accepts oppression, even if the oppressor regime is historically progressive compared with the regime it has replaced. It is also an objective economic judgement. We know that it is impossible to achieve optimal and harmonious planning through the bureaucratic road; that socialist democracy and free control by the masses, the broadest self-management, are indispensable to achieve this end.

Second, it can easily be demonstrated that—contrary to claims that the relations of production in the Soviet Union are essentially capitalist—capitalist relations of production cannot at all be reduced to 'domination by masters of the means of production over the direct producers', but imply a whole series of additional features: notably, that the means of production be commodities, that these means of production circulate among units of production in the form of the buying and selling of machines, raw materials, etc. Moreover, most of the long-term laws of development of the capitalist mode of production are already inherent in the fundamental contradiction of the single commodity, the contradiction between use-value and exchange-value. It was not by accident that Marx constructed the first volume of *Capital*, and everything in his economic analysis that followed from it, in this way. And none of this applies to the socio-economic reality of the Soviet Union.

Third, if one were to assert that the relations of production in the

Soviet Union are neither socialist nor capitalist but those of a new society dominated by an exploiting class, one would have to demonstrate the origins of this mysterious new ruling class, which is completely non-existent as a class up to zero hour, when it seizes power. One would have to uncover the dynamic, the laws of development of this society—something which none of the proponents of this theory have ever been capable of doing. It would also have to be shown that these relations of production, allegedly characteristic of a new mode of production, have the stability and capacity for self-reproduction common to modes of production, which is contrary to everything we know about Soviet society, not to mention the 'people's democracies'. Moreover, let us note in passing that any Marxist who affixes the label 'new class' to the Soviet bureaucracy must recognize the progressive character of this bureaucracy relative to the bourgeoisie, and must credit it with the enormous economic and cultural achievements of the USSR, just as the achievements of the nineteenth century must clearly be credited to the bourgeoisie.

If we reject these three hypotheses, there is only one way out: we are dealing with the specific, hybrid relations of production of a specific country (or group of countries). In other words, we are faced with the analysis of relations of production peculiar not to the period of transition from capitalism to socialism in general, but to a society which, although it is passing through this stage, has experienced particular processes of development in a given historical context. This implies both a pronounced fragility of the relations of production, compared with those characteristic of stable modes of production, and a greater stability than could have been foreseen under the assumption that the phenomenon would be very short-lived.

The Laws of Motion of the Soviet Economy

You mentioned that proponents of the theory that the Soviet Union is neither socialist nor capitalist but that its relations of production are characteristic of a new class society would have to uncover the particular laws of development of this society. But don't advocates of the Trotskyist analysis face the same task? After all, you maintain that the Soviet Union is not capitalist, which implies that the laws of capitalist economic development described by Marx do not pertain there. At the same time, you insist that the relations of production in the USSR are not socialist. But the Soviet economy must function in accordance with some set of laws. And they would have to be analysed whether one characterizes this economy as a 'mode of production' or as merely a hybrid set of 'relations of production'. What are the specific laws governing the operation of the Soviet economy?

It is surely true that we face this task, and we have indeed tried to grapple with it. I would mention, for example, that much of the second volume of my book *Marxist Economic Theory* is devoted to an examination of the Soviet economy and of the economics of the transition period in general. Obviously, I cannot go into great detail in a brief interview, but I will try to summarize the central elements of our analysis.

Let me begin by emphasizing our contention that the Soviet economy is no longer capitalist. This is demonstrated by a number of empirical observations. To start with, all large-scale industrial, transportation, and financial enterprises—in other words, the means of production and circulation—are state-owned. Further, this state ownership is complemented by three additional features: prohibition of the right of private appropriation of these means of production and circulation; centralized economic planning; and the state monopoly of foreign trade. All this means that generalized commodity production no longer exists in the USSR and that the law of value no longer *rules* there. There is no market for large-scale means of production or for labour-power. Both the means of production and labour-power have therefore ceased to be commodities.

On the other hand, because of the pressure of the world market, the insufficient level of development of the productive forces, the persistence of conflict of interest between social classes (like workers and peasants) and social layers (the bureaucracy), the enormous structural disparity between industry and agriculture, town and country, and manual and intellectual labour, commodity production inevitably survives in some areas—particularly in the production of means of consumption. It is therefore impossible to free the economy completely from the *influence* of the law of value. This survival of commodity production means that the economy is not yet socialist. The central contradiction and prime law of motion of the Soviet economy—and indeed of all economies during the phase of transition from capitalism to socialism—is therefore the continual conflict between the logic of the plan on the one hand and the influence of the law of value on the other.

The abolition of the *rule* of the law of value in the USSR has had enormous consequences. The development of the economy, for example, has not been afflicted by the sort of profit-determined sector priorities and inequalities that international capitalism has imposed on all less developed economies throughout the era of imperialism. It is also because of this abolition that the Soviet economy has been able to avert the business cycle, periodic over-production crises, and conjunctural massive unemployment. The USSR has been marked by long-term average growth rates superior to those of the industrialized capitalist countries, even after the achievement of basic industrialization. On the other hand, the survival of partial (though not generalized) commodity production, the pressure of the world market, and the other factors I have mentioned place objective limits on the effectiveness and impact of comprehensive economic planning. Over-production of those goods that are still commodities remains possible. These contradictions cause periodic fluctuations in growth rates and generate various sources of tension, even crises, peculiar to societies in transition from capitalism to socialism. But these tensions and crises, while quite real, are qualitatively different from those that afflict capitalist countries or would afflict a socialist economy.

The survival of commodity production in Department II (manufacture of means of consumption) has a momentous corollary: labour-power continues to be remunerated in the form of a money wage. This means that the workers' access to consumer goods continues to be governed primarily through exchange against money. This establishes—and again this is true of every society in transition from capitalism to socialism—a particular contradiction between the non-capitalist relations of production on the one hand and the essentially bourgeois norms of distribution on the other. That contradiction is not only felt within the sphere of distribution, but also has repercussions in the sphere of production and even affects the techniques of planning. For example, it leads to an inclination towards independent book-keeping at the enterprise level and towards the financial autonomy of enterprises as a result of the generalized use of money in national book-keeping.

As I have pointed out, under this sort of partial commodity production money cannot play the role it does under capitalism, or even under simple commodity production. It cannot become big capital, and only in marginal cases (like 'black market' production) does it become a means of direct exploitation of labour-power. Never does it become an instrument for the genuine private appropriation of major means of production. It *can*, however, become an instrument in the partial private appropriation of the social surplus-product (interest and rent), and it *does* stimulate a spontaneous tendency towards primitive accumulation of private capital, but within strict limits. It also remains a central factor in the consolidation and transmission of social inequality (inheritance, for example). This is another central contradiction and basic law of motion of the Soviet economy.

Everything you have said so far would apply to any society in transition from capitalism to socialism. All these contradictions are, as you put it, objective. But are there not particular contradictions— and laws of motion—of the Soviet economy which result from the form of political rule, namely the rule of the bureaucracy? If there are, how do they relate to the question of whether this bureaucracy constitutes a ruling class—in other words, whether we are dealing with a mode of production or a specific, hybrid set of relations of production?

These fundamental contradictions, which would be faced by any social formation in transition from capitalism to socialism, are enormously aggravated in the USSR by the consequences of the political counter-revolution that triumphed in the late twenties, leading to the monopoly on the exercise of power and administration in all spheres of social life now held by a materially-privileged social layer, the bureaucracy. Just as the law of value reigns in the most 'natural', unhindered manner under *laissez-faire* capitalism, a system based on the socially-planned investment and distribution of major economic resources functions normally and freely only if the entire economy is under the control and management of the associated producers themselves. The administration of productive units and of all basic economic processes by a privileged bureaucracy inevitably introduces great distortion and waste in the planning process.

Those distortions born of the survival of partial commodity production, the pressure of the world market, and the other factors I have cited are compounded by the additional contradictions introduced by the bureaucratic system itself. Many of the specific crises the Soviet economy has suffered over the past half century have been caused by these sorts of bureaucratic distortions. This is another basic law of motion of the Soviet economy.

The masses of producers have a dual interest in optimizing the planned use of economic resources. On the one hand, they want to reduce mechanical, non-creative labour inputs to a minimum; on the other, they want the greatest possible satisfaction of their needs and desires as consumers. Any waste of economic resources runs counter to one or both of these interests. There is no evidence, whether theoretical or empirical, to demonstrate that a centrally-planned, collectivized economy under genuine, democratic workers' management would utilize economic resources less efficiently than a capitalist economy based on competition and the race to maximize profits.

In the absence of democratic control of planning, production, and distribution by the associated producers themselves, however, a centrally-planned, collectivized economy can be run only through a contradictory combination of the drive for material self-interest on the part of the 'managerial' layer of the bureaucracy on the one hand and the political control exercised by the state apparatus on the other. (The party apparatus and the state apparatus have long since become one and the same.) Experience has confirmed what Marxist theory could have predicted: given such a combination, the Soviet economy will constantly function below its optimal rate of growth; periodic and explosive disproportions will arise between various branches of the national economy.

At the same time, it must be kept in mind that the bureaucracy's material privileges are essentially restricted to the sphere of consumption. (I am leaving aside its non-material privileges, such as 'social prestige', the 'thirst for power', and so on. These are not expressed in material advantages and are irrelevant to *economic* analysis.) Given the specific nature of the Soviet economy, these privileges take two main forms: higher monetary incomes (including income illegally acquired through corruption, bribery, theft, and 'black' or 'grey' market operations) and non-monetary advantages consequent to the position occupied in the hierarchical structure of the bureaucracy (for example, access to special shops, personal use of state-owned automobiles, relatively lavish apartments or villas, and so on). In both cases, the effect is that the bureaucrat has greater access to consumer goods (of higher quality) than the average worker, let alone the average peasant. Nevertheless, this leads neither to private property in the means of production nor to the accumulation of huge money fortunes.

All this introduces yet another highly explosive contradiction into the functioning of the Soviet economy. On the one hand, the material self-interest of the bureaucracy is the central instrument for realization of the plan. Given the bureaucracy's monopoly of administration throughout the entire economy, it is the major mechanism through which economic growth is socially mediated. On the other hand, there is *no economic mechanism whatever*—let alone a spontaneous and automatic one—through which fulfilment of this bureaucratic self-interest can be brought into line with optimal economic growth—at least not once an initial threshold of industrialization has been crossed.

This, by the way, is one of the important theoretical objections to the idea that the bureaucracy constitutes a new ruling *class*. Those who uphold this idea face a great paradox, which they have never resolved: they are unable to demonstrate the essential characteristic of any ruling class in a class society, namely the correspondence, the correlation, at least on a general level, between the interests and motivations of the so-called ruling class and the internal logic of the given economic system. There can be no contradiction between the motivation and behaviour of the bulk of the capitalist class and the internal logic of the capitalist system. Otherwise, the whole Marxist analysis of social classes becomes totally incoherent and we would be dealing with a disembodied, reified mode of production completely divorced from living social forces and playing the role of Hegel's *Zeitgeist*.

Now, it is manifest that no such correspondence exists in the Soviet Union. Not only does it not exist, but everything we know about the behaviour and motivation of the bureaucracy, especially those layers of it most closely linked to economic administration, which are supposed to control the social surplus product, runs counter to the logic of the planned economy. One of the strengths of the revolutionary Marxist—Trotskyist—analysis of the social character of the USSR is that it has been able to highlight precisely this aspect of things, on the basis of a specific conception of the bureaucracy and its contradictory role in Soviet society. This analysis has grasped the essential fact that we are dealing with a phenomenon which differs, qualitatively and structurally, from that of a ruling class. Because there is no private property in the means of production in the Soviet Union, because the advantages the bureaucrats enjoy are essentially privileges related to their functions and positions in the hierarchy, and because these advantages always remain precarious as a very result of the absence of property, it has been impossible for a system of administration founded on the individual interests of the bureaucrats to develop any genuine intrinsic rationality. Indeed, we may say that all the major economic reforms of the Soviet economy since the second five-year plan— from the principle of *khozrachot* (autonomous profitability of each individual enterprise) introduced under Stalin to Khrushchev's *sovnarkhozi* to Liberman's proposed 'restoration of the profit indicator of overall economic performance' to Kosygin's system of 'combined indicators' to the latest counter-reforms now eliminating some of the effects of the Liberman reforms—have been aimed, unsuccessfully, at overcoming this contradiction.

There is a quite fundamental reason for this lack of success. By its very nature as a social layer commanding material privileges in the sphere of consumption, the bureaucracy *cannot* countervail its tendency to subordinate general social priorities to *separate* sectoral advantages (which are acquired on the level of individual factory, enterprise, locality, region, industrial branch, nationality, and so on). In other words, there is no way to permit simultaneous satisfaction of both the private interests of the bureaucrats and the needs and requisites of a socialized and planned economy. Hence, every one of these reforms has led to a new form of contradiction, which leads in turn to a new reform, which leads to a new manifestation of the contradiction, and so on *ad infinitum*. This fact in itself should suffice to indicate that the bureaucracy is not a ruling class, and that the Soviet Union has not produced a stabilized mode of production of any sort; for such a situation is unthinkable under a stabilized mode of production. At any rate, there is no historical precedent for such a situation.

For in so far as the bureaucracy attempts to accumulate private advantages, it cannot adequately manage a planned economy. And in so far as it has to manage the planned economy at least adequately, it cannot give priority to the accumulation of its own material privileges. The error of those who view the bureaucracy as an incarnation of 'the will to accumulate', 'production for production's own sake', 'the rise of production in heavy industry at the expense of light industry', or anything of a similar kind is that they have a mystified image of the real Soviet bureaucracy. There may have been some planners, and probably a few political leaders, who had the passion of production for its own sake, of production for accumulation. The real bureaucrats, the flesh and blood ones who inhabit the real world, are doubtless motivated by many passions, but these are much more mundane than production for production's sake. Their passions are strictly linked to the particular position the bureaucracy occupies in Soviet transitional society and to its very special and contradictory articulation with the system of planned economy.

Bureaucratic management—in whatever form—will therefore always lead to waste of resources in a variety of ways: concealment of reserves, transmission of false information, inflation of input requirements, production of low-quality outputs unrelated to consumer needs, theft of productive inputs for use in 'grey' or 'black' market production, etc. Neither systematic recourse to terror, as under Stalin, nor partial restoration of market mechanisms, as during the post-Stalin period, can eliminate the ultimate root of this waste, which is the conflict between the material self-interest of the privileged managerial bureaucracy on the one hand and the need for optimal use of the economic resources freed by the abolition of private property in the means of production and of the rule of the law of value on the other hand. The collective interest of the overwhelming majority of the producers, however, requires just this optimal utilization of resources. Only democratically-associated producers receiving equalized 'social dividends' from stepped up economic growth or increased labour productivity would have a genuine, material interest in global *social* optimization of the use of economic resources.

But is it not the case that the sort of self-managed system you are talking about requires a certain level of development of the productive forces, that would allow the preconditions for the functioning of such a system to be assembled? And does Marxist theory not have something to say about the economic, political, social, and cultural preconditions that would permit these new relations of production to be stabilized, and crystallize into a mode of production?

This question really boils down to two problems. What are the preconditions for withering away of the market economy and money economy? And what are the preconditions for withering away of the social division of labour between producers and administrators? In my view, the present wealth of the most industrially advanced countries would permit rapid attainment of a level of development such that basic material needs could be satisfied to the full. This is the most obvious criterion for the possibility—indeed necessity—for market and monetary categories to wither away. For under these conditions, such categories can be applied only with perverse effects. We can already see evidence of this in the attempt to 'organize' the agricultural abundance of the Common Market on the basis of the market economy. I also believe it would be possible immediately to introduce half-day working. Moreover, this is the material condition—not in itself sufficient, but certainly necessary—for making self-management a reality rather than a mere slogan. If the producers do not have the time to manage their factories, their neighbourhoods and the state—not to mention federations of socialist states—you can proclaim self-management as much as you want, but there will still be professional politicians, and therefore functionaries, and therefore potential bureaucrats, who will control this management. Well, the conditions for half-day working and for generalized, compulsory university education now exist in all the great industrial countries.

But did they exist in 1920?

No, I am speaking of today.

So in 1920 they did not exist?

Certainly not in Russia.

How about Germany, in 1920?

In the very short term, no. In the medium term, probably. What could the Germany of 1920 have become if there had been a victorious socialist revolution and a merger with the Soviet Union? It is not easy to say. I mention in passing, because it is little known, that preparatory work for manufacture of the first electronic computer was under way in Germany back in the thirties—and this under an extremely reactionary economic and political regime. Given the intellectual forces of Germany, if there had been a socialist regime in the early twenties, it is my guess that fifteen or twenty years could have been gained over capitalism, so far as the third technological revolution is concerned. Let us not forget that Einstein was in Germany, and that the development of nuclear energy—with all its contradictions but also promise for humanity, provided security is given strict priority over cost (not to speak of 'profitability')—could have permitted enormous progress in the context of a socialist Germany and socialist Europe. But all this is guesswork. It is not possible to build hypotheses on if's. Let us talk about what is possible today. Today the potential is there.

Any dialogue between those who indict a betrayed or bankrupt revolution and those who sing the praises of a revolution that has yet to occur must obviously remain uncertain, undecided, doubtful. The hard evidence needed to really convince the sceptics would be a model born of a victorious revolution qualitatively superior to what exists in the Soviet Union, Eastern Europe, or the People's Republic of China today. In a sense, this is what explains the difficulty even for Marxist theory to pronounce the last word on the nature of the USSR, the nature of the transitional stage, the nature of the problems to be solved, and the means by which to solve them. For the test of practice has not yet occurred, in either direction; and the last word in theory will be spoken only after the last word in practice. It is very difficult for theory to anticipate fully what practice has yet to resolve in real life.

The Social Character of the Bureaucracy

Let us return, then, to the reality of the USSR. The nature of the Soviet regime has been the subject of increasing debate and discussion in the Left in recent years. Some forces have claimed that

Soviet reality now reveals signs of economic crisis, that unemployment has arisen there, that the productive forces have stagnated, that there has been no rise in the standard of living of the masses, etc. On this basis they have argued that the USSR is indeed subject to problems analogous to those of the capitalist countries. Others have pointed to the stability of bureaucratic rule, the actual widening of the bureaucracy's sphere of intervention, its increased role in the economy, and so on. If these observations are correct, would the combination of economic and social crisis plus stability of bureaucratic rule suggest the existence of a ruling class?

To start with, this discussion in the West is often marred by great light-mindedness. More precisely, most of those who discuss the USSR have been unable to approach the socio-economic reality of the country with what Lenin considered one of the basic characteristics of the materialist dialectic, namely *die Allseitigkeit* [all-sidedness] —the process of taking account of all aspects of a problem, and not isolating certain aspects from others. A whole history of western Sovietology—and I include under this rather pejorative term all the various currents and subcurrents of Marxist thought itself—could be written from this standpoint. Now one aspect, now another has been emphasized, depending on the moment, the pragmatic exigencies of the political struggle, and even personal whims and vulgar self-interest. At one point, stress is laid on the limited character of the productive forces, at another on waste, at another on the contradiction between the low living standards of the population and the immense industrial potential, at yet another on the leaps forward in technology, at another on the enormous technological backwardness, and so on.

Moreover, this is not so much a question of lack of information. In order to develop a view that at least aims at being comprehensive, the essential thing is to take the trouble to examine the whole, and to constantly strive to integrate often contradictory elements into a dynamic, overall view of Soviet reality. I am struck, for example, by the really light-minded, even irresponsible way in which many western observers speak of the economic crisis supposedly 'striking the Soviet economy, just as it has struck the western economy'; and by the way in which others (including some who claim to be Marxists) consider unimportant the little difference that although there has been a terrible new rise of unemployment in all the industrialized countries of the West, there is no unemployment at all in the industrialized countries of Eastern Europe. They escape these difficulties with formulas that are actually nothing but frivolities, diversions without serious theoretical content. They say, for example, 'Yes, but there is concealed unemployment, hidden within the factories, in the Soviet Union'. The only 'difference' is that the Soviet workers continue to be paid, while the unemployed workers in the West are out on the street. And why does the ruling class in the industrialized capitalist countries, even though these are richer than the Soviet Union, lack the will or ability to eliminate 'manifest' unemployment by replacing it with hidden unemployment? Clearly, all these questions go back to a method of general analysis, and to the inability of all those who refuse to apply it to understand the very complex reality of the Soviet Union.

Take another example. I think we must reject as incompatible with reality, as a distortion, any idea that there has been a stagnation of the productive forces in the Soviet Union, a waste that has totally neutralized the effects of planning. I believe that even though there have been repeated crises of declining Soviet economic growth rates, even though there is indeed frightful waste (undoubtedly the second count in the indictment of the Soviet bureaucracy, the first being the fact that it stands in the way of self-management of the producers, the toiling portion of the population), the very duration both of the regime and of its economic growth have finally had cumulative effects that it would be absurd to deny—particularly since they represent one of the essential sources of contradiction in the system today.

I would add that arguments based on the low living standards of the population, on the inadequate level of consumption, although they do contain a kernel of truth, must be used cautiously. Above all, standard of living must not be identified with ease in obtaining food supplies. Since the Soviet Union has become a great industrial power, the modification of the demand and consumption pattern of the workers that occurred in the western capitalist countries has taken place in the USSR too, although with some delay. This means that the permanent shortage of quality agricultural products is considered especially absurd and unacceptable. But it does not mean that living standards have stagnated as a result of this shortage. In the case of many industrial consumer goods—and especially housing (which is not the least important factor), where the situation was disastrous under Stalin and immediately after his death—the cumulative changes of the past twenty-five years have finally had real effects. The demands of Soviet workers today, even in the realm of consumption, are quite different from those traditionally raised in Stalin's day; they point in directions far more comparable to those taken in the industrialized capitalist countries.

In this sense, I believe we must emphasize—and I know this provokes indignation and hilarity among all revisionist currents—that the relations of production in the Soviet Union are based on a planned organization of large-scale production, a planned organization based on state property (which is a form of social property) in the means of production. There is no doubt about the superiority of this aspect of the Soviet economy, at least in the light of a long-term view that is able to distinguish this general observation from dithyrambic conclusions claiming that what is involved is socialism, that the socialist paradise has come to pass, and other such idiocies. To claim, as do Bettelheim and his school (for they are at the root of it all), that property in the means of production is collectivized only juridically and that the enterprises actually own a good portion of their means of production is to misunderstand the reality of Soviet planning and its results. It is to lend phenomena like the black market, or the bureaucracy's illegal appropriation of goods through parallel circuits, decisive weight in the economy. Although these phenomena are undoubtedly real, they do not command such decisive weight.

Finally, one must be cautious in speaking of stability. I would prefer to say that the reign of the Soviet bureaucracy has been characterized by a combination of stability and instability. For those who had hoped for a political revolution or a collapse of the regime in the short run, there has been stability. But if we draw the balance-sheet of the twenty-five years since the death of Stalin, there has not been a single year without changes in the Soviet Union of a very important nature, compared with the old image of monolithic immobility. Can it be said that the Soviet Union with the Stalin cult and the Soviet Union without the Stalin cult are exactly the same thing? That the Soviet Union with a living standard for workers comparable, say, to that of Turkey is exactly the same thing as the

Soviet Union with wage levels that are now approaching those of Italian workers? Can it be claimed that the Soviet Union which produced only 30 million tonnes of steel is the same thing as the Soviet Union which is now the world's largest steel producer, producing 20 per cent more per year than the United States? Can it be said that the Soviet Union in which oppositionists were found only in Gulag camps and the Soviet Union today with its ferment of political currents, *samizdat*, and discussion at all sorts of levels (not only among intellectuals, but also in the unions), are one and the same thing? From this standpoint as well, the problem is more complex. But here, in contrast to what I said on the previous point, what is lacking is not so much a method of integrating all this information as the information itself. We have little knowledge of anything in the Soviet Union that is not macro-economic or macro-social. We know the general outlines, the aggregates: things like the industrial production figures, the national income, even the bureaucracy's share in the distribution of the national income, are not so difficult to calculate. All this is more or less known. But we are dealing with a country of 250 million people. This society contains many mini-societies within it. And here we are obviously much less informed. We only perceive certain aspects of reality through sudden revelations; through the light that may be shed from time to time, by some source or other, about what is happening.

As you say, there has been a cumulative growth of the Soviet economy over the past half century, despite all the bureaucratic waste. In fact, the USSR has been transformed from a relatively backward country into a major industrial power.

Not just a major industrial power, but the second-largest industrial power on earth, at least from the standpoint of total, absolute production figures. Even the industrial productivity of labour has now risen to the neighbourhood of Italian and British averages. All this, of course, constitutes an achievement made possible by the overthrow of capitalism.

One result of this kind of economic growth has been a dramatic increase in the social weight of the Soviet proletariat. Its level of cultural and technical skills has also risen. But this has not had the effect of bringing down, or even significantly eroding, bureaucratic rule. Is that in contradiction, at least implicitly, with the Trotskyist analysis?

On the contrary. The growth of the Soviet economy and the corresponding increase in the social weight and technical and cultural skills of the working class does not automatically make the overthrow of the bureaucracy's monopoly of power and management of society any easier or more rapid. The relative stability of the rule of the bureaucracy—or at any rate, its relative longevity—is basically a result of the fact that the overthrow of this regime requires *conscious* political action, a political revolution. This in turn requires maturation not only of objective but also of subjective conditions. The major reason for the duration of bureaucratic rule in the USSR is that these subjective conditions for political revolution have not yet ripened.

Two, interrelated factors account for this. On the one hand, one of the central effects of the long period of bureaucratic rule—and I include in that category not only Stalin's reign of terror, but also Khrushchevism and Brezhnevism—has been a process of continuous atomization and de-politicization of the Soviet working class. This places enormous obstacles in the way of a political revolution. Communism, Marxism, and socialism have been discredited in the eyes of many Soviet workers, for they have been systematically prostituted into an apologetic state religion in the service of the ruling bureaucracy. This is particularly important in view of the lack of a victorious social revolution in the West or political revolution in an East European country, either of which could offer the Soviet proletariat an attractive alternative model.

On the other hand, the very growth of the Soviet economy in spite of all the waste caused by bureaucratic mismanagement has laid the basis for a slow but steady increase in the living standards of the Soviet workers. The bureaucracy has therefore been able to encourage a phenomenon that could be called 'reformist consumerism', which has become a sort of alternative to political action within the working class. True, this provokes new tensions and contradictions, as a result of rising expectations among the workers: for quality consumer goods, access to higher education, better quality health care, free travel abroad, and so on. But it has also helped to maintain the de-politicization and atomization of the proletariat and has therefore acted to curb any rebirth of systematic mass action or organization. (The only exception to this—and it is partial—is the ferment among the oppressed nationalities; but here mobilizations have tended to be restricted to struggles for national goals.)

But it is important to bear in mind that the relative lack of ripeness of subjective conditions for political revolution does not mean that bureaucratic rule is reproduced smoothly or automatically. It merely introduces another contradiction into the Soviet economy. The more the rising objective weight of the proletariat collides with the continued exclusion of that proletariat from meaningful decision-making processes in management and planning, the more *generalized indifference* to the outcome of productive processes tends to permeate all levels of the activities of the workers. This in turn becomes a source of slowdown of economic growth (and a vast reservoir of potential additional growth in the event of a victorious political revolution).

The Working Class, the Bureaucracy and the State

Despite this contradiction—or perhaps because of it—the working class has succeeded in determining a number of upheavals, even political ones, at least in some of the countries of Eastern Europe. The proletariat is now intervening in increasingly massive fashion.

I would be cautious with the term 'increasingly massive', because this could almost lead to the idea that we are on the eve of qualitative or automatic corrections. But it is obvious that the situation is very different from that which prevails in the industrially advanced capitalist countries, both in terms of the relationship of social and economic forces and in terms of the bureaucracy's very inability to elaborate its own ideology—which obliges it not to acknowledge its own power, but to present itself as the representative of the power of the working class. I have already had occasion to call attention to another fundamental paradox of this situation: the fact that the working class, which is proclaimed as the ruling class in all official propaganda, is in reality devoid of all political rights. At the same time, although the working class does not participate in the management of the economy and the state, it nevertheless does command *de facto* powers and rights, resulting from the October Revolution, which remain considerable. This contradiction must be understood, mastered, and its consequences grasped.

Because there is no labour market in the USSR; because it is formally illegal and usually indeed impossible for a Soviet factory director, unlike the head of a capitalist enterprise, to fire a worker; in other words, because job security is infinitely greater in the USSR (though we should not exaggerate, it is not absolute), Soviet workers find it possible to impose a number of realities in the factories, such as a slower work pace, which do not exist in the capitalist countries. And there is a bizarre blend, once again hybrid, of great indifference to individual effort and great interest in individual skill—which to some extent is the opposite of what occurs in capitalist society.

The two aspects of this contradiction must not be underestimated, because they have a very clear social dynamic. According to official figures (and even though these are exaggerated, they do have some relation to reality), there are ten million people in Soviet factories today—ten million—who hold university degrees or degrees from post-secondary technical colleges. This is a considerable percentage of the total number of workers (seventy million) and it is rising from year to year. This must inevitably have an effect on the self-confidence of the working class. It must inevitably shift the relationship of forces with the bureaucracy, in the context of a society in which the monopoly of knowledge was initially an immense weapon in the hands of the privileged. That monopoly is now being undermined by this extraordinary effort at cultural and technical education on the part of the Soviet working class.

How is it that, under such conditions, there should at the same time be indifference to productive effort? This too is not hard to explain. Indifference exists precisely to the extent that the mass of producers are deeply convinced that it is useless to make any real effort, when everything is on the one hand strictly controlled from the centre, and on the other infinitely disorganized by the bureaucracy's waste and privileges. There is too much risk involved in making any move. So people opt for the status quo, and simply try to get by as best they can. Another factor may also be mentioned, which although secondary is not without importance (probably it is more important in Eastern Europe than in the Soviet Union, but even in the latter it has some weight). This is the gap between reality and statistics, due to the fact that a good quantity of labour is invested in commodities traded through parallel circuits. The slow work pace in the great enterprises is partly due to the fact that many skilled workers do other jobs after they go home.

All this said, however, it is nonetheless true that the Soviet working class, with its skills, its much higher level of culture and its manifest desire to perfect its technical capacities, is deeply frustrated, deprived as it is of any real participation in the management of the state and the economy. The few, less than modest reforms introduced during the sixties were at most aimed at introducing a degree of co-management on a few social questions, like work rules and wages. Moreover, this was co-management between the trade-union apparatus (in other words a fraction of the bureaucracy) and the factory managers; it did not involve general assemblies of union members, which would have been quite another thing—taking us back to an indirect form of working-class participation in the exercise of power such as existed in the twenties.

Why have there not yet been more explosive demonstrations of protest by the Soviet proletariat against this state of affairs, which must be increasingly intolerable to it? I think there are two main reasons for this. First is the lack of an alternative model, which I have already mentioned; in other words, ideological and political scepticism, which must be extremely deep. The Soviet working class has been profoundly disappointed by the way the October Revolution turned, through the Stalinist degeneration, towards a model of social leadership which does not meet the workers' needs. The workers have not been attracted to the capitalist model either. But they see no alternative in the world today, no third model. There are no cadres within the Soviet working class able to propose a different model of management. Here Stalin's radical extermination of all Communist opposition tendencies, of all Communist cadres, has had a really disastrous effect. In the absence of any such alternative model, there has been a withdrawal towards private life, immediate demands, higher living standards, even towards individual social advancement through education (the negative side of the race for education, which must not be ignored). All these forms of withdrawal are practically inevitable. The second major reason is that there has been undeniable progress in the standard of living and working conditions of the Soviet workers. This progress, nearly constant since the death of Stalin, i.e. over the past twenty-five years, has generated what may be called a climate within the working class that is more reformist than revolutionary. Temporary explosions may erupt around particular questions, for example when the shortage of food products or the intensification of repression is especially severe. Normally, however, the Soviet workers hope to improve their lot by exerting pressure within the framework of the system rather than by challenging it comprehensively.

It is the combination of these two factors which accounts for the present political passivity of the working class (factors, by the way, which we have seen at work also in advanced capitalist countries). An additional detonator may well be necessary to trigger broader explosions: a revolutionary victory in the West; or the development of a more articulate and effective political opposition among non-workers in the Soviet Union, that could succeed in establishing contact and dialogue with the working class; or very deep and explosive contradictions within the bureaucracy itself; or new, more explosive crises in Eastern Europe. Other possibilities could be added, but some supplementary detonator is probably required to alter the situation.

There is one other great unknown: what do young Soviet workers think and how do they see society? I mean workers who have graduated from technical and professional schools during the past five or six years, and who never experienced not just Stalin and de-Stalinization, but even the invasion of Czechoslovakia, which was the last great internal crisis in the bureaucracy's system of domination. This is a big question mark. There may be some surprises here, but for the moment we must not have excessive short-term hopes.

What you have just said about the Soviet working class again raises the question of the nature of bureaucracy. There are those who agree that the bureaucracy cannot be compared to a ruling class in a classical mode of production—the bourgeoisie, for example—but who would wonder—not in general, but in the context of the specific Soviet social formation—about this: given the prominent role of the state, particularly in the economy, as you have stressed, and given

the atomization of the working class, has the bureaucracy accumu-
lated a body of powers in the economic, social, and political domains
such that it now stands outside the working class? And would that
mean that the position of Trotsky, who spoke of a workers' bureau-
cracy, a fraction of the working class through which the dictatorship
of the proletariat was exercised in a deformed but real manner, is no
longer valid?

If one were to define the bureaucracy as solely the topmost layers of
the hierarchy, then it is obvious that any kinship with the working
class, either psychological or social, would become increasingly
difficult to demonstrate. The relationship would then become purely
historical—at best! The only element of Trotsky's definition that
would remain—though I think even this would still be decisive, in
spite of everything—would be the mode of remuneration: the fact
that the bureaucracy, since it does not own the means of production,
participates in distribution of the national income exclusively as a
function of remuneration for its labour-power. This entails many
privileges, but it is a form of remuneration that does not differ
qualitatively from remuneration in the form of a salary. However,
although this definition may satisfy theoreticians, above all Marxists
who attach key importance to economic phenomena, I would at once
concede that it is not very convincing from the psychological and
pedagogic standpoint. To explain that the bureaucracy is a workers'
bureaucracy solely because the people receiving twenty times the
wage of an ordinary worker are still receiving a wage is a highly
abstract argument. Even so, as I say, its validity must be recognized,
and above all the implication that the bureaucracy would cease to be
a workers' bureaucracy as soon as it acquired essential sources of
income deriving from property, etc.

But in fact this restrictive definition of the bureaucracy is quite
arbitrary and therefore false. Certainly it is not Trotsky's definition,
contrary to what is claimed by some of his critics. Such a definition is
utterly unable to account for the reality of the bureaucracy's
domination. If the bureaucracy could really be reduced to these
individuals, a few hundred thousand at most and perhaps only a few
tens of thousands, then the enormous control it continues to exercise
over society as a whole would be difficult to explain. For the
principal instrument of this control during the Stalin era—permanent

and bloody terror; real fear of loss not only of liberty but of life—manifestly no longer exists to the same extent. As soon, however, as we extend the notion of the bureaucracy to include as it should all the layers in Soviet society that are privileged in one way or another, then we are talking about millions of people: between five and ten million, if not more. This total would include the entire trade-union bureaucracy; the whole officer corps of the armed forces, not just the generals and marshals but also the junior officers; the entire hierarchy of production, not just the directors but also the engineers; and the great majority of the intelligentsia (except teachers, who are paid less than workers and have no material privileges).

As soon as we apply this correct definition of the bureaucracy, then the premises of the previous argument vanish. For it is absolutely certain that a good number of today's bureaucrats, in this broad and real sense of the term, are not merely the sons and daughters of workers but even former workers themselves. The upward mobility I referred to earlier, which—with all its negative aspects—underlies the thirst for education and skills that characterizes a good part of the working class, is essentially mobility towards the bureaucracy. One of the principal weapons the bureaucracy has used to maintain its dictatorship has been precisely this mobility; the fact that it has been able to 'skim the cream' off successive generations of workers, by offering them something the capitalist system cannot. The most that can be offered a worker under the capitalist system is a position intermediary between the proletariat and the bourgeoisie. He is certainly not offered the property that would allow him to become head of a great enterprise. The particular structure of society in the Soviet Union enables the bureaucracy to absorb the sons and daughters of workers, and even workers themselves, into the apparatus. Not into the summits of the apparatus, but into positions much higher than those of the so-called middle classes in the advanced capitalist countries.

There is a very interesting and concrete sociological problem connected to this. After the period of industrialization and the first five-year plans, and after the upheavals of the Second World War and de-Stalinization, has this upward mobility continued to function during the past fifteen years in the same way that it did before? Or has it begun to slow down—especially above a certain level of the hierarchy? There is some interesting evidence about this subject, although I do not know of any statistical data. In particular, all questions related to access to university studies, and to the need—in almost all sections of the bureaucracy—for university degrees in order to move beyond a certain level, arouse enormous passion. Since the bureaucracy, powerful as it is, is barred from accumulating the private property that could guarantee its privileges, it attempts to transmit these privileges to its own sons and daughters (more, incidentally, to the sons than to the daughters) by assuring their access to its own ranks by virtue of their access to university degrees. This is now introducing a source of deep social conflict. The struggle for admission to universities has become intense. Soviet literature, for example, provides descriptions of this. The day entrance examination results are announced is a day of real social tension in all the university towns of the Soviet Union. The charges of corruption, bribery, and nepotism that are made by workers and popular layers on such occasions are much more violent than any charges made about lack of access to the management of enterprises. For this is a more tangible, phenomenological, and immediately visible aspect of the bureaucracy's privileges, since it closes off what has hitherto been the essential mechanism of compensation: namely, education and access to upward mobility. Here we can expect even more violent reactions and conflicts in the future. Once again, this shows that although the bureaucracy may try to sever entirely the umbilical cord with its past, the working class and Marxist ideology, it is one thing to try and quite another to succeed. What is involved here is an ongoing process which is far from completed; and it is obvious that there may be very violent reactions.

As you say, there is evidence pointing to a slowdown of social mobility. Upward mobility has been declining for the past fifteen years, perhaps even since the death of Stalin . . .

No, no, the period of de-Stalinization saw a massive purge of the apparatus which made room for young blood again, though it is only recently that we have received figures on this.

In any event, this reduced upward mobility has occurred around a structural nucleus, which is the entirety of the apparatus of the state and the party. This raises a slightly different question, but one that points in the same direction as the previous one. Under these conditions, does the term 'workers' state' have real meaning once the central nucleus around which power is articulated tends to be external to the working class, which has no political rights whatever? What is the validity of the term 'workers' state' under such conditions, given the expropriation of the working class?

For the past forty years, we in our movement have no longer used the unqualified term 'workers' state' except on a few, limited occasions. We say 'bureaucratically degenerate' or 'bureaucratized workers' state', which is not at all the same thing. Trotsky spoke of a broken-down automobile that had crashed head-on into a wall. The difficulty here is the difference between science and pedagogy. The formula 'bureaucratized workers' state' refers to criteria of the Marxist theory of the state. For Marxism, there is no such thing as a state that stands above classes. The state is in the service of the historic interests of a given social class. If one drops the adjective 'workers'', it can be replaced by one of two other terms. It can be called either a bourgeois state, or a state of a bureaucracy that has become a new ruling class. I have already indicated why these definitions are absolutely false, and even more confused—more heavily laden with totally irrational confusion—than that of 'workers' state'. Let me take just one example. If we allow that the bureaucracy is a new class, are the Communist Parties in power then 'bureaucratic' parties? Does the class struggle in the capitalist countries then become a triangular conflict among the working class, the bourgeoisie, and the bureaucracy? Or is the bureaucracy the only class in history that becomes a class only after seizing power, although it was not a class prior to the seizure of power? Was the Chinese Communist Party a workers' party—or a workers' and peasants' party, it matters little—up to the time it seized power, and did it become a bureaucratic party after seizing power? All this leads to absurdities, to a lack of comprehension of world reality today. It makes it impossible to orient oneself in the day-to-day class struggle on a world scale. And this is infinitely more dangerous than the pedagogical or political-pragmatic disadvantage of using the term 'workers' state' to apply to the Soviet state. That said, when the Fourth International—following Trotsky—asserts that there is still a bureaucratically degenerate workers' state in the Soviet Union, and that in this sense the Soviet Union still preserves a form of dictatorship of the proletariat, it does so in a quite precise way which implies no more than it says. Up to now this state has objectively continued to defend the structures, the hybrid relations of production, born of the October Revolution. Thus up to now this state has prevented the restoration of capitalism and the power of a new bourgeois class; it has prevented the re-emergence of capitalist property and capitalist relations of production.

It is only in this sense that we use the adjective 'workers' '. But it nevertheless does, of course, have a profound historical meaning, which can be clarified through comparison to other systems, other transitional situations. Let us take a particularly revealing historical example. If we draw the balance-sheet on what has been called, somewhat superficially, the epoch of absolute monarchy, we find incontestably that in a good part of Europe this was also the era of the primitive accumulation of capital and the rise of the young bourgeoisie, the epoch of the strengthening of this bourgeoisie; in other words, the epoch that paved the way for the bourgeois revolution. At the same time, however, if one views the problem from another standpoint, from the vantage-point of what remained of the semi-feudal aristocracy, it is equally incontestable that absolutism saved this decrepit and degenerate class, enabling it to continue to exist for another two centuries or more. It did this in an extremely simple manner: since the landed incomes of the semi-feudal nobility were less and less adequate to enable the nobility to maintain its lifestyle and habits, the absolute monarchy acted as an enormous 'financial pump' extracting income from the other classes of society, primarily the peasantry and the bourgeoisie, and transferring it to the court nobility in the form of stipends and contributions. It may thus be said that the state of the absolute monarchy was a semi-feudal state, that defended the historic interests of the aristocracy. But to interpret this to mean that this state defended the feudal nobles such as they were or wanted to be—I am referring now not to the twelfth century, but to the sixteenth or seventeenth—is obviously an absurdity. On the contrary, the state attacked them, crushing the Frondes of these nobles throughout Europe with a violence and severity that was not much less intense—when all the relevant allowances are made—than the anti-worker repression by the bureaucracy in the Soviet Union. Thus, there is a very big difference between, on the one hand, maintaining certain socio-economic structures historically linked to the interests of a particular social class and, on the other, defending the immediate, daily interests of a social class in the sense of what it itself sees as—and wants to be—its place in society. This is what makes our definition of the Soviet Union as a bureaucratically degenerate workers' state correct both historically and theoretically.

It is, nonetheless, true that this definition is difficult to understand and assimilate for anyone who approaches the problem not with these criteria but with simple common sense. Obviously, for simple common sense it is absurd to say that the dictatorship of the proletariat exists in the Soviet Union, since the immense majority of the proletariat exercises not only no dictatorship but not even any power. And if one interprets 'dictatorship of the proletariat' to mean 'direct government by the working class', then this dictatorship certainly does not exist. For us, the dictatorship of the proletariat exists in the Soviet Union only in the derived, indirect, and socio-theoretical sense of the term. Here again, though, I think the dispute is purely semantic and not very interesting. For as soon as the labels are abandoned and one is compelled to use more detailed and nuanced circumlocutions, one returns to the real problems, which are not problems of labels. What is the place of the bureaucracy in Soviet society? Is it the same as the place of a ruling class? By what methods can the bureaucracy stabilize its power and privileges indefinitely? Are these the same methods as those employed by a ruling class? Is it possible for the working class to alter the situation? Does it need a thorough overturn of the whole economic system or is it sufficient to modify the system of power, which will certainly entail considerable economic consequences but is still different from a social revolution? When one becomes more concrete, specific, and precise, the differences do not at all disappear. On the contrary, their real meaning emerges. Then it is not a matter of differences in labels, terms, or concepts, but differences in interpretation of contradictory aspects of Soviet society and in the political conclusions drawn from the assessment of these phenomena.

Capitalist Restoration
or Political Revolution?

But didn't Trotsky raise the possibility that the bureaucracy might sever even its historic links to the working class and effect a restoration of capitalism? Certainly one would not want to argue that the sole threat of restoration comes from outside the Soviet Union, in the form of imperialist military attack or economic penetration. If one says that the USSR is a transitional society, that the Soviet economy does not embody a fully articulated 'mode of production', and that the bureaucracy is not a ruling class, does it not follow that subsequent evolution could be in either direction? To take up the analogy you made earlier: when walking across a bridge one can always stop, turn around, and go back to the other side. There is nothing in the nature of the bridge as you have defined it that would prevent this kind of change of direction.

The point is well taken. But we should look carefully at the factors pressing in one direction or the other. For about twenty years now the Soviet bureaucracy has been faced with mounting problems arising from the need to shift from extensive to intensive industrialization. This fundamental need results from the gradual exhaustion of the large-scale reserves in land, agricultural labour, and raw materials that fueled the industrialization of the first few five-year plans. So far, all the attempts to solve these problems have failed to achieve a qualitatively higher degree of efficiency in the use of economic resources, although some progress has been made.

There are two basic stumbling blocks that cannot be overcome by the bureaucratic leadership. First, as I pointed out earlier, it is impossible to forge a rational link between the material self-interest of the bureaucracy and the optimization of economic growth. Second, there is no way to overcome the relative indifference to production on the part of the direct producers themselves. The first stumbling block could be removed only if a permanent tie of material interest were re-established between the individual bureaucrats and the particular enterprises—in other words, if private property in the means of production were re-established, in the economic, although not necessarily simultaneously juridical, sense of the word. That, of course, would mean restoration of capitalism.

The second stumbling block could be overcome only through the conquest of generalized workers' control, workers' management, and workers' political power in the economy and society. The first change would represent a victorious social counter-revolution, the second a victorious anti-bureaucratic political revolution.

Now, within the bureaucracy, especially its 'managerial' wing, there are undoubtedly tendencies striving to link the drive for security of social status, income, and privileges to *permanent* ties to given enterprises or groups of enterprises. These tendencies are simply a reflection, probably conscious in part, of the historically demonstrated fact that without such ties (that is, private property in the economic sense of the word), there is no guarantee that material privileges and enhanced social status can be rendered secure and transmitted to new generations. In addition, these efforts dovetail nicely with the dictatorship's objective tendency to seek a unifying rationale linking bureaucratic material self-interest to the need to streamline the functioning of the system. They also dovetail with the pressure of the world market, the trend towards primitive, small-scale accumulation of capital, the operation of 'grey' and 'black' market sectors of production, and so on.

If all these tendencies unfolded fully, we would probably see a staged disappearance of central planning, an erosion and dismantling of the state monopoly of foreign trade, and a rising symbiosis between a number of Soviet enterprises, freed from the iron control of the plan, and their counterparts in the imperialist countries. Trotsky himself called attention to this danger long ago. In fact, it may even be the case that he underestimated the degree of attachment of the majority of Soviet bureaucrats to collective property. But if so the mistake was simply, as so often, one of timing; he noted an embryonic trend and too rapidly considered it already generalized. At all events, it is striking that although on the whole the demands of, say, Soviet managers do not centre on the question of private accumulation, they have nevertheless for more than twenty-five years now been raising a series of questions whose logic undermines the planned economy. When the managers speak of greater rights for directors, what they are aiming at is the right to lay workers off, to set prices, to modify production schedules in conformity with market incentives. It seems quite obvious that demands of this sort contradict the logic of the planned economy, and constitute nothing other than a transitory phase on the road to re-establishment of private property. Clearly, the directors of the great automobile or electrical equipment trusts are not going to wake up one day and say 'give us the factories'; it would occur through a whole series of intermediary phases. This is another reflection of the contradiction between, on the one hand, the planned structure and socialized, collective, state character of large-scale production and, on the other, the maintenance of bourgeois norms of distribution—which result essentially from the survival of market and monetary categories in the sphere of the means of consumption, and which are the foundation of the bureaucracy's privileges.

But before all these tendencies could lead to an actual restoration of capitalism, they would have to overcome the resistance of the key sectors of the state apparatus that oppose this whole trend. This, incidentally, is the objective justification for our use of the scientific formula 'degenerated workers' state' to describe the USSR, in spite of all the anti-working-class measures and the total lack of direct working-class power, or even political rights. Even more important, though, they would have to overcome the resistance of the proletariat itself, which has a lot to lose through such a process of capitalist restoration, particularly what is undoubtedly the major remaining conquest of October from the standpoint of the workers: a qualitatively higher degree of job security than exists under capitalism.

The gradual restoration of capitalism in the Soviet Union through a 'cold' process (or through the 'palace revolution' detected by the Maoists, Bettelheim, and some other theoreticians) is equally as impossible as the gradual overthrow of capitalism in Western Europe through a series of reforms. To believe otherwise is, to use an apt phrase of Trotsky's, 'to unwind the reformist film in reverse'. In sum, the restoration of capitalism could occur only through new and disastrous defeats for the Soviet and international proletariat, through violent social and political upheavals.

The manifestly contradictory situation of the bureaucracy, and in particular its internal contradictions, pose a very practical question (though it is unfortunately not a burning one right now): what is the nature of the anti-bureaucratic revolution? Here again a number of problems arise, particularly in connection with the term 'political revolution'. Trotsky advanced a single definition, but with points of reference that were not always identical. In The Revolution Betrayed *he compared the political revolution to 1830 and 1848 in France and to 1918 in Germany. He made other comparisons too, but he kept coming back to these. In other words, changes effected with a certain mobilization of the masses, but without fundamentally modifying the structures of the state apparatus. On the other hand—and this was the object of a rather lively discussion in the Fourth International, at least before the war—during the same period Trotsky argued that the bureaucracy must be expelled from the regenerated soviets. This raises the problem of whether use of the term 'political revolution' has not been the source of some ambiguities. For in the past a number of comrades—most of whom, incidentally, were moving away from Trotsky's definition—have suggested that transformation of the Soviet Union will come about through pressure on the bureaucracy, and even through its self-reform. Consequently, is it not crucial to insist on the content of this revolution, which will eventually lead, whatever the intermediary steps, to the destruction of the state apparatus as it presently exists; to elimination of the bureaucracy from the soviets; and to the establishment of a new formula of management and therefore of planning—while at the same time maintaining centralized planning. Is it not better to stress the content of this anti-bureaucratic revolution, rather than the term 'political revolution', which can give rise to ambiguity?*

I think the ambiguity lies not in the term 'political revolution', but in the peculiarity of a political revolution in a workers' state, which by definition, even if it is bureaucratized, is a state whose economic weight is exceptional. As a result, even a revolution that is 'purely political' (an absurd concept in any event) will obviously have socio-economic effects infinitely greater than those of a bourgeois political revolution. The latter at most replaces one faction of the bourgeoisie in power by another, and in no way modifies the system of private property, capitalist competition, exploitation of the working class, etc.

I must say that the characteristics you ascribe to the political revolution remain a bit imprecise. In my opinion, the best definition of political revolution would be simply this: a take-over of the management of the state, the economy and all spheres of social activity by the mass of producers and the toiling masses, in the form of the power of democratically elected workers' councils, soviets. The term 'expulsion of the bureaucracy from the soviets' is itself ambiguous, for its meaning depends on how broadly the notion of bureaucracy is defined. It threatens once again to limit the freedom of choice, the political freedom, of the workers. I believe that this freedom must not be subject to any limitation. As the Transitional Programme says, the workers must be free to elect anyone they want to the soviets, without restriction or exclusion. This requires a multiparty system and the establishment of political and personal freedoms much broader than have ever existed in the Soviet Union, except during the initial period just after the October Revolution. It implies, among other things, experimentation with a whole series of new forms of the exercise of power. It matters little to talk about 'dismantling' the state apparatus. Self-management, even democratically centralized and planned self-management, is inconceivable unless a good part of the central state apparatus that now exists in the Soviet Union is dismantled; but the state apparatus is not solely this central apparatus.

Once this content is defined, we can see whether there are basic differences or mere terminological disputes. The latter are uninteresting, for they remain abstract. The basic differences are related to different analyses of Soviet reality, to different views of what workers' power and the real dictatorship of the proletariat should be. One of these differences probably relates to the capacities and limits of the working class. Here too, the historical dimension, historical relativity, must never be forgotten. There is no comparison between the working class of the Soviet Union today and the working class of 1937, 1927, or 1917. It is different not only numerically, where there has been considerable growth, and from the standpoint of political and class consciousness, where there has been an enormous regression. It is also different in its educational level: its technical, cultural and administrative capacity to take over management of the economy and the state. What was extremely difficult after the October Revolution, with the working class of that epoch, is much easier today.

It remains to be seen which detonators, external and internal, can set the Soviet proletariat on the road to class consciousness again. If this does not occur at all, then the debate 'political revolution or social revolution' becomes absolutely useless anyway, because then the real problem will be counter-revolution, trying to prevent a counter-revolution. If, however, our expectations turn out to be realistic—and there are many indications that they are in fact realistic—then the question of whether what we shall have seen was actually a political revolution, a social revolution, a combination of the two, or neither the one nor the other, will be of no real interest. We will simply have to note the close of this historical chapter with great pleasure and a sigh of relief. It is an interval of history that has cost humanity dear, the international communist movement most of all; one which continues to cost the world socialist revolution dear; but one which the Soviet and world proletariats will have then brought to a definitive close.

Eastern Europe

So far we have been talking mainly about the Soviet Union. It seems evident that the general points you have made about transitional society and the class nature of the Soviet state would apply equally well to the East European states. But isn't there a sense in which these states have a political specificity of their own? Capitalism was overthrown in Eastern Europe not by mass revolutions (except in Yugoslavia and Albania) but by the action of the Soviet state and its army. These states did not suffer a process of degeneration but were bureaucratically deformed from the outset. On the other hand, the governments in several of these countries—Hungary or Poland, for example—now seem significantly more 'liberal' than that of the Soviet Union. And opposition movements, in Hungary, Poland, and Czechoslovakia at least, have gone much further than in the Soviet Union. This poses three related questions. First, is it likely that the process of anti-bureaucratic political revolution will occur in Eastern Europe before it does in the Soviet Union? Second, is that revolution likely to take different forms in Eastern Europe? And third, how can the threat of Soviet intervention be countered—or indeed, can it be countered, or must the political revolution in Eastern Europe await the victorious political revolution in the Soviet Union?

I agree that it is semantically incorrect to call the East European countries degenerated workers' states. It would be more accurate to say bureaucratically deformed workers' states. But this formula creates another problem, namely how to distinguish them from, say, the Soviet Union in 1921, which was also bureaucratically deformed (as Lenin pointed out), but where the workers still exercised incomparably greater direct political and economic power than they do in Eastern Europe today. I would prefer to use a single formula to apply to all the states in which the bureaucracy holds a monopoly of power: *bureaucratized workers' states*, or *bureaucratically-ruled workers' states*. This formulation avoids that confusion.

It is obvious that opposition to the bureaucracy is now much stronger in Poland and Czechoslovakia than in the USSR. Even though the opposition is quite heterogeneous, the working-class, socialist-communist component is already stronger and more class conscious than it is in the USSR. The reasons for this are manifold: more favourable social structure; less complete physical destruction of the historic working-class cadre; stronger roots of the socialist-communist tradition in the *existing* working class. (We should never forget that today's Soviet working class is literally a new working class, in which the workers of 1927 or even 1939—not to mention those of 1917—represent an insignificant minority. This is not true to the same extent in East Germany, Czechoslovakia, or Poland.)

It is therefore quite likely that the political revolution might break out in one or more of the 'people's democracies' before it erupts in the USSR (after all, we already have the precedents of Hungary and Czechoslovakia). I do not believe that future upheavals will take forms fundamentally different from those of Hungary in 1956 and Czechoslovakia in 1968. But whether we will see the same striking maturity of both organizational forms (workers' councils!) and political content in Russia remains to be seen. At this point, it is useless to speculate on the subject; our knowledge of what is really happening in the Russian working class is too fragmentary. As to the best way to counter the threat of a Russian intervention, that is evident: internationalization of the opposition movement. In other words: mutual contacts and co-ordination among the East European countries and with the USSR; internationalist propaganda and agitation directed towards the Soviet peoples and workers; internationalization of the mass struggles themselves. It is unfortunately little known that the occupation of Czechoslovakia had a deep impact on many of the Soviet troops, some of which had to be withdrawn as 'politically unreliable'. If the Kremlin had to occupy several countries at the same time—especially at a time when the opposition in the USSR itself was more advanced than in 1968—the impact of such counter-revolutionary interventions could actually ignite the political revolution in the Soviet Union itself.

The Chinese Revolution

This entire discussion has left one major phenomenon out of account: the Chinese revolution. In one respect, the Chinese revolution was superior to the Russian, for it actively mobilized greater masses of the population, including, of course, the peasantry. On the other hand, the proletarian component was vastly less important. This contradiction has marked the Chinese workers' state ever since. Its political life has been more 'healthy' in the sense that mass participation in politics has never ceased; the Chinese masses have never suffered the de-politicization that afflicted the Russian. On the other hand, there has never been a real Bolshevik tradition in China, and in this sense working-class political life has always been more 'primitive'. Does this mean that the process of anti-bureaucratic revolution in China will be different from that in the Soviet Union and Eastern Europe?

I do not accept the assertion that the Chinese revolution actively mobilized a greater portion of the population than the Russian. Not because I underestimate the scope of the mass mobilizations of the Chinese peasantry, which were indeed momentous, but because I believe that your statement implies a serious underestimation of the scope of the mass mobilizations in Russia in 1917 and 1918, which in my view remain unmatched, even if you include the Chinese peasantry. It is true, however, that the subsequent dynamics of the mass movement in Russia and in China were quite dissimilar.

In Russia there was a continuous process of de-mobilization and de-politicization after 1920-21; it lasted more than a decade. Then, after the monstrous purges of the thirties, this process led to a qualitatively deeper demoralization. In China, on the other hand, although there were ups and downs to the peasant mobilizations and although the mass movement in the cities and towns was always more restricted, even in 1947-1956, than had been the case in Russia from 1917 to 1921, there was never any historic breakdown of political activity of the type brought about under Stalinism. Indeed, there have been successive upswings in mobilization: in the mid-fifties, the mid-sixties (the Cultural Revolution) and again in the seventies (the Tien An Men demonstration of 1974, followed by the big upsurge after the purge of the 'gang of four').

In that respect, the situation is more favourable in China than in the USSR, although you are right to point out the much greater weakness of communist tradition and, I would add, the much less favourable relationship of social forces. Again, this is speculation, but it is not impossible that the political revolution could break out in China before it does in the USSR. It certainly will take quite different forms from those in Eastern Europe or the USSR, forms that reflect the combination of more and less favourable conditions we have mentioned. But isn't it remarkable that in the first waves of mass political struggles that have occurred so far, the demand for soviets has been raised each time, even in 'backward' China, with its 'meagre Bolshevik tradition'?

The specific features of the Chinese revolution are too complex and numerous to discuss in any great detail here. I would, however, like to emphasize one vital aspect of that revolution, namely the role of the peasantry in the mass struggles of 1945-1949, which brought down the Chiang Kai-shek regime. Does the role of the peasantry in the Chinese revolution challenge one of the basic theses of the theory of permanent revolution?

I would begin by noting in passing that the relatively limited participation of the urban working class in the 1946-1950 revolutionary upsurge was not predetermined by objective factors. It is true that the Chinese working class had suffered crippling blows in its traditional centres—the city of Shanghai, for example—as a result of the Japanese occupation, the atrocities committed by both the Japanese army and the Kuomintang forces, the partial disorganization of economic life, and so on. This was less true, however, in northern China and especially Manchuria. In this area Japanese imperialism developed industry, for its own military purposes. And while it is true that living standards were dismally low and the repression ferocious, illegal struggle was not impossible; it did indeed develop, stimulated by both national oppression and economic super-exploitation. Furthermore, immediately after the war there was an upsurge of urban struggles against the Chiang regime, although it did not achieve the pitch of the second Chinese revolution, of 1925-27. This upsurge was promising, but was throttled by the policies of the Chinese Communist Party, which wanted no independent development of working-class struggles. Then, in the final phases of the civil war, runaway inflation and ferocious repression by the Chiang bandits made the urban struggle exceedingly difficult.

Even with this proviso, however, it is undeniable that the main forces involved in the revolutionary battle that brought Chiang down and made the establishment of a workers' state possible were based in the countryside. Is this surprising? I would say no. In fact, in Trotsky's summary of the theses of the theory of permanent revolution, he states quite explicitly that the peasantry, as the overwhelming majority of the population in the backward countries, would occupy an 'exceptional place' in the revolution, not only because of the agrarian question itself, but also because of the national question. This is true in all those countries in which the peasantry does constitute the overwhelming majority of the population. Nowadays, this is increasingly rarely the case (although it remains so in a number of important countries, like Indonesia, Nigeria, India, and Egypt); but it certainly was the case in China in 1945. The massive participation of the peasants in the revolutionary battles of 1945-50 is therefore not at all surprising.

The real analytical problems, however, are these: What social force held the political leadership of these struggles? How can one account for the peculiar organizational form in which the revolution triumphed, namely the armed confrontation between the People's Liberation Army (PLA) and the guerrilla forces on the one hand and Chiang Kai-shek's army on the other?

The answer to the first question seems indisputable to me. The leadership of the PLA was in the hands of *urban* social forces, namely the apparatus and militants of the Chinese Communist Party. (I say apparatus *and* militants because there was a constant flow of urban militants to the guerrilla forces and the liberated areas from 1937 right through to the conquest of the large cities themselves, a flow first of thousands and then tens of thousands.) To characterize these forces as 'petty-bourgeois' is to place in question a basic tenet of the theory of permanent revolution: that the petty-bourgeoisie is incapable of playing a political role independent of the bourgeoisie and the proletariat. Particularly in the light of subsequent events, such a characterization of the Chinese Communist Party bureaucracy seems untenable. Can there be a petty-bourgeois party that destroys private property, establishes the dictatorship of the proletariat (albeit in highly bureaucratized conditions from the very outset), and wages a large-scale (and generally successful) war against the major power of world imperialism, in Korea? No. The only reasonable conclusion is that the Chinese Communist Party, independent of its often opportunist and even treacherous tactical twists and turns, was striving to destroy capitalism and therefore represented a fundamentally proletarian social force. The apparatus of the party represented a bureaucracy which was privileged in relation to the mass of the proletariat from the very beginning; but it was a formation within, and not external to, the Chinese working class.

The answer to the second question is more complex. No social revolution involving the overturn of the property relations that govern the lives of millions of people can triumph by military means alone. The agrarian revolution that transformed the property relations in an area inhabited by several million people north of the Hwang-ho (if not north of the Yangtse-kiang) was certainly not limited to the military conflict between two armies. There is a good deal of evidence that mass uprisings in the countryside in northeast China actually *preceded* the all-out war between the PLA and the Kuomintang army and were probably an important factor in undermining the negotiations aimed at establishing a coalition government between the leaders of the Kuomintang and the Communist Party leadership. There is equal evidence that in northern and central China such rural uprisings—a genuine popular agrarian revolution—accompanied rather than followed the military victories of the PLA, making them much easier if not actually accounting for them. In southern China, of course, the situation was reversed. There agrarian revolution followed the proclamation of the People's Republic of China, and was even consciously curbed for some time by the party bureaucracy.

The unprecedented mass explosion in the countryside of northern

China after World War II, the revolutionary thrust of which went far beyond the traditional peasant uprisings of Chinese history, must be analysed objectively. Rural society in this region had been thoroughly wrecked by ten years of constant warfare: civil war, Japanese imperialist exactions and repression, plunder and repression by counter-revolutionary Kuomintang forces, massive guerrilla operations against both the Japanese occupation and the Chiang forces, and so on. All this caused the emergence of a layer of millions of uprooted poor peasants, jolted out of their traditional life and system of production and practically reduced to the status of semi-proletarians, even semi-paupers. This social transformation explains the massive scope of the permanent guerrilla warfare, the massive recruitment to the PLA, the spontaneous uprisings, the phenomenal resistance to Chiang's attempts to impose 'normal' tenant-landlord relations again after August 1945 when his forces occupied northern China, and the radical form assumed by the agrarian revolution at the village level from the very beginning. It also explains why the Communist Party leadership was able to make the transition from a radical land reform to the suppression of the private property of the capitalist class without meeting significant resistance from the rural population. A large part of the rural bourgeoisie had already been expropriated and eliminated by the rural poor themselves *before* the expropriation of the urban capitalists.

In all these respects, the character of the Chinese workers' state obviously differs from the Russian, not to mention the East European countries, and independent analysis of it is undoubtedly a necessity of revolutionary Marxist theory. But despite these important differences, it seems evident that our analysis of the fundamental character of Soviet society as a society in transition from capitalism to socialism, halted in that transition by the usurpation of power by a privileged bureaucracy that can be removed only through an anti-bureaucratic political revolution, is also essentially applicable to China.

'Centuries of Transition'?

Let us conclude by raising another possibility, which again you may consider excessively speculative. If we accept the Trotskyist analysis that the states in which capitalism has been overthrown have become bureaucratized workers' states, and if we also analyse the post-bourgeois stage of development in the framework of class struggle on a world scale, we arrive at the conclusion that October 1917, the first victorious socialist revolution, inaugurated a period of world-wide transition whose duration, although it cannot be predicted exactly, threatens to be relatively long compared with the predictions of Russian revolutionaries just before the seizure of power—or for that matter compared with some of Trotsky's own writings. Do you agree with this?

Yes and no. You know that the question of so-called 'centuries of transition' has played a certain role in the history of the Fourth International. I do not want to be misinterpreted, and above all I would not like to give the impression that a specific historical process was somehow fated to be, or governed by an innate tendency within the proletariat, structurally or organically linked to it. For in fact that process must be understood in the context of the test of strength between the classes that was joined when the era of capitalism's decline began. What we have seen in the Soviet Union, the ossification of the bureaucracy over half a century, does not correspond to any objective necessity, to any fate. It is the product of a combination of unique historical circumstances. The fact that this system spread into Eastern Europe, and profoundly influenced the structures of domination and organization of the workers' state even in China, Vietnam, and Cuba, does not invalidate this analysis. For it is obvious that what occurred in all these countries was a by-product of what occurred in the Soviet Union, and did not develop independently of the power of the Soviet bureaucracy or of the world context in which the Soviet bureaucracy arose.

What remains open is the question of whether the victory of the proletarian revolution in the industrially advanced countries, or in the countries in which the proletariat already represents the absolute majority of the nation, will unleash—both within these countries and on a world scale—a process that can 'de-bureaucratize' the experience of the proletarian revolutions of the twentieth century with a rapidity much more disconcerting than the duration of the phenomenon of bureaucratization itself. Here, history will have the last word. Should it confirm that revolutionary Marxists have been harbouring illusions on this subject, then it would be necessary to draw conclusions about the deeper historical and social roots of bureaucratization different from those generally drawn in the analysis of Marx, Lenin, Trotsky, and the Fourth International. But it is unjustified, impressionistic, and irresponsible to draw these conclusions prematurely, before the evidence is in: especially for Marxists, who are not simply theoreticians or historians, but above all militants, people who intervene with the aim of consciously altering the course of history.

Personally, I continue to think that we will have some very happy surprises in this regard. Given today's conditions, given the relative richness of the economy and the overwhelming numerical weight of the proletariat, with its democratic political traditions and high level of technical and cultural skills, I find it hard to conceive of the repetition in countries like France, Italy, Spain, or Britain, not to mention the United States, of anything that could even remotely justify the idea of a transition lasting for centuries, or a centuries-long bureaucratization (even one more benign than that of the USSR), between the fall of capitalism and the advent of a socialist society.

4

The Politics of Contemporary Internationalism

We would like to begin by asking a number of questions about the Second World War. On the eve of the outbreak of the war, Trotsky and the revolutionary Marxists regarded the impending conflict essentially as an inter-imperialist war, an attitude that was carried over into the early stages of the war itself. Comparisons were frequently made with the First World War. Is it not true, however, that as the war unfolded it assumed a more complex character, certainly different from the First World War, and that this shift was partially, although not sufficiently, reflected in the slogans and actions of the Trotskyists at the time. The Fourth International, for example, had supported Chinese resistance to Japanese imperialism even before the war; it supported the Soviet Union against the Nazi invasion; in many countries its militants participated in the resistance to fascist occupation; in Britain and the United States the Trotskyists did not advance the 'classical' slogans of revolutionary defeatism, but instead advocated a struggle against the fascist states that was in many respects original, best exemplified in James P. Cannon's writings and his speeches at his trial for sedition in the United States in the early forties. Didn't all this amount to a new characterization of the war, at least implicitly, and wouldn't the Trotskyists have been better placed to exploit the potential revolutionary dynamic of the anti-fascist struggle if they had been equipped with a more accurate and coherent strategic conception?

In my view, the question of the nature of the Second World War is closely linked to that of the character of the major driving forces of world revolution as they emerged from the First World War. I agree with you that the question is complex and that there was a danger of dogmatic schematism. The greater danger, however, was opportunist capitulation to bourgeois public opinion in the 'democratic' imperialist states, particularly as expressed in the class-collaborationist manoeuvres of the labour bureaucracies in these countries, for those manoeuvres condemned the revolutionary potential of mass movements against fascism to defeat in advance.

Before dealing with the Second World War, I would like to point out that even Lenin's struggle against social patriotism during the First World War was based on a more subtle characterization of that war than is expressed in the simple formula 'imperialist war'. In several of his articles, which appeared in a collection, co-authored by Zinoviev, entitled *Against the Stream*, Lenin emphasized that the imperialist war was accompanied—and this, he said, was inevitable—by just wars of national liberation by colonial peoples and oppressed nationalities. Further, the very slogan 'turn the imperialist war into a civil war' implied that there could well be a third type of war coexisting with the first two. After all, Lenin did not expect that the imperialist war would be transformed everywhere and simultaneously into a civil war. Implicit in his analysis and action slogans, then, was the notion that the 'imperialist war' could well become an imbrication of three wars in one.

Now, Trotsky was no dogmatist. After Hitler's seizure of power, when Trotsky began trying to prepare the vanguard of the international working class, especially his own comrades and sympathizers, for the inevitable world conflagration, he took these sorts of considerations into account. In the theses entitled 'The Fourth International and the War', an amazing document written in the early thirties and unfortunately little known today, even among militants of the Trotskyist movement, these considerations are not only cited, but are integrated with another, even more formidable change in the world situation, namely the existence of a workers' state, the Soviet Union, and the need of the workers to defend that state against imperialist onslaught from any quarter. This document contains an entire chapter dealing with the different tactics to be applied by revolutionary Marxists in those countries engaged in direct aggression against the Soviet Union and in those allied to it. In the imperialist countries that attack the Soviet Union, Trotsky said, it will be the duty of revolutionaries not only to oppose the war politically, but also to attempt to sabotage the arms industries, to prevent weapons from being delivered to the front, and so on. In countries allied to the Soviet Union, it would be absurd to sabotage the shipment of arms to the Soviet front, or even to interfere with their production.

Second, the same document is also quite clear about the need to defend bourgeois, and even pre-capitalist, states engaged in wars of independence against imperialist powers. Once again, this was a concrete problem, and revolutionary Marxists took a clear position in support of the Ethiopian war against Italian imperialism and the Chinese war of resistance to the Japanese invasion.

From the analytical standpoint, then, Trotsky's supporters were rather well-placed to understand the unfolding of the Second World War, which became, I would say, *five* wars in one: an inter-imperialist war between plunderers, to which the working class could extend not even an iota of support; a just war of self-defence by the Soviet bureaucratized workers' state against imperialist aggression by Nazi Germany and its allies; a just war of self-defence by semi-colonial China against Japanese imperialism; just wars of national liberation by oppressed colonial peoples against their imperial overlords, whether Japanese, English, or French; and finally, a just war of resistance by the masses of workers and the oppressed in the occupied countries of Europe against the super-exploitation and national oppression imposed by the Nazis. Now, conceptually, insofar as these wars were distinct—and to some extent they were—the political position to be taken is clear enough, and the overwhelming majority of the Trotskyist movement understood this and did take the correct positions, although I admit that there were some comrades, although not many, who failed to understand it.

The difficulty arises—and this difficulty is the result not of inadequate theoretical analysis of the war, but of the complexity of reality itself—from two additional problems: first, while conceptually distinct, and distinct in reality to a large degree, these five wars were evidently *inter-related* in a highly complex manner; second, although four of these 'five wars' were intrinsically just from the viewpoint of the international working class in the sense that they *should have been fought*, they were in virtually all cases led by social and/or political forces that had no interest whatever in waging them in a manner in conformity with the objective historic interest of the world proletariat and the masses in the colonial and semi-colonial countries. The problem for revolutionaries then became: how to support these just wars while simultaneously extending no political confidence to the forces leading them. The tactical difficulties in terms of slogans and actions arose from these two problems, which were thorny ones by any standard, and not from any theoretical inadequacy in our conception of the character of the Second World War as a whole.

Indeed, as far as the fundamental analytical problem in the imperialist countries themselves was concerned, there was a striking parallel between the First and Second World Wars, confirmed by the practical experience of what happened immediately after both wars. Within the imperialist countries, any wrong characterization of the nature of the inter-imperialist war, any notion that because of the specific nature of Nazi, Italian, or Japanese imperialism, there was an element of justice in the war of British, French, American, Belgian, or Dutch imperialism against the opposing imperialist camp, would lead only to systematic sacrifice of immediate working-class interests, to systematic class collaboration, and to the strangling of revolutionary possibilities at the end of the war. In the Second World War, as in the First, there was a direct line between acceptance of 'national defence' by an imperialist government and class collaboration with the bourgeoisie in halting the revolutionary uprisings of the workers at the end of the war. All those who accepted the premise also accepted the conclusion. It is no accident that the political forces that held that the Western imperialist powers were waging a just war against Nazism ended up forming coalition governments at the end of the war to reconstruct the bourgeois order, the capitalist economy, and the bourgeois state apparatus.

I can give you a personal example that expresses this quite strikingly. During the war, as a representative of our very small revolutionary forces in Flanders (we had only a dozen comrades in the Antwerp branch of our section in the underground), I had occasion to meet some representatives of the left wing of the Socialist Party, among whom were some left Zionists who were extremely militant in the Resistance to Nazi occupation. They were trying to convince us to join a sort of national front, which in Belgium, as in all the other European countries, was emerging as a kind of umbrella group of the various tendencies in the Resistance. I remember telling them: you propose that we work together today against the common enemy—and I agree that there is a common enemy. Today we are organizing strikes against the occupation (the first big strikes in Belgium occurred as early as March 1941 in the Liège coal and steel industry; we had important influence in the coal industry in Charleroi, which is why these people were so eager to have us participate in this umbrella organization). Moreover, we are eager to see these strikes spread. But what will be your attitude the day the German troops leave Belgium and are replaced by British and American soldiers? What will you do about strikes then?

They simply snorted. If you think you will convince the Belgian workers and people to continue the fight against the Allies after the Nazis are defeated, they told us, you are kidding yourselves; that is a utopia, and a reactionary one at that, because if it did happen it would be bad. History has shown, however, that it was not a utopia, and it was certainly not reactionary. Strikes did break out in Belgium on a very broad scale just after the Allied troops ousted the German occupation forces. In France, Italy, and Greece there were more than just strikes—there was incipient civil war, the beginning of a potential socialist revolution. Any lack of clarity on the nature of the inter-imperialist war and on the class character of the states and governments conducting it, any confusion on the historical tasks facing the working class in these countries, could lead only to counter-revolutionary, class collaborationist policies. This is not a matter of theory—it was proven in reality.

There was also a second consequence of any failure to grasp the imperialist character of the war of the Western imperialist states against Germany, Italy, and Japan. If the war of Britain against Germany, for example, is regarded as a just war, then any uprising of the Indian masses against British rule during that war must be opposed. The reason for this is evident. Even if one regarded an Indian uprising against Britain as equally just, one would have to recognize that the war between Britain and Germany was the 'main war' in the sense that it involved more forces, was more extensive, and was, by almost any reasonable standard, 'primary'. One would then have two just wars, the problem being that the side of the 'just' in the first war was the side of the 'unjust' in the second. Once one establishes that sort of logical structure, it follows inevitably that one of the two 'just' struggles must take precedence over the other, and in this case it is evident which would have to be granted the priority. Again, this is not an abstract argument. The world Stalinist movement consistently denounced any and all uprisings of colonial peoples against their 'democratic' imperialist masters during the Second World War. In many cases—probably most, if not all—this was not because the Stalinists actually favoured imperialist rule in the colonies. Nor was it because of their wholly justified concern to defend the Soviet Union, since the USSR certainly had no stake in British rule in India, for example. Nor was it even primarily because the British were 'allies' of the Soviet Union, although that argument was demagogically advanced from time to time. No, the real reason was that the Stalinists believed that the British imperialists were fighting a just war against Nazi imperialism and that this war, since the stakes were highest, had to take priority over all other conflicts. The logic is ironclad; it is the underlying premise that was false. History has shown, I believe, that this was the major danger for revolutionaries in the Second World War: the trap of regarding the inter-imperialist war as just. We are still paying for the consequences of that 'mistake'.

Now I am certainly willing to grant that some comrades of the Fourth International—very few in Belgium, a minority in France, perhaps the majority in Greece—fell into an opposite error. In emphasizing the danger of this trap, they underestimated the importance of the other aspect of the war: the historically just character of any form of mass resistance to the super-exploitation and oppression—indeed in some cases the actual genocide—introduced by the Nazi occupation of Europe. To this day there is a wing of the Trotskyist movement in France—the comrades of Lutte Ouvrière—that completely rejects this second aspect and maintains that the Trotskyist movement (and even Trotsky himself, because his very last article, the one he was working on when he was murdered, begins with the words 'France in turn has now become an oppressed nation') capitulated to social patriotism and bourgeois ideology by participating in the Resistance. This, of course, is completely wrong, both theoretically and politically. It is absurd to maintain that in the midst of the super-exploitation, oppression, and genocide going on in the occupied countries there were no specific and immediate tasks of self-defence, just because of the general nature of the war as a whole. Not only absurd, but even suicidal. The uprising of the Warsaw ghetto was a thousand times justified, and any revolutionary on the scene who refused to participate in it either on the grounds that its leadership was pro-Western Allies (with a significant Zionist component) or on the grounds that the Second World War was an inter-imperialist war in which the proletariat should not take sides, would be beneath contempt.

We do not choose sides between imperialists, but we surely defend ourselves against murderers (whichever side they may be on). The same is true of the super-exploited masses of workers, peasants, and petty bourgeois in all the occupied countries. Even in the countries in which there was no genocide, the standard of living of the toiling masses was lowered to one-half or one-third of what it had been before the war. Why should people relinquish the right to struggle against that situation by any means necessary? I consider all these movements absolutely justified inasmuch as they were *mass* movements of self-defence. Again, the difficulty arose when there were combinations of autonomous mass movements and attempts by bourgeois political apparatuses to integrate these movements into projects, plans, and operations linked to war decisions being made in London or Washington. Then the separation is not easy to realize in practice, especially for small revolutionary groups without significant mass influence. But it can be realized conceptually, and can be put into practice to some extent.

There is no denying that the tactical difficulties were immense, and that we made quite a few mistakes. But the Belgian Trotskyists were certainly the people in the underground who had the most nearly correct position and who made the fewest mistakes. This was due in large part to the outstanding political and theoretical acumen of our comrade Abram Leon, the undisputed political giant of our organization in Belgium at that time, murdered by the Nazis at the very young age of 26. It was he who developed the strategic formula of our work in the Resistance: to support and stimulate all mass movements by workers and poor peasants against super-exploitation and national oppression arising from the occupation and to fight to transform them into a movement for socialist revolution, the overthrow of the capitalist order, and the establishment of workers' states. There would have been little point in trying simply to exclude all bourgeois forces from the Resistance by decree, on the abstract grounds that revolutionaries refuse to associate with bourgeois politicians. Conversely, it would have been—and was—disastrous to weld the Resistance into a programmatic united front with the capitalist class of the occupied countries. The proper strategic line, admittedly complex to implement, was to wage the Resistance according to the formula Leon developed.

I said that this strategy was difficult to implement. Small revolutionary groups, like the Trotskyists, for example, lacked sufficient strength to put it into practice. All we could do was to try to set an example, and I think we did that rather well, all things considered. But it was not at all impossible to implement, especially for parties with mass support. Indeed, in one case in occupied Europe it *was* implemented successfully, although with bureaucratic deformations: Yugoslavia. Although the leaders of the Yugoslav Communist Party paid lip service to the 'national front' ideology of the world Stalinist movement, their actual practice was quite different. As early as 1942 they were organizing not only resistance against the Nazis, but also civil-war actions against the bourgeois order—and were roundly denounced by Stalin for just this reason. In the villages of Yugoslavia, fighting was going on not between collaborators and non-collaborators, but between those who favoured socialist revolution—which meant a variety of things in the villages—and those who opposed it. It is no accident, for example, that the Yugoslav Communist Party organized proletarian brigades and issued internationalist appeals to the Italian, and later even the German, soldiers. This should be emphasized, because too little attention has been paid to it: by the end of the war, there were *thousands* of Italian and German soldiers fighting in Tito's army.

Now, we do not have sufficient time to discuss the reasons why this development occurred in Yugoslavia and what its limits were, namely the bureaucratic deformations of the Yugoslav Communist Party and the Tito leadership. But the important point is this. If it was possible for a heavily bureaucratized Communist Party of Stalinist origin, still very strongly influenced by Stalinist methods, to achieve this success, the same potential surely existed on a much broader scale in countries like Italy and France. This shows that the strategy we developed was theoretically correct and politically realistic, despite whatever secondary tactical errors we may have committed. More than that: it was a historic tragedy for the world proletariat that the traditional working-class parties, Socialist and Communist, rejected this sort of strategy in favour of a continuation, or rather resuscitation, of their Popular Front policies of the middle and late thirties.

Trotsky and the Aftermath of the War

Let us turn to a related question. On the eve of the Second World War, in addition to presenting an analysis of the character of the impending conflict, Trotsky made a number of predictions about the course that events would take at the war's conclusion. Nearly all of these turned out to be false. Soviet democracy was not restored in the USSR through a political revolution, nor was capitalism restored through a victorious counter-revolution (which was the alternative Trotsky foresaw). On the contrary, Stalinism not only survived the war, but emerged strengthened in certain respects and underwent an expansion. Meanwhile, again contrary to Trotsky's predictions, the capitalist world experienced a new phase of accelerated economic development, the proletarian revolution winning no victories in the advanced West. Do such sweeping errors of prognosis imply deficiencies of theoretical analysis? Can they be explained without challenging the entire revolutionary Marxist analysis of contemporary social reality?

Generally speaking, the classical political pronouncements of Marxism may be divided into two categories: first, what may be called *short-term predictions*; second, theoretical efforts to uncover the fundamental trends of development, in other words, the attempt to grasp the underlying character of a historical epoch and the major contradictions that define it.

Innumerable errors have been made in the first category—by Marx, Engels, Lenin, Trotsky, and everyone else. Let us recall, for example, that at the end of 1916 Lenin gave a speech to a meeting of Swiss workers in which he drew a sombre and pessimistic balance-sheet of the situation after the defeat of the Russian revolution of 1905. In effect, just two months before the February 1917 explosion he argued that although 1905 had unleashed a process that would eventually lead to a new revolution, his generation would probably not live to see it. The list of these sorts of errors could be extended virtually at will. Their fundamental origin is that the course of events in the short term is determined not only by great historical trends, but also by a myriad of secondary factors which not only cannot be adequately integrated into an exhaustive analysis but frequently cannot even be known beforehand, simply because full information is unobtainable. Trotsky, like Marx before him, often said that the function of theoretical analysis is not to produce materialist prophets or seers, a contradiction in terms in any event, but to discover and codify these broad historical trends.

Why, then, do we nevertheless see repeated excursions into the business of short-term predictions, not only by Trotsky, but by all other Marxists as well? What is the source of this apparently irrepressible penchant for sooth-saying, in spite of the disclaimers? It is more than anything else a consequence of *revolutionary politics itself*. If revolutionaries desire to change the world—and this is, after all, their main function—they must act within the confines of a series of short- and medium-term possibilities in order to be able to determine their actual line of action. Revolutionary theory analyses underlying, essential historical trends, but revolutionary action is practised within the constraints of immediate reality. To resolve this difficulty from the conceptual standpoint, we must distinguish between the formulation by revolutionary Marxism of the scientific laws of development of modes of production or of particular social formations on the one hand and the positing of what can only be considered *working hypotheses*, and not scientific laws, about the short-term evolution of events on the other hand. Without these working hypotheses about short-term evolution, it is simply impossible to act; but at the same time, their constant verification in reality is required if they are to be sufficiently grounded to determine correct action. In that sense, these short-term predictions, although frequently false, are an exigency of revolutionary action—*provided they are verified and corrected on the basis of experience*. Dangerous as they may be, without them there can be no revolutionary action, but only broad historical theory.

Now, this digression is required if we are to understand the following, apparently paradoxical assertion: In his understanding of the grand lines of development of our century, Trotsky was not only correct, but demonstrated such great lucidity that his faulty short-term predictions were often the result precisely of his extraordinary lucidity about the long-term tendencies of history. Ever since the decline of the world revolution became evident in the late twenties and thirties, when the phenomena of fascism and Stalinism began to acquire increasingly barbarous dimensions, lucid revolutionary Marxists have faced three questions that are basic in determining the long-term evolution of our epoch.

First, had the world revolution suffered a lasting defeat such that the world would plunge into a protracted period of barbarism? This question may sound alarmist nowadays, but it was perfectly apposite in the thirties. One could amass an impressive list of quotations from many Marxists, from reformists like Rudolf Hilferding, the last great Social Democratic theorist, to quite a few ex-Trotskyists, who were convinced that Hitler would win the Second World War and that Europe would be ruled by fascism for a century or more. Trotsky, on the other hand, answered this question differently, arguing that the defeats suffered by the world revolution were weighty indeed, but limited in time. There would, he said, inevitably be a new rise of revolutionary struggles by the proletariat and the oppressed peoples at the end of the war. He predicted that neither Hitler, nor Mussolini, nor the Japanese dictatorship, nor the regime of Chiang Kai-shek, nor that of Stalin, nor the imperialist colonial empires would survive the war and its aftermath. With the exception of Stalin, this prediction was accurate. The new rise of world revolution after the Second World War is an incontestable fact.

The second question: was this extraordinary interlude of reaction and decline not only of the workers' movement but of all the conquests of human civilization (symbolized by the horrors of Auschwitz and Hiroshima) a mere accident of history? Here again, Trotsky's answer was clear, and it has been confirmed by history: No, this was not an accident. The decadence of bourgeois society and the decomposition of the capitalist mode of production, whose richness, technological achievements, and unprecedented material progress had carried humanity forward for two centuries, would be marked by reactions that would get worse as time went on. The more powerful the wounded beast, the more frenzied and destructive its death agony, with increasingly devastating consequences for the human race. Rather than ceding to the beatific optimism of the gradualists and reformists, who believed that things would eventually work themselves out more or less automatically, Trotsky insisted on the extraordinary costs humanity would pay for the survival of the capitalist system. Here again, he has been proven correct. Today, in spite of twenty years of expansion of the productive forces and a constant rise in material production, a greater and greater sector of the vanguard of workers and intellectuals are aware of these dangers, which take different forms—not only fascist or brutal military regimes, not only the alarming rise of torture as a regular form of institutionalized political practice throughout the world, but also the threats to the world's ecological balance, the blind plunder of natural resources, the lingering threat of a third world war, the proliferation of nuclear weapons and weapons technology, and so on.

Third, if on the one hand there will inevitably be fresh and protracted upsurges of revolutionary struggle, and on the other hand the proletariat faces an enemy which is quite capable of defending itself and which presides over a system that will not collapse automatically as the result of its internal contradictions, severe as they may be, what is the central question of revolutionary strategy? Trotsky's answer: the problems of the political leadership of the proletariat and of the revolution, the tactical and strategic problems linked to the class consciousness of the toilers, become the crucial historical problems of our epoch. Indeed, Trotsky held, the crisis of humanity itself is ultimately reducible to the crisis of revolutionary leadership of the proletariat, not only in the organizational but also in the broader, political, sense of the term. In the context of the historical crisis of a society which is in decline but which will not disappear automatically in face of the periodic, but not linear or unlimited, rise of revolutionary mass struggles, the success or failure of these struggles is decisive for humanity as a whole and depends upon the construction of an adequate revolutionary leadership. If these struggles do not produce victories, the death agony of bourgeois society will drag on, and if it does, the consequences of our response to the second question acquire increasing actuality.

This third question also had a corollary, of which Trotsky was well aware. In the manifesto of the emergency congress of the Fourth International, held in May 1940 (which may be considered Trotsky's political testament in certain respects), he wrote, in response to the question of whether the revolutionary opportunities opened by the Second World War would be wasted by the traditional bureaucratic apparatuses, that the question was improperly formulated. A revolutionary upsurge, he continued, is not a short-lived event but a process that will last for many years, even decades; there will be ups and downs, wars, revolutions, counter-revolutions, armistices, and new wars. Such an epoch—and at that point Trotsky was speaking of decades, and not merely the years immediately following the war—will be propitious for the construction of revolutionary organizations. This prediction, too, has been confirmed on a historic scale.

We may sum up, then, by saying that on these three questions, which were the decisive ones in understanding the epoch in which we live, Trotsky was not at all mistaken. On the contrary, he demonstrated that the Marxist method of analysis was capable of grasping the general trends of historical development regardless of conjunctural optimism or pessimism. There was, then, no deficiency of theoretical analysis, and the course of history since the Second World War in no way suggests that the revolutionary Marxist analysis of contemporary social reality was fundamentally faulty.

This, however, is only part of the answer to your question, for the fact remains that many of Trotsky's short-term predictions on the eve of the war were indeed quite erroneous. In what was he mistaken, and what was the source of the error? I will leave aside alleged mistakes that are actually based on dishonest quotation-juggling, such as the claim that Trotsky asserted that the Soviet Union as such would inevitably be defeated in the war, when his writings actually show that he argued no such position. First of all, he overestimated the short-term impact on the consciousness of the workers' vanguard of the new rise of world revolution. Here he had been guided by a historical analogy: the isolation of a handful of internationalists within the workers' movement in 1914 had given way to an extraordinary rise in the strength of the internationalists in the latter days of the First World War and especially after the victory of the October Revolution. In making this analogy, Trotsky fell into a serious underestimation of the cumulative effects of twenty years of defeats not only of proletarian revolutions, but also of the organized workers' movement as a whole. In a sense, this was paradoxical, for he did not make this mistake when examining particular national cases, such as Germany and Russia. He never suggested that Nazism would be a brief interval followed by a rapid new rise of the German workers' movement to a level superior to that of 1918-1923. On the contrary, he stressed the long-term effects of Hitler's victory as a factor demoralizing the workers and lowering their consciousness. He was certain that there would eventually be a new rise of the movement, but under conditions more arduous than those which prevailed before the rise of fascism.

His analysis of Russia was even sharper. He pointed to the disastrous effects of the events of the late 1930s and the atomization of the Russian masses on the average level of consciousness of the workers, and to the extraordinary difficulties in reconstituting the forces of the class after the historic disappointment of the victory of the Stalinist bureaucracy. In both cases Trotsky strongly argued that the terror and the consequent physical repression and elimination of cadres, as grave as they were, did not constitute the principal cause of the difficulties of a forceful re-emergence of the revolutionary movement. The real obstacles, he wrote, were the lack of perspectives, the demoralization, and the lack of self-confidence of social classes that had suffered historic defeats of such scope as the victory of fascism or Stalinism.

The paradox is that Trotsky advanced widely varying assessments on the national and international scale. In his analysis of particular countries like Germany and Russia, he evinced great lucidity. On the other hand, he was mistaken in his international predictions, because he based his reasoning on the assumption that the post World War II period would closely parallel the post World War I period.

An international upsurge did occur. In some respects it was even broader than the post-war wave of struggles from 1918 to 1923, if we include Britain among the countries in which the workers showed that they desired a socialist transformation in 1944 and 1945. *But these forces were much more confused politically, and therefore more easily manipulated by the traditional apparatuses.* The result of the inter-penetration of these two factors was that the revolutionary upsurge was halted much more quickly and therefore never attained the political scope of the earlier upsurge.

In other words, Trotsky underestimated what I would call the break in continuity of the revolutionary socialist tradition. It is here that the differences between the situations of 1944-45 and 1918-19 are most striking. In 1918 and 1919 revolutionaries were speaking a language easily comprehensible to the masses of organized workers, since 1914 had been but an interruption in a general upward swing of class consciousness. The mass of European workers believed in 1914 that the socialist revolution would occur soon. They had been educated in the same manner as leaders like Luxemburg, Karl Liebknecht, Lenin, or Trotsky, and all the internationalists. They had a common tradition, and the internationalists had never lost direct contact with the masses of workers, even after the events of 1914, except perhaps for a brief period up to 1916, for after that date, the centrist wing, which opposed continuation of the imperialist war, began to overtake the most chauvinist reformists in most of the Social Democratic Parties. (Even Kautsky's supporters, for example, attended the Zimmerwald conference and voted for Trotsky's resolution, but against Lenin's.) This continuity is clearest in the critical case of Germany. Except for the two first years of the war, the Spartacists found themselves in a generally positive situation. Their decision to join the Independent Social Democratic Party (USPD) when it was founded in 1917 was not accidental, nor was it a tactical error. It was a product of the fact that the Spartacists spoke a common language with many of the militants and even a good number of the leaders of the USPD, who were supporting the Russian revolution at the time. Shortly afterwards, Socialist parties in a number of countries in which revolutionary traditions were not exceptionally strong applied for membership in the Communist International: the Italian and Czechoslovak Socialist Parties, for example, and don't forget that the majority of the French Socialist Party voted for the Communist International at the Tours congress of 1921.

Thus, the situation faced by revolutionaries in 1944 was wholly unlike the 1918, or even 1914, situation. They were isolated in a workers' movement whose internationalist tradition had long been broken. The class-collaborationist policy of the Socialist and Communist parties was not a four-year aberration but the culmination of at least twenty years of evolution (taking 1927, the year the Left Opposition was expelled from the Soviet Communist Party, as the beginning of the extirpation of internationalism, although in many cases the date must be placed even further back). Under these conditions, revolutionaries had scant possibilities of significantly augmenting their forces, even though there was a conjunction of an accentuated radicalization of the workers and an outrageously class-collaborationist policy by the Social Democrats and Stalinists.

To this misestimation of the ability of revolutionaries to win hegemony over the post-war upsurges, we must add two supplementary factors that played a great role in the analysis both of Trotsky personally and of the Fourth International—two factors that are important but could lead us into circular reasoning if they are isolated from the more general context.

The first of these factors was the absence of any revolution in Germany at the end of the Second World War. The German revolution had occupied a position of prime importance in all the predictions of Trotsky and the Fourth International. There was, of course, a decline in working-class consciousness in Germany, but there was also a qualitative weakening of the grip of the traditional apparatuses on the working class. The situation offered the possibility of a spontaneous explosion that would rapidly escape the control of the Socialist and Communist parties. As an eye witness in Germany at that time (I had been deported there as a political prisoner and worked for some time at the huge synthetic oil plant of Wesseling near Cologne), I still believe that this prospect was less unrealistic than one might be inclined to think, at least until the spring of 1944. But social decomposition took hold in Germany at a certain point. The mass of producers was actually made up of prisoners of war, political prisoners, concentration camp inmates, and deported foreign workers. The disorganization of collective life was nearly total, even simple co-operation in the workplaces breaking down. Under these conditions, the prospect of a revolutionary upsurge in Germany began to evaporate, for a myriad of objective reasons: the 'total mobilization' and accentuated Nazi terror, especially after 20 July 1944; the massive bombings of the cities by the British and American air forces; the terrible effects of intimidation, followed by the occupation and dismemberment of the country; the collapse of the means of communication.

To all this were added the effects of the defeat on the population: famine, misery, dispersion of the urban population. Equally devastating were the political consequences of Stalinism and reformism. The German Communist Party had preserved more working-class cadres than one might have thought. But although the party was not in an extremely weak position at the outset, it had to adapt itself to Stalin's policy, which meant endorsing the most counter-revolutionary theses imaginable. In particular, the Communist Party supported the dismantlement of the factories of the Ruhr and sabotaged the strike against it. Meanwhile, the Social Democratic Party, viciously anti-communist, supported the line of the western imperialists to the hilt, despite some instances of rebellion that were more nationalist than leftist. The consequences of all this on a working class that was already reeling from the debilitating blows of the events of 1929-33, the years of Nazi terror, the war, and the dismemberment of the country, were incalculable.

What is the balance-sheet of this whole analysis? It would be false to reduce it to the catch-phrase 'imperialism and Stalinism strangled the German revolution'. That sort of formulation would imply that Trotsky and the Fourth International underestimated the counter-revolutionary capacities of imperialism and Stalinism, which is just not true. The fact of the matter is that we expected a German revolution *despite* this. What voided that working hypothesis was the concatenation of circumstances I have described (which would have been difficult to foresee in 1940, or even in 1943), which made any mass uprising impossible as of the summer of 1944. (It is interesting, though idle of course, to speculate about what could have happened had the German general staff succeeded in getting rid of Hitler on 20 July 1944 and had the war been brought to a rapid end.) In any event, the absence of a revolution in Germany, or even of a more limited revolutionary upsurge comparable to France, Italy, or Greece, weighed heavily on the course of events both in Europe and throughout the world.

The second factor unforeseen by Trotsky and the Trotskyists was that the Communist Parties exerted considerable attractive power among the European working class because of the role played by the Soviet Union in defeating fascism, and even because of the social transformations in Eastern Europe. In 1948 and 1949 it was not easy to explain to a Communist militant that Stalin had opted to attempt to preserve the bourgeois order outside the borders of the USSR. The organized workers and youth falsely identified the victories of the Yugoslav and Chinese revolutions with the Soviet Red Army. Then, during the peak years of the Cold War, from 1949 to 1952, the most radicalized layers of workers and youth were drawn spontaneously to the Communist Parties and the Stalinist youth organizations, not because of the class-collaborationist policy being followed by these parties, but because of the world political division of 'two camps' created by the Cold War.

In this regard, it is important to note that the Fourth International was the first force in the workers' movement to have understood—from the time of its Third World Congress in 1951—that the consolidation and extension of Stalinism was only apparent, even in the geographical zone brought under the control of the Soviet Army. The reality was a very contradictory mixture of extension of the rule of the Soviet bureaucracy beyond the borders of the USSR and genuine instances of socialist revolutions that would eventually strike at the very roots of Stalinism and provoke its historic world crisis, leading to the gradual decomposition of the Kremlin bureaucracy's control over entire sectors of its domains. But these two conjunctural factors—absence of the German revolution and apparent consolidation of Stalinism in the international workers' movement—had these disastrous effects on the course of the revolution, especially in the Western countries, only because of the general context of the historic decline of class consciousness. If, for example, the apparatus of the French or Italian Communist Party had been outflanked by the mobilization the way the Social Democratic apparatus was overtaken in Germany after 1918, the effects on Stalinism would have been shattering. But this did not happen, because after the cumulative effects of twenty years of defeat, the spontaneity and capacity for self-organization of the working class were vastly less than we had anticipated in 1940, or even 1944.

These cumulative effects were the fundamental cause of the limitations of the revolutionary upsurge of 1944-48 in Europe. I want to be clear that I am not at all saying that this situation was predetermined as of 1923, which is only the year in which the string of defeats began. In reality, many victories were still possible, despite the German defeat of 1923, as is shown by the Chinese and Yugoslav revolutions and the events in Spain and France in the thirties. Even Hitler's victory could have been prevented. By the end of that twenty year period, however, we were dealing with the effects not only of the defeat of 1923, the annihilation of the Chinese revolution in 1926-27, the continued isolation of the USSR, the lack of international perspectives for communists after the victory of Nazism, the defeat of the French mobilizations of the mid-thirties and of the

Spanish revolution in the bloody civil war, but the *cumulative* effects of all these setbacks. It was the misestimation of the importance of this phenomenon that was most fundamental in Trotsky's erroneous predictions. That is what enabled the Communist and Social Democratic parties in Western Europe to successfully play the role they did in the reconstruction and consolidation of the bourgeois order in Western Europe in the aftermath of the Second World War.

The Cold War and the Long Boom

One of the major reasons why the Communist Parties played the role they did in Western Europe in the aftermath of the Second World War was, of course, that the Soviet leadership was striving to maintain its wartime alliance with 'democratic imperialism', viewing this alliance as the foundation of a 'new world order'. Some Communist Parties, the American for example, took this notion so seriously that they actually dissolved. But the war was not followed by an era of international co-operation between imperialism and the Soviet Union. Instead the Cold War broke out. Why did imperialism reject Stalin's bid for long-term collaboration? What was behind the policy of the Cold War and 'containment'? Was it a genuine attempt to restore capitalism in the Soviet Union and Eastern Europe?

Uninterrupted co-operation between imperialism and the Soviet bureaucracy collapsed in 1947 and 1948 for a very simple reason: the rise of world revolution outside the control of either Washington or Moscow. The two best examples, of course, are Yugoslavia and China. In both cases there is overwhelming evidence that Stalin genuinely and sincerely wanted coalition governments that would rule over capitalist states in which pro-Moscow and pro-Washington political tendencies would divide the posts on a more or less equal, fifty-fifty basis. This is what was agreed to at the conferences held in the closing stages of the war, and there is not the slightest evidence that the Kremlin ever attempted to violate those agreements. The Yugoslav and Chinese Communist parties, however, unfolded their real strategy (and by real strategy I mean what they were actually doing, as opposed to their verbal fealty to 'Comrade Stalin') by breaking with some of the key tenets of Stalinism. In particular, they refused to give up their independent structures of power and refused to disarm their partisans. That is why coalition governments failed in both cases and why, under the mounting impact of mass mobilizations, the institutions of the bourgeois state (and eventually, although not simultaneously, bourgeois property relations) were swept away. One of the lessons the imperialists drew was that the Kremlin was no longer able to deliver on its promises to thwart revolutionary upheavals everywhere in the world. The will was there, but not the power.

On the other hand, the imperialists were under great pressure to reconstruct their markets and fields of investment on the widest possible scale. I would not say that they had definitively decided to strive to restore capitalism in the USSR even at the price of a third world war, although some elements in the American military certainly toyed with that idea and received some support from significant circles of bourgeois politicians. There was, however, no imperialist consensus on this. But they had certainly decided to probe, to test how far they could go. Once the capitalist state had been salvaged and the bourgeois economy set in working order again, the Communist Parties were ousted from the government in Italy and France. A successful effort was made to 'recuperate' Finland and Austria from what was fast becoming the 'Soviet bloc'. A similar effort was made with regard to East Germany, but this failed, only West Berlin being reintegrated into the 'free world'. Similar operations were mounted against Yugoslavia and Czechoslovakia. In Korea, a clear attempt was made to annihilate the North Korean workers' state; what is not completely clear is whether the American ruling class had definitively opted to try to roll back the Chinese revolution as well. Some American bourgeois politicians certainly had that line, and they probably had a good deal of support within the ruling class.

In other words, having rescued the bourgeois system in the West European heartland through collaboration with the traditional workers' parties and the Soviet bureaucracy, having 'lost' Yugoslavia and China despite Stalin's best efforts, and requiring the most extensive possible territory for economic expansion in order to forestall the post-war depression that had been feared, imperialism launched an international offensive. The ideology of 'containment' was simply a cover through which to sell this policy to the population of the advanced capitalist countries (especially in the United States), by casting the Soviet Union as a world power bent on imperialist expansion. This ideology in turn served as the basis for a sweeping witch-hunt, again most especially in America. The result of all this was the Cold War, which in turn compelled Stalin to react defensively by consolidating the bureaucracy's control over the East European countries under its domination. That, however, required the overthrow of capitalist property relations in these countries and the establishment of bureaucratized workers' states. It is important to note, by the way, that Cold War ideology was of major importance in the ideological fortification of bourgeois rule in the advanced capitalist countries and thereby continued to hold sway long after the Cold War in the proper sense of the term had ended. Indeed, we still see not a few aspects of that ideology even today. But once it became clear to both sides that a new equilibrium had emerged from the Cold War, imperialism began to scale its offensive down, at least on a global scale, and began responding to the Kremlin's overtures of 'détente' and 'peaceful coexistence'. The latter, of course, had always been the *fundamental strategic* goal of the Soviet bureaucracy, even at the height of the Cold War, and it remains so today. When attacked, however, that bureaucracy has to defend itself, for despite everything it still rests on a class base different from that of the bourgeois states.

The period of the Cold War was also the period of capitalist restabilization and economic boom in both Western Europe and the United States. What were the driving forces of this boom and how was imperialist policy towards the workers' states related to it?

I do not believe that there was a direct correlation between the Cold War, the capitalist restabilization in Western Europe, and the post-war economic boom. Or rather, a decisive element is left out in presenting this sort of causal chain, namely the defeat of the post-war workers' upsurge in Western Europe and of the wave of trade-union struggles in the United States between late 1945 and early 1947. I would insist that this defeat be seen as an autonomous factor decisively influenced by the policies of the Stalinist and Social Democratic leaderships. To leave that factor out of account is to offer a lop-sided picture of what really happened after World

War II, one which could result in a real falsification of history.
It is important to remember that despite all the negative factors we
were discussing earlier, the years 1945-1948 were a time of tremendous economic, political, and social *instability* in countries like
France, Italy, West Germany, and Japan. In Britain the bourgeoisie
was in disarray after the sweeping Labour Party victory of 1945,
while the labour movement was at the apogee of its historical
strength. Even in the United States, the picture was far from
tranquil; 1946 saw the biggest strike wave in American history. The
picture in 1953 is strikingly different. Now we have the Europe of the
Tories, of Adenauer, of De Gasperi in Italy, of a divided and disoriented working class in France. In the United States Eisenhower
has been swept into office, with his secretary of state John Foster
Dulles, and the country is in the grip of McCarthyism. The passage
from the first picture to the second required more than merely the
effects of the Cold War and the Marshall Plan. It also needed the
defeat of the strike wave in France in 1947-48; the effects of the lost
opportunity of the political general strike in Italy on 14 July 1948,
deliberately curbed by the leadership of the Communist Party; the
betrayal of the great Ruhr strike against the dismantlement of
industry, which broke the back of the West German Communist
Party; the betrayal of the mass movement against re-militarization
by German Social Democracy, which initiated the long downward
trend of political activity by the working class; the dismal capitulation of the American trade-union bureaucracy to the Cold War and
the McCarthyite witch-hunt; the deliberate refusal of the British
Labour Party to break with capitalism in 1945-50, even though it
surely had the strength to do so. Subsequent events become under-
standable only in the light of all these events. It would therefore be
quite mistaken to assume that the launching of the Cold War in itself
was responsible for the re-stabilization of capitalism and the
economic boom.

As for the mechanism of that boom, I would refer you to my book
Late Capitalism, where this question is analysed in detail. It is
impossible for me to repeat such a long analysis here. The important
point, however, is that political and social stabilization preceded the
economic boom and provided the preconditions for it. In Europe the
boom began with a rate of exploitation inherited from fascism, in
other words, with a rate of profit much higher than during the

short-lived 'boom' of 1923-29. In the United States the Taft-Hartley Act and McCarthyism had similar effects. This in turn explains why there was a much higher level of capital accumulation. Hence the possibility of a third technological revolution, which in turn accounts for the long duration of the boom. The 'business cycle' did continue to operate during the expansion (that is, there were periodic over-production crises), but they were much shorter and milder than during the inter-war period.

Finally, the working class, although it had suffered serious defeats after 1947, was not at all crushed. It retained its organizational strength and therefore had to be reckoned with. This is the main factor that accounts for the 'reformist' aspect of the boom (for example, the fact that it proceeded through an expansion of the internal market rather than through the reconquest of the workers' states), for which the very length of the boom in turn provided the material resources.

The Sino-Soviet Dispute

Capitalist stabilization began to show signs of erosion as early as the beginning of the sixties. Even though there was no fundamental change in the world situation, we did see such events as the Cuban revolution and the related US-Soviet confrontation, the beginnings of the radicalization of youth in the advanced capitalist countries and the rise of the 'new left', the opening phases of what was to become the third Indochina war, and so on. If we look at Washington's response to the Cuban revolution, the Laotian crisis, and the anti-western shift of a number of the nationalist regimes in the 'third world' (Nasser, Nkrumah, Sukarno, etc.), we see a fairly clear continuity of imperialist Cold War policy. On the other hand, it was just at that time that the hitherto united 'Communist bloc' began to show signs of serious fissure, with the outbreak of the Sino-Soviet dispute. What were the underlying reasons for that fracturing? Was the origin and later development of the dispute based on real conflicting material interests of the Soviet and Chinese leaderships?

To start with, the cycle of class struggle, the cycle of anti-imperialist struggle, and the long wave of economic development should be considered separately to a large extent. The three are, of course, interrelated, but not in a mechanical way. In the imperialist countries, the 'expanding long wave of economic development' (commonly known as the 'post-war boom') came to an end in the late sixties. (Some would say the early seventies, but I will not go into that.) Around the same date, the cycle of anti-capitalist, proletarian class struggle began to pick up again, May '68 being the thunderbolt that symbolized this upturn. It is important to note, however, that the rise in class struggle began *before* any major over-production crisis, at a time when there was no massive unemployment and real wages were still rising. The crisis of the world imperialist system, however, had been mounting without serious interruption since the late forties, continuing through the fifties and sixties despite the ups and downs of mass mobilizations in the various dependent countries. That crisis exploded with the victory of the Chinese revolution, and there is a direct link between that victory, the second Indochina war (leading to the consolidation of a workers' state in North Vietnam), the beginning of the Algerian revolution, the launching of the guerrilla movement in Cuba, the subsequent victory of the Cuban revolution, the spread of revolutionary movements to several Latin American and African countries, the conquest of national independence in Algeria, the beginning of the third Indochina war, the intensification of the liberation struggle in the Portuguese colonies in Africa, and so on.

By and large, the worldwide youth radicalization and the rise of the 'new left' were at first by-products of this wave of world revolution centred in the 'third world'. Many of the specific idiosyncrasies of the new left current, such as 'third worldism' and the rejection of the urban proletariat as a 'revolutionary subject', were typical products of a unique combination of circumstances: relative quiescence for a long period in the advanced capitalist countries and continual waves of struggle in the dependent capitalist countries. The events of May '68 in France, however, abruptly altered these circumstances and thereby changed the themes and expressions of the radicalization in a lasting manner.

Throughout this period, the Soviet bureaucracy adhered firmly to its fundamental line of attempting to collaborate with the colonial bourgeoisie and to block any tendency of the colonial revolution to 'grow over' into a socialist revolution. This was the strategic orientation of the Kremlin in all countries, from China to Vietnam, Algeria to Cuba, Indonesia to India, Egypt to Iraq. Wherever local Communist parties held hegemony over the mass movement and adhered to this orientation, shattering, often bloody, defeats occurred. On the other hand, wherever local Communist parties (or independent revolutionary forces, as in Cuba) broke with that strategy, even if only empirically, the revolution was able to triumph.

Under these circumstances, which were widely perceived, if not fully understood, a deep ideological crisis erupted within the 'international communist and anti-imperialist movement'. Key questions of strategy such as the problem of relations with imperialism and the national bourgeoisie, the forms of struggle, and the dynamics of revolution in these countries ('two-stage' revolution or uninterrupted revolution) were suddenly being discussed more openly than they had been in decades. This ideological crisis was sharpened by a number of striking contrasts in the fate of mass struggles: the Cuban victory and the Brazilian defeat, the Chinese and Vietnamese victories and the Indonesian slaughter, to give just two examples. Under these conditions, several currents among 'third world revolutionaries' began moving towards a break with the traditional Menshevik-Stalinist strategy of 'revolution by stages' and alliance with the national bourgeoisie in the dependent capitalist countries. However, either because of their Stalinist origins and the ideological remnants of their original education or because of their one-sided emphasis on *forms* of struggle as opposed to *political* strategy, this break with classical Stalinism remained only partial. A reversal towards class collaboration was therefore always possible, although the ideological ferment among these currents was quite real for a long period.

The reaction of imperialism to the anti-imperialist liberation struggles has been rather more complex and diversified than your question would suggest. It is true that for a whole period the main thrust of imperialist policy was towards open counter-revolutionary military intervention, economic blackmail, and overt and covert political intervention; but at the same time, political manoeuvres with the colonial bourgeoisie and broad sections of the nationalist petty-bourgeoisie never really ceased. Indeed, in some cases these manoeuvres were more successful than the more open interventions, as is indicated by imperialism's defeat in Vietnam and its success in Egypt. Since the early seventies, in fact, there has been a trend in imperialist policy towards these sorts of manoeuvres and away from direct military interventions. The most decisive factor in this shift, of course, was the movement in the United States against the war in Vietnam, which was not only successful in forcing Washington to withdraw its ground troops and halt the bombing, thus creating the preconditions for the Vietnamese victory, but also prevented the Ford administration from intervening to save the Thieu regime at the last minute and has created political conditions such that the American ruling class is now unable to engage in the sorts of massive and overt military adventures that were its stock in trade during the fifties and early sixties. This does not mean that U.S. imperialism has abandoned the policy of vigorous counter-revolutionary intervention on a world scale, nor does it imply that massive military commitments of the Indochina type will remain impossible indefinitely. But the combination of the political effects of the anti-war movement and the recent successes of imperialism in more subtle manoeuvring has given rise to an evident shift in imperialist strategy towards the third world.

There remains the question of the link between all these developments of the sixties and the emergence of the Sino-Soviet conflict. Let me begin with some methodological remarks. If we are to understand the origins and dynamics of conflicts between the leaderships of bureaucratized workers' states, we must constantly combine the relative autonomy of the political and ideological conflict and disputes based on contrasting immediate material interests. To neglect either aspect is to abandon the classical revolutionary Marxist analysis of the character of the ruling bureaucracy in these states, in this case the Soviet and Chinese bureaucracies. To concentrate exclusively (or even nearly exclusively) on the political and ideological conflict would be to treat the bureaucracy as a collection of people lacking material interests distinct from those of both the working class and the bourgeoisie. On the other hand, to concentrate exclusively (or nearly exclusively) on the material interests would be, in effect, to identify the bureaucracy as a new ruling class. The peculiar, 'intermediate' position occupied by the bureaucracy in Marxist sociology—not a new ruling class, but a privileged layer of the proletariat with its own specific material interests to defend—implies exactly this unique combination of politics and material interests, which is the ultimate source of conflicts between different ruling bureaucracies. This is reflected in the particular manner in which each bureaucracy rules, in other words, in the manner in which it maintains and guarantees its privileges through the exercise of a *monopoly of power*.

Exactly because the bureaucracy is *not* a new ruling class, because it has no necessary social role to play and no subjective legitimacy in the eyes of the workers and peasants, it can defend its privileges only if it strictly maintains its monopoly of power. The bureaucracy is therefore compelled to guard this monopoly jealously and rigidly—hence the nexus between nationalized property, the maintenance of a formal communist tradition, and the one-party system and political repression.

Ultimately, the roots of the Sino-Soviet conflict lie in the fact that it is objectively impossible for the Soviet and Chinese bureaucracies to maintain a common political-ideological orientation (whether internally or in foreign affairs), because of the quite different socioeconomic conditions of the two countries. There is a simple reason why this political-ideological difference inevitably escalated into a rift at the state level: Mao could not tolerate a pro-Kremlin faction in the Chinese Communist Party any more than Khrushchev or Brezhnev could have tolerated a pro-Mao faction in the Soviet Communist Party. Since the party apparatus is identical to the state apparatus in both countries, the dispute had to be reflected in a conflict between two state powers. The Kremlin tried to bring the Chinese leadership into line by means of pressure on the Chinese state; Peking was then compelled to retaliate at the state level.

The conflict, then, is not of purely political or even ideological origin, but is a reflection of the inability of the Moscow or Peking bureaucrats to tolerate 'polycentrism' or 'factionalism' in their own ranks, since this would challenge their monopoly of power and therewith their material privileges. The differences in ideological and political orientation thus ultimately reflect differing tactics of bureaucratic self-defence under varying objective circumstances. This, however, does not imply 'competition' in the capitalist sense of the term. Moscow has not attempted, for example, to 'conquer' inner Mongolia so as to exploit its wealth, nor has Peking any interest in 'conquering the wealth of Siberia'. There is nothing in the structure of either country impelling its ruling group to expand in this manner. It is therefore important to note that the 'material roots' of the Sino-Soviet conflict differ qualitatively from the material roots of inter-imperialist conflicts or of conflicts between imperialist countries and bureaucratized workers' states. Inter-imperialist conflicts derive from the economic competition that is built in to the capitalist mode of production itself. Such conflicts can be mediated and regulated short of military conflict under given political and military conditions, but they cannot be eliminated so long as the capitalist system survives. Conflicts between imperialist and bureaucratized workers' states ultimately reflect the contradictory socio-economic structures of the countries concerned, and again can be mediated and halted short of military conflict in many cases, but cannot be eliminated until the major capitalist states are overthrown. The conflicts among ruling bureaucracies, however, while they are an inevitable consequence of the bureaucracy's monopoly of power, are in no way inevitably generated by the socio-economic structure of the workers' states. It is in that sense that they may be considered 'political and ideological' in a way that these other conflicts cannot.

The next question is a rather lengthy one, but of great importance. In the sixties the Fourth International gave critical support to the Chinese position in international affairs as opposed to the Russian. It was claimed that the Chinese leadership was playing a role in world politics that, although not at all proletarian internationalist, was significantly more positive than that of the Kremlin. In recent years, with the turn of Chinese foreign policy, the position of the FI has shifted too, now presenting the role of the two largest workers' states as equally deleterious, although continuing to place the historic responsibility for the original Sino-Soviet division on Moscow.

Consider, however, the following argument. The counter-revolutionary role of the Kremlin has generally been asserted in a negative way. In other words, the Soviet leaders have counselled forces under their influence to restrain themselves, not to seize revolutionary opportunities, to support the 'lesser evil' in conflicts between bourgeois political forces. On a growing number of occasions over the past eight years, however, the Chinese leadership has not simply restrained and derailed revolutionary movements, but has actively supported the counter-revolution. Take the example of the Bangladesh war in 1971. The Soviet leadership played a counter-revolutionary role in the more or less 'classical' Stalinist sense, uncritically supporting Mujibur Rahman's Awami League and doing everything to ensure that the war would halt at achieving political independence and not 'grow over' into socialist revolution, which would have posed a real threat to the stability of the pro-Soviet Indian regime. But Peking actually gave active aid, not only political but also military, to the armed forces of the Pakistani dictatorship. Iran presents a similar case. The Kremlin did seek accommodation with the Shah, and the pro-Moscow Tudeh Party did not wage an intransigent struggle against him. But Peking actually hailed him as a progressive figure and an anti-imperialist fighter.

Finally, in the advanced capitalist countries, we find the Chinese leadership offering open support to figures at the right of the bourgeois political spectrum: Nixon, Henry Jackson, Franz-Josef Strauss, the Christian Democrats in Italy, the Gaullists in France. All these forces have one thing in common: anti-Sovietism. They are all identified, in one way or another, with Cold Warism. The compass of Chinese foreign policy over the past eight years seems to have become opposition to the spread of Soviet influence. The Chinese leaders have therefore actively supported imperialist and pro-imperialist forces in all cases in which they have feared that the victory of revolution—or even of opposition—would objectively strengthen the Soviet leadership. Conversely, on a number of occasions you have pointed to signs of a resurgence of Cold War attitudes and policies on the part of imperialist governments, especially Washington. It seems clear that these new instances of Cold Warism, up to and including the current intensification of the arms race by Carter, are directed primarily against the Soviet Union. The Kremlin therefore has had to defend itself and has been embroiled in a growing number of conflicts with imperialism, in which Peking has generally supported the latter. In the light of all this, could it not be said, if such terms are at all permissible, that Soviet policy has evolved positively and Chinese negatively to the point that the latter is now palpably worse?

I do not agree that the question can be approached in this manner. Rather, we must begin with the more fundamental points. At the root of intra-bureaucratic conflicts lies the concept of socialism in one country, the fundamental tenet of Stalinism as a specific ideology of the bureaucracy, reflecting its specific material interests. This question is neither purely Platonic nor purely pragmatic; that is, it is not simply a matter of deciding whether the label 'socialist' can be applied to some particular country, or of deciding whether an effort should be made to achieve the greatest possible economic growth and social progress even under conditions of the relative isolation of an underdeveloped workers' state. It is rather a question of a *specific strategy for socio-economic development in a workers' state*. Socialism in one country embodies a strategy that *subordinates* everything that happens in the rest of the world to the needs of national development, which is described as 'building socialism in the main fortress'. This strategy therefore inevitably combines nationalism and national-messianism, since this sort of subordination is nationalistic by definition and since no communist outside the given country (and not many inside) would accept it unless they had been convinced that this particular country, and this country *alone*, represented the bastion of socialism on a world scale. An additional corollary of this strategy is 'peaceful coexistence' with imperialism, the abandoning of any genuine orientation towards world revolution.

Now, the exact implementation of this development strategy at any given moment depends upon a number of objective constraints over which the bureaucracy has little control. It is for this reason that the actual pursuance of 'socialism in one country' in the Soviet Union involved the Kremlin in a series of wild gyrations, from Bukharin's attempt to integrate the kulak into socialism peacefully to subsequent forced collectivization, from the slow industrialization of 1925-27 to the dizzying growth rates of the first two five-year plans, and so on. These policy shifts were paralleled by similar zigzags in foreign policy: the 'third period', the Popular Front, the Hitler-Stalin pact, the 'great anti-fascist alliance', Cold War sectarianism, renewal of Popular Front strategies, etc. These wild fluctuations do not reflect any fundamental shift in strategy by the bureaucracy, for socialism in one country and peaceful coexistence remain the determinant guidelines. On the contrary, they simply represent bureaucratic responses to shifts in objective circumstances (sometimes, of course, unintentionally brought about by the effects of the previous line). The application of the fundamental guidelines requires the various tactical shifts. It would have been surprising indeed if there had not been similar wild gyrations in the policy of the Chinese bureaucracy, which has been applying the same guidelines in very different objective circumstances.

Now, what are these various constraints on the implementation of policies of socialism in one country? We will mention five, but the list is not at all exhaustive (it merely outlines the general shape of the situation): the initial material and social base of the bureaucracy concerned; the attitude of imperialism towards this bureaucracy; the level of political and social activity (or even awareness) of the proletariat in the country over which the bureaucracy rules; the vicissitudes of the world revolution as a whole; the capacity of the bureaucracy to influence each of the sectors of world revolution through parties under its domination or control. If we examine the gyrations of Maoist policy in the light of these five factors as they concern China, all the various shifts begin to make sense.

After the death of Stalin, Mao was undoubtedly one of the leading authorities, if not the supreme figure, among most of the Communist party bureaucracies throughout the world. The policies he advocated were by no means wildly irrational. Even on the question of de-Stalinization, he kept his bearings at first, for his comments in 'On the Historical Experience of the Dictatorship of the Proletariat' and 'On the Correct Handling of Contradictions Among the People' were actually much more sophisticated attempts to explain Stalin's crimes than Khrushchev's crude theory of the 'personality cult'. In 1956 he supported the second of the interventions of the Kremlin's army in Hungary (on 4 November); but he, along with most Communist leaders throughout the world and some Soviet leaders too, had condemned the first intervention (of 23 October). He also strove to prevent a similar intervention in Poland, which won him much sympathy in Eastern Europe, and not only among the 'liberal', pro-Gomulka factions.

There is little doubt that at that time there were pro-Mao currents and leaders in most Communist Parties, probably even the Russian. We know that some previously pro-Khrushchev forces in the Western parties were leaning towards Peking at that time.

Contrariwise, we know that there was at least one pro-Khrushchev leader in the Chinese Communist Party, Marshal Peng Tehuai, who launched an all-out attack on Mao's policies at the Lushan Plenum of the Central Committee, at which a balance-sheet of the 'great leap forward' was drawn.

There is sufficient evidence today to delineate the main differences between the initial positions of the Khrushchev and Mao currents. They turned around alternative attitudes towards world imperialism; alternative strategies towards the anti-imperialist movement (and more generally, on how to advance the 'world communist movement'); alternative military policies; and alternative economic policies. Briefly, the Khrushchev faction stood for: broadened détente with US imperialism; alliance with the national bourgeoisie in the semi-colonial countries (including with their governments); less emphasis on the importance of the colonial revolution in general; greater 'consumerism' in the Soviet Union and Eastern Europe, combined with intensified technological competition with international imperialism; repetition of the Soviet pattern of economic development in the less developed workers' states (that is, initial construction of a few huge centres of heavy industry); concentration of sophisticated weaponry capable of matching US military power (nuclear weapons, for example) in the Soviet army alone. The Mao faction, on the other hand, stood for: 'bypassing' the imperialist power centres by relying essentially on armed struggle in 'third world' countries, which were said to be the real centres of world revolution; reliance on 'people's war' as a means of defence against imperialist aggression, with simultaneous decentralization of the disposition of nuclear weapons among the workers' states (which meant, in effect, that Moscow should provide the other workers' states with these weapons); a pattern of economic development based primarily on 'labour investment' (which meant small, decentralized, labour-intensive industries); a wage freeze for workers and peasants and a reduction of the degree of bureaucratic material privilege, relying on indoctrination ('putting politics in command') and mass mobilization as an instrument for the acceleration of economic growth.

The material roots of these political and ideological differences are not difficult to discover, for the objective conditions in which the two bureaucracies were trying to 'build socialism in one country' in the late fifties and early sixties were quite distinct. Four differences in particular should be emphasized: the qualitatively greater hostility towards China than towards the Soviet Union exhibited by world imperialism; the much greater backwardness of China in the socio-economic domain; the greater level of mass political activity in China (especially in the towns); the different geographic areas in which the two bureaucracies commanded important influence over local Communist Parties, China having significant weight nearly exclusively in Asia and some 'third world' countries in other continents, the Kremlin mainly in the imperialist countries. The alternative policies of the Khrushchev and Mao factions therefore flowed quite logically from the differing constraints on the application of the strategy of 'socialism in one country'. In the end, the temptation for both bureaucracies to attempt to settle these differences not simply through ideological debate but also through the use of state power ('great power politics') became irresistible. There is no doubt in my mind, however, that the decisive steps in this respect were taken by the Kremlin in 1960 and 1961. It is therefore the Soviet bureaucracy that bears the prime responsibility for the transformation of this dispute into a conflict at the state level. Moscow suddenly cut off all economic aid to China, withdrew its experts, and left the plants they had been building unfinished, thereby wasting much of the enormous investment China had made in them. These steps were soon followed by a radical reduction even of normal trade, amounting to a *de facto* boycott of China by the Soviet Union. At the same time, the Kremlin refused to give China nuclear weapons or to help it develop the technology to produce its own weapons. This was then followed by the concentration of military forces on the Sino-Soviet border in central Siberia. The Soviet Union even aimed missiles with nuclear warheads at major Chinese cities, industrial belts, and the nuclear experimentation centres in the Chinese northwest.

One has only to recall the international political context in which these actions were taken to realize to what degree they constituted foul crimes against the world working class and the struggle for socialism. US imperialism was busily building up its power bases throughout Southeast Asia. A large faction in the Pentagon had launched a campaign to use nuclear weapons against China before it developed a defensive capability. The imperialist aggression against the Vietnamese revolution was just moving to the stage of massive escalation, while aggression in various forms was being prepared against other Asian struggles. China itself faced a desperate economic situation in the wake of the collapse of the second stage of the 'great leap forward'. Under these conditions, the Kremlin's actions indicated that the Soviet bureaucracy considered China, and not imperialism, its primary enemy.

Another element must be taken into account too. At the Lushan Plenum of the Central Committee of the Chinese Communist Party, Mao found himself in a minority against the faction led by Liu Shao-chi and Teng Hsiao-ping. He then tried to reconquer the leadership of the party by launching the cultural revolution. But the mass mobilizations that were thereby initiated soon took on a dynamic of their own, some genuine left tendencies emerging from the Red Guards. An additional constraint was thereby placed upon the Mao bureaucracy, which now had to contend with motion among the Chinese masses and the possible emergence of left oppositionist tendencies.

If we combine all these elements, we can easily understand the reasons for the foreign policy pursued by Mao during the 1960s. This policy gradually evolved from its emphasis on hostility to US imperialism to a position of equal opposition to the two 'super-powers', as Mao became obsessed by the danger of a Soviet-American entente directed against China, an obsession which seems not to have been entirely unfounded. At the same time, Peking continued to express hostility to imperialism during that period, supporting anti-imperialist struggles as a 'general line' to be counter-posed to the Soviet version of 'peaceful coexistence'. The furthest to the right Mao went during this period was his rejection of a united front with Moscow in defence of the Vietnamese revolution, which cost Peking the support of the Japanese Communist Party and a number of other parties in Asia as well (the Communist Party—Marxist in India, for example). The watchword at the time was 'self-reliance', which was actually nothing but a rationale of China's economic isolation, caused by the dual boycott imposed by Washington and Moscow.

In the meantime, however, the Chinese bureaucracy was continually alert for possible openings. With the suppression of the turmoil of the cultural revolution, international manoeuvres became easier. When openings did come, they were not from the Kremlin. (Once again, this was Moscow's fault; the withdrawal of some of the military forces massed on the Chinese border and an offer of economic aid would have altered the situation significantly.) Rather, these openings came from imperialism, first of all the European and Japanese imperialists, who were seeking new trade outlets. Beginning with 1971, Chinese participation in world trade was on the rise, bringing an end to autarky. Then came the Nixon-Kissinger overtures, partly aimed at facilitating an end to the Vietnam war on terms favourable to American imperialism, but also at ameliorating Washington's long-term relations with China. Peking responded enthusiastically, developing a new theory and practice to accommodate that response: the 'three worlds theory' and the closely related conception that the Soviet Union had become the main enemy.

The current objective constraints on Chinese implementation of the strategy of socialism in one country (now expressed in the formula of the 'four modernizations') are substantially different from those which prevailed twenty years ago (an unknown factor being the degree of politicization and potential rebelliousness of the urban masses). There is therefore no reason to believe that the theory and practice of considering the Soviet Union the 'main enemy' will last for decades, any more than Peking's previous verbal opposition to the strategy of 'peaceful coexistence with imperialism' lasted for decades. There is simply no material basis for the protracted pursuance of that policy, which was merely a rationalization of a particular situation. China remains a bureaucratized workers' state, like the Soviet Union, and in the long run the Chinese bureaucracy will find it much more difficult to 'coexist peacefully' with Washington than with Moscow. Unilateral reliance on capitalist countries for trade and credit in the acceleration of economic growth threatens to damage seriously the planned economy which is the very basis of the power and privileges of the Chinese bureaucracy. The Yugoslav bureaucrats made that same discovery decades ago, and their Chinese colleagues will follow suit eventually. It would be much more rational for Peking to divide its trade between the 'two camps', to try to milk both of them for credits and aid, to play 'both ends against the middle' as the Yugoslavs have done, not without success. Such a shift in Chinese policy, of course, would require an adjustment of Moscow's attitude, as also occurred in the case of Yugoslavia. But in the long run, such an adjustment is in the interests of the Soviet bureaucrats too, although on both sides the shift may have to wait for a change in leadership personnel in both capitals. It should be clear that these remarks in no way imply any sort of justification for the counter-revolutionary actions and statements of the Chinese bureaucrats, which you correctly condemn and which the Fourth International has been condemning for many years now. They are indeed prime instances of bureaucratic cynicism and treachery. My intent here is to demonstrate that they are in no way exceptional departures from the normal behaviour of the bureaucracy; many parallels can be found in the past and present policies of the Soviet bureaucrats. You are in fact mistaken to restrict the counter-revolutionary impact of Kremlin diplomacy to instances of 'bad counsel'. The open support to Hitler's policy of imperialist conquest during the Nazi-Soviet pact; the material aid (in the form of oil) to Mussolini's invasion of Ethiopia; the strike-breaking actions of Moscow's allies during the last decade of the Franco regime (delivery of Polish coal to Spain during miners' strikes, for example); the open support to the Videla dictatorship in Argentina (by the Kremlin and its Argentine stooges); the initial support to Lon Nol against the Khmer Rouge, not to mention the crushing of workers' uprisings in East Germany, Hungary, and Czechoslovakia —these are just a few examples that go beyond the sort of 'negative' counter-revolutionary policy to which you refer.

To sum up, I would deny that we are entering a new cold war situation in which imperialism, more or less allied to Peking, is preparing an aggressive drive against the Soviet Union and in which the Soviet bureaucracy therefore has to defend itself by becoming more 'anti-imperialist'. It is true that Chinese *verbiage* is currently more reactionary than Russian. But their *actions*—outside Southeast Asia—have been of less aid to imperialism than has the policy of the Soviet bureaucracy, essentially because they are weaker in material resources, less able to act outside their borders. (There are, of course, exceptions: their criminal invasion of Vietnam, their training of Mobutu's troops, their aid to pro-imperialist forces in Angola.) Iran is a case in point. Moscow's active commercial, industrial, and technical collaboration with the Shah and the refusal of the Tudeh Party to take an aggressive part in the struggle against him certainly aided the Shah much more than Peking's treacherous and demented salutations to the Shah as an 'anti-imperialist fighter'.

There was, after all, very little Peking could actually *do* in Iran, which was not true of Moscow, despite its more prudent vocabulary.

The basic trend in the current world situation, I would argue, is not towards a new, full-fledged cold war between Moscow and Washington, but a continuation of the 'peaceful coexistence' that has been pursued for several decades now. In that context, subsequent to the weakening of US imperialism after its crushing defeat in Indochina, the Kremlin has been able to take some initiatives, particularly in Africa (and Afghanistan) to shift the relationship of forces marginally. Washington's response has been a stepped-up arms race and the preparation of counter-strikes in some parts of the world. But all this is occurring in the general framework of 'détente' and not of an aggressive alliance between Washington and Peking against Moscow. Indeed, ultimately, US imperialism remains more interested in peaceful coexistence with the Soviet bureaucracy, for it needs Moscow's counter-revolutionary assistance in key areas of the world (Western Europe, Latin America) where Peking simply cannot deliver. If that fundamental aspect of the world situation changes, we will of course have to reassess the reactions of the Soviet and Chinese leaderships. As yet, however, it has not occurred, and if I may formulate a prognosis, I do not believe it is likely to occur soon, for it would require a radical change in the social and political relationship of class forces in Western Europe, the United States, or Latin America.

The Situation of the American Working Class

Let us turn now to a different subject, another crucial factor in world politics. The economic crisis of the 1970s has had very different political effects in the various regions of imperialism. We have seen a deep radicalization of the working class in a number of countries in Western Europe and, more generally, a basic shift to the left in the politics of most European states. With the collapse of the Portuguese and Greek dictatorships and the crisis and liquidation of Francoism, capitalist Europe is now free of authoritarian right-wing dictatorships for the first time in about half a century.

There is, however, a major paradox in the imperialist world today, and that is the apparent political quiescence of the American working class, the largest proletariat in the world. Marxists have always placed tremendous hopes in the awakening of the US proletariat, a tradition that goes all the way back to Marx himself and includes Trotsky probably more than any other international revolutionary theorist. In your own essay 'Where Is America Going?', you predicted that we would see the end of the complete political integration of the American proletariat when the predominant position of the US ruling class on the world market was challenged. In debates with certain tendencies of the American 'new left' which had written off the proletariat as a revolutionary force back in the sixties, revolutionary Marxists generally predicted that a major economic depression was not necessarily required to awaken the revolutionary potential of the workers, that the American workers would react vehemently to any decline in their real wages, so used had they become to their economic gains of the post-war period. It was further argued that major political defeats and crises for the ruling class would have the effect of stimulating political awareness, leading the workers to challenge the complete hegemony of the Democratic Party.

The revolutionary Marxists have been strikingly vindicated so far as their predictions about the evolution of the objective situation were concerned. US hegemony over the world capitalist market has indeed been seriously challenged, if not completely obliterated. The real wages of the working class declined for several years in the mid-seventies, many of the social gains of the post-war period are under clear attack, and the American economy faces the worst unemployment of any major capitalist power. The ruling class suffered an unprecedented defeat in the Indochina war—the first war ever lost by American imperialism, largely because of the equally unprecedented massive opposition to the war in the United States itself—and this was followed by the Watergate crisis and the first resignation of a reigning president in the country's history, certainly the most serious political crisis faced by the US capitalist class since the Civil War.

Despite all this, the political radicalization of the American working class anticipated by revolutionary Marxists has not occurred. The class has not responded to these various objective developments in the expected manner. Why is this? What accounts for this anomaly and what future developments in the American labour movement are likely to alter it?

I would begin with a very general comment. The different effects of the general crisis of bourgeois social relations in the various imperialist countries are essentially a function of the varying *political* relationship of forces between capital and labour on the eve of the crisis. This relationship of forces is in turn the result of the entire historical evolution of these countries, in which the critical factor is the degree of political class consciousness achieved by the proletariat. Additional factors of great importance are the political experience and ability to manoeuvre of the capitalist class and the level of material reserves and economic margins it commands. In the case of the United States, there is not the slightest doubt that the fundamental key to the entire political situation is precisely the low level of *political* class consciousness of the working class, exactly the factor to which you have pointed.

Historically, I would maintain the prognosis I set out in 'Where Is America Going?' The situation has, in fact, begun to change, although you are correct that it has not changed as quickly as we had expected. Ultimately, however, I think it will be realized that the turning point came when American capitalism lost its leading position in industrial productivity. West German capitalism now holds first place in this decisive domain, and even Japanese capitalism has overtaken the United States, temporarily at least. This fact has been reflected in many important ways, not the least of which is that the wage differentials US workers have enjoyed for 40 or 50 years have been severely eroded and may even have disappeared entirely. It is difficult to judge this question accurately, because of the fluctuations in exchange rates, but it is clear that the American working class is losing its position as the proletariat with the highest standard of living in the world (I am speaking in terms of real purchasing power), and may well have already lost it. The direction of historical development in this respect is clear enough, and there are no signs that it will be reversed soon. In other words, the objective situation to which you refer is not a passing one, and I would maintain that the predictions of revolutionary Marxists about the subjective response of the workers will also be borne out, in time.

In fact, it is important not to overlook the clear signals that a radicalization of the US proletariat has indeed begun and is in its initial phases. The bourgeois press has commented extensively on the change in the mood in the trade unions, where there are mounting challenges to the corrupt bureaucracy whose rule has previously been impervious to threat. We know, however, that there is no automatic link between a rise in radical trade-union activity and a rise in political consciousness. The real question, then, is this: what are the obstacles in the United States that impede the transformation of an upswing in trade-union militancy into a qualitative politicization of the working class?

The answer is obviously complex, but I would emphasize three critical factors. To start with, it must not be forgotten that there has been an almost complete break in the continuity of socialist cadres and experience within the proletariat in the United States. Here we may make a striking comparison, despite the completely different historical circumstances, with the situation of the second-largest working class in the world, in the Soviet Union. The greatest paradox in the international struggle for socialism today is that the two largest working classes, which together total something like 160 million people, have both suffered this break in continuity and both stand—temporarily—outside the process of mounting political radicalization now occurring on a world scale.

What do I mean by break in continuity? The best way to explain this is to look briefly at the two previous mass radicalizations of the US working class, during the 1930s and immediately after the Second World War. On both occasions literally tens of thousands of political radicals, whether of proletarian social origin or not, played a central role in all the major struggles. In the thirties, revolutionary Marxists actually led the two mass strikes that did most to set the stage for the organizing drive that was later to produce the CIO, the Toledo Auto-lite strike and the Minneapolis truck drivers strike. It is probably no exaggeration to say that the cadres of the Communist Party were indispensable in the organization of the unions that came to make up the CIO. To a great extent, industrial unionism became a mass phenomenon in the United States as the result of the role of Marxists. This was also true of the strike wave of 1946-47, which involved even more workers than the strikes of the thirties. In the post-war struggles, significant currents arose in the unions in opposition to the line of the Communist Party from the left, forces that had drawn some conclusions from the blatant class collaboration the Stalinists had practised during the Second World War. This large presence of political radicals in the struggles of the American working class has much deeper roots than many people think. I have mentioned the previous two waves of struggle, but I could go back even further and discuss the role of the IWW (International Workers of the World) in the foundation of the American union movement and of the Socialist Party of Eugene Debs, one of the few leaders of international Social Democracy to oppose the First World War. Debs was jailed for his anti-war views and received more than a million votes in the presidential election of 1920, in a campaign he conducted from his prison cell.

It is not true, then, that the American working class had no socialist tradition or that this proletariat has always been foreign to political radicalism. What happened was that the repression associated with the Cold War and McCarthyism destroyed this political capital almost completely. This break in continuity was expressed in a quite physical form: socialists, communists, radicals were driven from the trade unions by the thousands and tens of thousands; the apparatuses of the unions were purged of radicals, and the layer of sympathizers of radical organizations or ideas, which surely numbered in the hundreds of thousands, was intimidated into silence by the severe action taken against these tens of thousands of activists.

The result was that when the general political situation began to change in the sixties with the rise of the civil rights movement and the first demonstrations against the war in Vietnam, the presence of radicals within the working class was minuscule, their influence in the trade unions virtually nil. Those few socialist activists who remained in the working class were not in a position even to speak out about the political issues being discussed in American society more generally, since the witch-hunt actually lasted longer in the union movement than in nearly any other sector of society. It is in this sense that I think it is correct to speak of a destruction of the socialist tradition in the American working class. The recovery of that tradition, which is essential if there is to be a genuine political radicalization, will involve a longer process than we anticipated ten or fifteen years ago. This, then, is the first point: we underestimated the scope of this break in continuity and its impact.

The second factor is in many ways related to the first: it is the complete identification in the minds of American workers of communism on the one hand with Stalinist repression and oppression on the other. The complete absence of any left alternative has effects in the United States very different from those in most West European countries. Because of the break in continuity, the organized Left in the United States, including the Communist Party and what is left of Social Democracy (those Social Democrats, that is, who have not become mere members of the Democratic Party, and not always left Democrats at that) is no larger, in absolute terms, than the far Left in countries like Spain. In relative terms it is even smaller, of course. The ruling class in all advanced capitalist countries attempts to identify socialism with what exists in the Soviet Union, well aware that Soviet society has long lost its attractive power to the masses of workers in the West. (In a sense, this is the greatest contribution Stalinism has made to the preservation of capitalism.) In most countries of Western Europe, however, there are mass Socialist or Communist parties that do not wholly identify with the Soviet Union and, in many of these countries, a far Left that has succeeded in establishing itself as an anti-bureaucratic presence in national political life.

In the United States this is not the case. Because of the absence of a significant Left, and because a good portion of the organized Left that does exist (namely the Communist Party) continues to maintain that the Soviet Union is indeed a model of socialist democracy, the American masses tend to be not merely anti-Stalinist, but anti-communist. For the US working class, communism simply means the Russia of Brezhnev. Not only is there no alternative model outside the United States, but there is not even a mass party calling itself socialist or communist with which the American workers could identify as representing their interests. The result is that socialism is much less attractive to the workers than it was in the thirties and forties—and it is difficult to have a serious political radicalization of the proletariat if the masses of workers regard the very notion of socialism as abhorrent. One of the consequences of this is to reinforce the lack of class politics in the organizational sense. In the absence of any socialist alternative, even in the broadest sense, the workers tend to be attracted to various substitutes for class action. This is one of the reasons for the enormous influence of 'lesser evil' politics in the United States, and for the concomitant phenomenon of the attractive power of the left wing of the Democratic Party.

Then, there is a third factor which should not be underestimated. In many ways the American ruling class is less politically sophisticated than the European. It often tends to be more brutal and cynical, and there is little doubt that the personnel of the bourgeois parties are generally less adept than their European counterparts. (This is probably another result of the lack of a mass working-class party; bourgeois political leaders are not compelled to confront representatives of the proletariat in political debate, but simply compete with each other for posts in the state apparatus; since there are few if any policy differences among them, election campaigns tend to become mere personality clashes conducted through the most garish imaginable advertising techniques.) But despite this, the US ruling class commands one enormous asset which all the other ruling classes in the capitalist world lack, and that is the fantastic reserve of wealth accumulated during sixty years of industrial supremacy on a world scale. The American rulers lost nothing in World War I; indeed, they made great material gains. They suffered no destruction of capital in the Second World War and even expanded the geographic territory under their domination. Thus, despite its relative lack of political sophistication, this ruling class has been quite clever in drawing on these reserves to integrate and coopt rebellious social forces, especially the leaders of those forces. This is the fundamental mechanism through which the major illusion of the more politically conscious workers is maintained: that much can be achieved through the operation of the two-party system.

I say that this is an illusion, but it must be acknowledged that the illusion is not a pure mystification. If it were, it would not have held such complete sway for so long. Because of these great reserves, the American ruling class is able to make concessions to movements of social dissent that would be much more difficult for the European ruling class to make. The civil rights movement is a case in point. Undoubtedly, blacks remain a super-exploited and oppressed section of the American population, and will so remain until the socialist revolution. But there is equally little doubt that genuine gains were made by the civil rights movement in the sixties, that not unimportant changes were introduced into American society because of it. It is symbolic, for example, that Andrew Young, who was one of the leaders of the civil rights movement, a close associate of Martin Luther King, now holds cabinet rank in the Carter administration. This ability of the ruling class to 'buy off' leaders of dissent has had enormous effects in the trade-union movement. Any radical unionist who begins to think in terms of national politics—that is, who begins to go beyond the problems of union strategy in the strict sense—becomes subject to a great temptation to try to work through the Democratic Party, or at least through the two-party system.

Once again, in the long run the effect of this factor will be eroded by the loss of American hegemony in the field of industrial technology. It is even likely that we will see a conjunctural reduction in the margin for manoeuvre of the US ruling class, since the current trend is towards the elimination of concessions and not towards greater reforms. But there is no disputing the fact that this remains the ruling class with the greatest reserves in the capitalist world, and it is probable that we have also tended to underestimate the effects of these reserves.

When you speak of the reserves of the American ruling class, you seem to be talking in primarily economic terms. But could it not also be said that the American bourgeoisie commands great political reserves, despite the relative lack of sophistication to which you refer? It is a peculiarity of the United States, for example, that the present state institutions have evolved directly from the phase of bourgeois revolution, with no intervening period of counter-revolution and restoration. The American political establishment seems able not merely to 'buy off' dissent in the manner you describe, but often genuinely to integrate those demands that fall within the purview of democratic, individual equality. On virtually all questions of democratic rights, for example, the American ruling class seems willing and able to adopt much more sweeping solutions than its European or Japanese counterparts. This 'democratic resiliency', if one can use the term, was reflected even in the Watergate crisis. Severe as this crisis may have been, it was, after all, resolved through the removal first of the vice-president and then of the president; the personnel of the government were turned out, but there was not the slightest crisis of the institutions themselves. If one compares this sort of solution to the manner in which European governments have responded to such crises, it is difficult to resist the impression that in the American bourgeoisie we are dealing with a class that commands formidable political reserves and presides over a system so flexible that even challenges from bourgeois third parties seem enormously difficult.

It is difficult to answer your question without going into detail about many specific problems of American history. I will therefore limit myself to one general observation, which will lead me to a fourth factor in the delay of the political awakening of the American proletariat.

First, however, I would argue that your assessment of the continuity of bourgeois-democratic institutions in the United States is rather incautious. Let us not forget that slavery continued to exist in the United States for about seventy-five years after the victory of the revolution and that the slave-owning class was the dominant component of the ruling bloc during most of that period. The first American revolution actually made the fewest changes in social relations of any major bourgeois revolution in world history, and left intact the most powerful non-capitalist ruling class. It was precisely for this reason that the second American revolution—the civil war—was far the most *radical* bourgeois revolution in world history, by any reasonable standard. It was the opposite of the first revolution in this respect. Let us not forget that millions of dollars worth of private property in the form of slaves was expropriated without compensation, that the entire set of social relations in the slave South was violently overturned, and that for eleven years after the civil war, most of the southern states were ruled by coalitions in which ex-slaves played a not at all negligible role, the federal government having been brought under the sway of the radical wing of the Republican Party, which, by the way, had the enthusiastic support of Karl Marx.

This second American revolution was indeed followed by a counter-revolution, a sort of restoration, which was also one of the most sweeping and violent in bourgeois history. All the governments of the ex-slave states were again overturned, the radical Republicans were ousted from their positions of power in the federal government and eventually destroyed. In the southern states, this counter-revolution was implemented to a large extent by a counter-revolutionary terrorist militia that unleashed a genuine white terror in the southern countryside: the Ku Klux Klan, an organization that is still with us today. The laws instituted during that counter-revolution to re-establish the oppression of the black population were the very laws that came under attack, and were eventually rolled back, by the civil rights movement in the 1960s, a full century after the civil war. The historical reality is therefore more complex than you tend to indicate.

I would agree with you, however, that the American political system, given the underpinnings of its economic strength and the reserves we have been discussing, has demonstrated much greater flexibility and success than the political systems of the European bourgeoisies. In that sense, the US capitalist class does command great political reserves, on which it has freely drawn. The coalition forged by Roosevelt around the Democratic Party in the thirties is the most important recent example of this. The New Deal may be considered the American version of the Popular Front, and it is no accident that while the European version entailed a *bloc* between bourgeois and workers' parties in which the former held political hegemony, the American version entailed the political dissolution of the trade-union movement into the major party of the bourgeoisie.

The question is whether these political reserves are being eroded along with the economic. Here I would call your attention to a very impressive fact. Since the Vietnam war and the Watergate crisis, all opinion polls in the United States have pointed to a striking decline in public confidence in the two-party system. This disenchantment has been expressed in a constant decrease in the turn-out at elections. Only about 50 per cent of those eligible now vote in congressional elections, which must be the lowest rate of participation in the imperialist world. Even in presidential elections, the turn-out rarely exceeds 65 per cent of those eligible. Among oppressed sectors of the working class, blacks for example, the abstention rate consistently exceeds 50 per cent. This is an expression of another of the major contradictions of American political life. It is true that US workers have a lower level of political class consciousness than most European workers. But precisely because of the lack of a mass working class party, the US proletariat has tended to have fewer electoral illusions than the European. It is my opinion that perhaps the most important consequence of the constant betrayal of election promises—beginning with Lyndon Johnson's 'peace' campaign in the 1964 elections and extending through the Watergate crisis and Nixon's resignation—is that the American population has become disenchanted not simply with the two-party system but also with *electoral politics in itself.* There is no doubt that there is a negative side to this attitude, for, other things being equal, it tends to aggravate the workers' lack of inclination to involve themselves in politics, since another fact of US political life has been that politics has become identified in the minds of the masses with *electoral* politics. But there is also a potentially positive side, which is that when the workers do begin to react politically, as they surely will, to constantly increasing inflation, soaring prices of housing, continuing massive unemployment, the erosion of living standards, and so on, they will have a greater tendency than the European workers to opt for forms of direct political action not based exclusively on electoral politics. That, of course, will make it much more difficult for reformist organizations to control the politicization of the American workers, since strict reliance on electoral politics is one of the greatest sources of reformist hegemony. Thus, these very political reserves of the US ruling class, while they no doubt exist, may well prove to be more easily overcome than the lesser political reserves of the European bourgeoisie.

There is, however, an important kernel of truth in what you say, which I would formulate somewhat differently. This is the fourth obstacle I was talking about, which could be called technical, organizational, or perhaps institutional. I refer to the practical conditions under which American elections are held and the structure of the American congressional system. The political parties consist of huge machines with a nearly complete monopoly of access to the media. The expenses involved in election campaigns are astronomical, despite the post-Watergate 'reforms'. The possibilities for fraud and voter manipulation are virtually limitless. The legislative districts are drawn in such a way that huge numbers of electors are involved in even the smallest districts. Finally, the elections are structured on a state basis, even the presidential elections. The result of all this is that only an initiative that is massive from the outset, covering most of the national territory and very heavily funded has any hope of seriously challenging the two-party system. The phenomenon we have seen in France, Spain, or Italy, where the far Left has been able to make a significant impact in national electoral politics, is more or less impossible in the United States. It is even highly unlikely that there could be a repetition of the experience of the early American Socialist Party, which started small and gradually increased its vote totals to attain some degree of national significance.

There are various important consequences of this, the most crucial of which is that the only force with the potential strength to launch a serious break with the two-party system in the medium term is the organized trade-union movement. This brings us back to our starting point: the beginnings of radicalization and politicization in the American union movement and the eventual emergence of a credible left wing strong and principled enough to act independently in the political domain and to press for a break with the Democratic Party. It is here that lies the key to the formation of a mass labour party in the United States, which, for the reasons I have cited, would likely be much more radical and militant, and much less reformist, than the mass working-class parties in Western Europe. The law of combined and uneven development may then find a new and striking confirmation. The American workers will have taken much longer to come to political consciousness and to organize their own party. But once they do so, that party will grow much more quickly and collide much more radically with bourgeois society than the parties of the European working class. Let us not forget that when all is said and done, the American proletariat remains the most powerful and largest in the world.

Japan

The second or third most important imperialist country, Japan, plays a role in the worldwide system of bourgeois political power that appears as something of an enigma. The struggles of the Japanese workers' movement are largely unknown in the West. Possibly for cultural and linguistic reasons, there is little exchange of experience or theoretical dialogue between the Japanese proletariat and the rest of the international movement. Has the Fourth International itself been able to overcome that relative isolation to any significant extent?

I would agree that one of the major obstacles here is the cultural and linguistic problem. This barrier operates in both directions, although there are more people in Japan able to read European languages than there are Europeans who read Japanese and follow Japanese political, economic, and social developments. Only in one field—economics, where there is a distinct Japanese school—has Japanese intellectual production become reasonably well known in Western Europe. The Trotskyist movement has probably made more progress in correcting this deficiency than any other tendency of the workers' movement, but we are still very far from a real solution. The dynamics of the Japanese class struggle are still largely uncharted territory for the international revolutionary movement.

It is possible, however, at least to cite some of the particular problems with which we must deal. To begin with, the expansion of Japanese imperialism since the Korean War has been spectacular. In an even more striking manner than German imperialism, the Japanese bourgeoisie has to a large extent achieved peacefully what it failed to achieve militarily in the Second World War, becoming the dominant power in the economic life of wide areas of Asia. Japan is now a bigger trading partner of Australia than is Britain or the United States; Japanese capital has crossed the Pacific and conquered a significant position in the American market and has moved into Mexico and Brazil. In general, we can say without exaggeration that Japanese capital today commands positions of economic power in the world that exceed even the dreams of the warlords at the time of peak military power, with the exception of its failure to control the Chinese market. But that, of course, is a result of the Chinese revolution and not of competition from other imperialist powers.

It should be noted, however, that many of these positions are highly vulnerable, a fact generally overlooked by Western analyses, which are often misguided by jealousy when dealing with Japan. The financial structure of some of the major Japanese-controlled multinationals is quite precarious. According to some reports, Mitsubishi, the second-largest trading house and financial broker in Japan, would be threatened with bankruptcy if even one of its major foreign projects collapsed. (It may be noted in passing that one of the largest such projects is in Iran.) This weakness is partly a result of the credit financing and investment through credit inflation that was forced on post-war Japanese industry during the reconstruction under American occupation, when many of the old trusts were broken up, at least according to law. Partly, it is also a result of the breathtaking pace of economic growth, which outran the normal process of capital accumulation in the sixties and early seventies.

Politically, the Japanese state has been prevented by a number of factors from playing a role commensurate with its economic strength. The difficulties here are similar to those that would have been faced by West German capitalism had it been compelled to go it alone. The West German bourgeoisie had the good fortune, partly thanks to the intelligent choices of its political leaders, not to be compelled to operate independently but to be able to act through the Common Market and all its institutions. These institutions have been shaped so as to allow German capitalism to play a significant role despite its great discredit in the eyes of the people of Europe. What could have appeared as open German hegemony has been camouflaged by a certain equilibrium and partnership between Bonn and Paris. Japan has been unable to function in this manner in East Asia, for it has had no partners that could have played the role of France, Italy, and Britain in the case of West Germany. There are now moves to establish a sort of Common Market in Asia consisting of Japan, South Korea, Hong Kong, Taiwan, and possibly the Philippines. Such a formation, however, would have more the appearance of a network of satellites around Japan than a league of roughly equal partners. Because of the experiences of the Second World War, resistance to Japanese imperialism remains a powerful factor in the consciousness of the masses in East and Southeast Asia, and this, in the absence of a Common Market type cover, has acted to limit the political strength of the Japanese state outside its borders.

Another difficulty faced by the Japanese ruling class in acquiring an international role commensurate with its economic strength is the internal resistance to militarization. The Japanese people have been alone in the world in actually experiencing nuclear holocaust, and this has created an anti-militarist spirit that has tied the hands of the ruling class to a much greater extent than in any other imperialist country.

In sum, then, the Japanese role in the world is characterized by three basic features: enormous economic and industrial strength; limited political influence incommensurate with this economic power; and an almost complete absence of any military strength at all. This, however, should not be interpreted to mean that the Japanese state itself is weak. On the contrary, for a variety of historical reasons, not the least of which is the manner in which capitalism first arose in Japan, the state has played a more active role in influencing, directing, and controlling economic and monetary affairs in Japan than in any other imperialist country. In a number of fields—international trade, for example, oil being a particular instance—the Japanese government has backed up its private corporations much more decisively and vigorously than any of the West European governments. One of the reasons why Japanese companies can actually try to outstrip the Americans in the field of computers, to take another example, is that there is a very intensive programme of state aid to private research and development. (Whether they will succeed or not is another matter.) The state has also played quite an active role in limiting wage increases, which has been one of the factors fuelling the economic expansion. Finally, in the wake of the US defeat in Indochina and the reduced ability of the American ruling class to intervene directly in other countries, particularly in Southeast Asia, Tokyo's political influence is now rising in what it regards as its proper 'sphere of influence'.

The conditions of the Japanese labour movement are also contradictory. On the one hand, the trade-union movement is quite well organized, and is surely much more political than the North American movement. The mass parties of the working class, the Socialist and Communist Parties, carry great weight in political life, more than in many European countries. At the same time, this movement, which seemed so powerful only a few years ago, especially during the time of peak economic growth, now seems increasingly off balance and disoriented. There are undoubtedly many reasons for this, most of which we have yet to comprehend fully. Let me indicate, however, a few of the peculiarities of the Japanese workers' movement. The main strength of the class organizations, including the unions, the Communist Party, and the Socialist Party, lies in the enormous public sector. On the other hand, many of the industrial combines, which in certain branches of industry are the largest in the world, are organized by company unions that have remained outside the great class battles of recent years. This has not always been the case. Our Japanese comrades point out that the turning point came in the late forties and early fifties, when a number of important defeats were suffered by some of the industrial unions. But today this is the predominant pattern: significant working-class strength in the public sector, relative weakness in the private sector. This creates the paradox of a movement that looks stronger on paper—and in elections—than it really is in the factories and workshops on a national scale. In reality, the Japanese working class is less able to stand up to the Mitsuis and Mitsubishis than one would expect.

Closely linked to this is one of the strangest characteristics of Japan's industrial structure, a phenomenon we have had great difficulty in grasping completely: the bizarre seniority system that prevails in the giant corporations. Under this system, wage differentials are based neither on skill levels nor on productivity, but simply on the number of years of service to the company. This seniority system also entails a peculiar structure of job security in which workers are permanently tied to particular firms. The result has been that the Japanese working class has been among the least mobile in the world over the past thirty years, and this in turn has created obstacles to class integration, since the workers are encouraged, in a material way, to identify with specific firms rather than with the class as a whole. What is not easy to understand is why this system has not seriously impeded the rise of political class consciousness; but it has been a formidable obstacle to the development of what the French call 'inter-professional union struggles'. In other words, it has strengthened the corporatist, particularist aspect of union struggles and has introduced deep divisions in the union movement. Unless these divisions are overcome, it would be difficult to conceive of a general strike for economic demands, for example. Paradoxically, however, this division would be less an obstacle to a *political* general strike.

These are just a few of the peculiarities of the Japanese social formation that have yet to be adequately explained by Marxists. There are others as well. The Japanese Socialist Party, for example, was the only Social Democratic party in the world that had a significant-sized Maoist tendency within it. There was a more heated debate about Maoism in the Socialist Party than in the Communist Party, which did lean towards Peking in the early days of the Sino-Soviet dispute but never developed a full-fledged Maoist tendency. Today its political line closely parallels that of the Eurocommunist parties. For a long period, the Socialist Party held formal positions to the left of the Communist Party; the practice of the SP, however, was classically Social Democratic. This contradiction between words and actions is now being resolved in the classical manner, the previously leftist verbiage being brought into line with the reformist practice. The workers' parties, especially the Socialists, had a golden opportunity to bring down the Liberal Democratic Party, which has ruled continuously for more than thirty years now, when the Lockheed scandal broke out. But that opportunity was deliberately shunned, which is one of the reasons for the current confusion and disorientation in the workers' movement.

Finally, one of the most striking features of the evolution of Japanese political life over the past fifteen years has been the resounding failure of the radical student movement. In the sixties this movement was probably the most powerful of its kind in the world, and had the greatest opportunities to forge real links with the proletariat and thereby bring about a change in the relationship of forces between reformists and revolutionaries in the working class itself. Instead, this movement evolved in a shockingly sectarian direction, fragmenting into para-military factions that finally launched campaigns of physical attacks against each other. The far Left thereby degenerated into what can only be called gang warfare, which involved not merely beatings and intimidation, but murders of activists of rival groups. The Japanese section of the Fourth International was the only significant-sized far left group that stayed out of this process and condemned it. Once again, the reasons for this development remain obscure, and accounting for it is undoubtedly one of the important tasks of revolutionary Marxists in Japan today.

Three Sectors of World Revolution

It is especially appropriate to conclude these discussions of the evolution of world politics with a number of questions about the Fourth International. Let us begin with a general analytical point. Most of the resolutions of the FI since 1963 speak of 'three sectors of world revolution', the advanced capitalist countries, the bureaucratized workers' states, and the dependent capitalist countries. The criticism has been made that this sort of division of the world conflicts with the concept of the unity of the world proletariat and represents a concession to Maoistic notions of the 'three worlds'. How would you answer that?

I must admit that I have always regarded that particular charge as based largely on bad faith rather than serious political objections to our analysis. When we speak of three sectors of world revolution, what we are talking about are the different *strategic tasks* faced by the proletariat in the three areas you mentioned. This differentiation of strategic tasks goes back not to 1963 but to the Transitional Programme itself, the key document of the founding congress of the Fourth International in 1938. There it is pointed out that in the imperialist countries we are dealing with a dynamic of proletarian revolution in the 'classical' sense of the term. In the dependent capitalist countries what is on the agenda is a process of permanent revolution whereby the proletariat, supported by the peasant masses, must accomplish the tasks of the bourgeois revolution but can do so only by conquering state power, i.e. establishing the dictatorship of the proletariat, and overthrowing capitalist property relations as well. In the bureaucratized workers' states the proletariat faces the tasks of an anti-bureaucratic political revolution, which are distinct in quality from both those of the proletarian social revolution and those of permanent revolution. This specificity of tasks in the three sectors can be denied only if one rejects either the theory of permanent revolution or the Trotskyist analysis of the nature of the USSR and the other bureaucratized workers' states, or both. Only at the level of the greatest abstraction can it be seriously maintained that the workers face substantially identical tasks and will accomplish those tasks in substantially the same manner in the United States, India, and the Soviet Union.

The more interesting question is how the underlying unity of the world proletariat is asserted *through* this process of world revolution occurring simultaneously in the three sectors. Here there are two fundamental points. First, the *specific tasks* in each of these three sectors can be resolved only if a common precondition is fulfilled: in all three sectors, the proletariat must seize power and establish a genuine dictatorship of the proletariat, which means a state governed by the norms of socialist democracy. Second, the most basic task faced by humanity as a whole—namely the creation of a classless, socialist society—can be realized only on a world scale. There is therefore a progressive integration of the specific tasks and the general tasks through the very process of world revolution itself. But this does not at all mean the counterposition of abstract, literary ultimatism to the actual process of world revolution. It means that there must be a *real* integration of tasks in the course of a revolutionary process that takes the form of the seizure of power in particular countries. Let us recall that Trotsky's opposition to the strategy of socialism in one country had nothing whatever in common with the preposterous idea that the workers could not conquer power in a single country, even a relatively backward one, or with the equally absurd notion that the seizure of power had to occur simultaneously in a series of key countries. On the contrary, the theory of permanent revolution argues precisely that the seizure of power must occur country by country, in conformity with the different tasks and conditions in each state, but that the revolutionary process can be completed only through the continual extension and integration of the tasks of socialist construction. Finally, the unity of the world proletariat is also asserted in the course of the process of world revolution by the *unity of its class interests*. No revolutionary struggle waged by any proletariat in any of the three sectors is contrary to the interests of the international working class as a whole, nor must it be subordinated, retarded, or curbed in the name of some 'higher interest'. This point is of particular importance in the cases of the anti-bureaucratic political revolution and the struggles of the toiling masses in the dependent capitalist countries.

These observations imply a twofold dialectic that must be taken up by revolutionary Marxists and of which the Fourth International is the programmatic, political, and organizational expression.

On the one hand, the law of uneven and combined development, which governs objective reality in the epoch of imperialism, also governs the actual process of the world revolution, which does not advance continuously and simultaneously on all fronts. Revolutionaries must make every effort to unify it, but they must subordinate neither their tasks nor their support for ongoing revolutionary processes to this prior unification. Concretely, this means that the *unevenness* of the world revolution implies a *combination* of tasks. In each country, the proletariat and its revolutionary vanguard have the task of supporting revolutions going on elsewhere in the world, but at the same time must actively prepare to make the revolution in their own country. To abandon the second task in favour of the first is to become a brake on the revolution, but to abandon the first in the name of the second, even if under such edifying formulas as 'the only adequate aid to the revolution elsewhere is to make the revolution here', is to abandon the banner of proletarian internationalism, to retreat to national communism.

The second aspect of this objective dialectic relates to the actual geographic extension of the revolution. This is in no way pre-determined by any 'immanent logic', and especially not by the exist-ence of the three sectors of revolution. Rather, it is determined by a multitude of factors which themselves evolve over time: geographic proximity, political links, economic interdependence, historical traditions, similarity of political situations, attractive power of particular revolutionary movements, and so on. For instance, the revolution in the Portuguese colonies in Africa had deep repercus-sions in Portugal—and through Portugal, in Spain—before having important effects in Ethiopia, Eritrea, Zimbabwe, and Namibia. May '68 in France found powerful echoes in Czechoslovakia, and its effects in Yugoslavia were not wholly unlike its effects in the rest of capitalist Europe. There is no objective law that a colonial revolu-tion can spread only to other semi-colonial countries, or that a political revolution can spread only to other bureaucratized work-ers' states, or that a proletarian revolution can spread only to other imperialist countries.

The unity of the world proletariat therefore determines the inter-national interaction of all the various revolutionary processes, albeit in a de-synchronized manner and to varying degrees. It is for this reason, more than any other, that the underlying unity of interests of the world proletariat must find organizational expression in a united world party if that unity is to be manifested consistently in real life.

The Fourth International

This raises another point. Despite its insistence on the need for a united international organization, the Trotskyist movement has gone through quite a number of splits since its formation. Indeed, the Trotskyists have frequently been ridiculed by other tendencies of the workers' movement for this. What were the most important of these splits, and were they justified? And do you think that the reunification of the main forces of world Trotskyism in 1963 put an end to this apparent fissiparous tendency of the Fourth International?

I would begin by saying that the explanation for the splits that occurred in our movement in the late forties and early fifties lies essentially in the protracted isolation and slowness of growth of the Trotskyist movement after the Second World War, in direct contradiction, as we have said, with the predictions and expectation of Trotsky. As I pointed out earlier, the most fundamental reason for this unforeseen delay in the rise of consciousness of the international working class was the accumulated effects of the terrible defeats suffered by the world revolution in the twenties and thirties.

Several currents in the Trotskyist movement, however, decided that the failure of the Fourth International to grow was the consequence not of objective factors but of some particular subjective factor—a wrong theory of the nature of the Soviet Union, wrong tactics, an incorrect attitude towards the Communist Parties, an excessive emphasis on the proletariat in the advanced capitalist countries, there were many variations on this theme. And in a weak movement there is an evident tendency for minorities to decide to go it alone, to split and attempt to apply whatever theory or tactic they believe will induce rapid growth. The balance-sheet on all these various attempts is now definitive. In no case did any of the split groups achieve a substantially higher rate of growth than the Fourth International—for the very simple reason that the real explanation for our failure to grow during this period lay not in our subjective weaknesses but in the objective conditions.

Now, the major split suffered by the Fourth International—in reality the only really important one, since the others involved only marginal forces—was the split of 1952-53, which was initiated in France by the current that is now called the Internationalist Communist Organization (OCI) and later spread to include the Trotskyist organizations in the United States, Britain, Canada, Argentina, and several other countries. It is this split that led to a division of the main forces of the Fourth International for ten years. This was the major split not only because it involved the largest number of forces, but also because it concerned some of the historic cadres of the International, especially but not exclusively in the United States.

The political origins of the scission lay in different ways of interpreting the changes in the world situation after the beginning of the Cold War and the meaning of these changes for the future of the world revolution and the Fourth International. The problems faced at that time were the most difficult ones in the history of the International, involving a completely unforeseen turn in the world situation. Take just one example: the largest country in the world, China, was witnessing a victorious socialist revolution led by a Communist Party, whereas for years Trotskyists had been educated in the idea that the Stalinist parties had definitively gone over to the bourgeois order on a world scale.

I personally remain convinced that the resolutions we adopted at our Third World Congress, in 1951, to which Comrade Michel Pablo made a great personal contribution, were fundamentally correct and enabled the Fourth International to weather the storm. It is quite true that some of our analyses were faulty, that mistakes were made. But Pablo's essential—and positive—contribution, which was thoroughly misunderstood for a whole period, was to assert that what was actually occurring, contrary to appearances, was not an expansion and consolidation of Stalinism, but an extension of revolution that would eventually provoke a tremendous crisis of Stalinism, a crisis within the international Communist movement, and a process of political revolutions in the countries in which the bureaucracy had monopolized power. It is my opinion that this fundamental assessment of the situation in the early fifties has been proven substantially correct.

Some comrades in the movement, either out of over-sensitivity to any form of change in analysis and prognosis or out of what I would call a certain inclination to vulgar Stalinophobia, suspected that this interpretation would lead to 'capitulation' to Stalinism. For years after the events, for example, they clung to the preposterous notion that China was still a bourgeois state after 1949 and that Mao was implementing a policy of capitalist coalition government. So long as these problems were not clarified, it was difficult to avoid growing suspicion on both sides. This was the political basis of the split.

Incorrect organizational methods by Pablo also played a role in this, but not a really decisive one, since some of these mistaken measures were supported by the forces that later split and were opposed by leaders of the Pablo current. In any case, these matters are all well documented in the publications of our movement, and there is no need to go into them in detail here. What is more important is that as early as 1956, only three years after the split, the two sides had virtually identical reactions to the Hungarian revolution, supporting the rebellion and the attempts of the Hungarian workers to establish workers' councils and condemning the Soviet military intervention. This demonstrated that any political basis for the split had disappeared and that a rapid reunification of forces was necessary.

Unfortunately, it took us six years to achieve that unification, and I believe that we all paid a very high price for this delay. On both sides serious centrifugal tendencies and programmatic aberrations began to develop, under the impetus of attempts to justify and rationalize what had obviously become an arbitrary separation. This is one of the deadly dangers of light-minded splits: those forces that wish to maintain separate organizational existence when the degree of political differences does not justify it are driven to invent 'principles' to account for their actions. The subsequent ugly degeneration of the Healy sect in Britain originated in this period, and probably could have been prevented by an early reunification of forces. Similar remarks could be made about the current led by Juan Posadas, which had supported the majority of the Fourth International in the split. The degeneration of this grouping caused us to lose hundreds of very valuable cadres, particularly in Latin America.

It is my opinion that even though various forces in the Fourth International today may assess the 1953 split and its aftermath differently, everyone has learned the lessons, if learning was necessary, of the negative consequences of unprincipled splits. Today the Fourth International has nearly ten times as many members as it did at the time of the reunification congress in 1963. We have not yet achieved the breakthrough Trotsky predicted on the eve of the Second World War, but the positive dynamic is clear. More important, in spite of a number of extremely vehement tendency and faction struggles over important political questions, the International has not suffered a single international split since 1965. We have been able to debate our differences freely, even publicly, and to preserve internal democracy, including the right of tendencies and factions to organize and fight for their ideas, without suffering splits. If we compare this to what has happened in the other tendencies of the international workers' movement, I think we can safely say that Stalinists, Maoists, and centrists should be rather more cautious in stridently accusing Trotskyism of being congenitally susceptible to destructive splits.

I would conclude by emphasizing this point about internal democracy. The most important organizational conclusion to be drawn from the past twenty-five years of the history of the Fourth International is that contrary to the deep-rooted myth upheld by Stalinists and Social Democrats, freedom to form tendencies and factions, and jealous defence of the rights of party members to express their opinions and to fight for them within the party (even to the extent of over-stressing those rights) have proven to be effective safeguards of the unity of the revolutionary movement and not at all a cause of splits. In this respect, as in others, the Fourth International today is defending the heritage of Lenin, of the Leninist principles of democratic centralism, including the right to form tendencies and factions in the party.

Critics of these Leninist principles of organization generally make two claims. First, that the historical evidence would tend to show that Leninist forms of organization exhibit an inherent tendency to degenerate in a bureaucratic direction, closing off the ability of rank-and-file members to participate fully in formulating party policy. Second, that the very concept of an organization consisting of professional revolutionaries effectively excludes ordinary workers, who lack the time to conduct internal debates and discussions on the extensive scale of full-time party leaders or others who have no job or family responsibilities. In this sense, tendency rights can become a pure formality, since the party membership is often physically unable to lend that form a democratic content. How has the Fourth International been able to deal with these sorts of problems?

I would answer along two lines. First, whatever the problems associated with Leninist democratic centralism may be, alternative forms of organization seem even more inclined to degenerate in the direction of bureaucracy. Take the most common form of Social Democratic organization, for example: the electoral district constituency party with a large 'paper' membership, an organizational form that has been largely appropriated by most of the mass Communist parties today. In practice these parties have shown themselves to be just as prone to bureaucratic manipulation as parties organized along Stalinist lines. The degree of control exercised by a corrupt bureaucracy well integrated into bourgeois society over a largely passive working-class membership is quite as great as that of a Stalinist bureaucracy. Indeed, it is even easier to reproduce this sort of bureaucratic structure, since it parallels the structure of the bourgeois state itself. In the worst of cases, then, it could be said that the labour movement has yet to devise any organizational form that offers lasting effective structural guarantees against bureaucratic degeneration. I would not reject that assertion out of hand. The essence of this problem, often overlooked by people who lend excessive importance to the purely formal aspects of the question, is that in the last analysis the only real guarantee against bureaucracy is a politically active working class, or at least working-class vanguard.

This does not mean that organizational rules and safeguards, the formal aspect of the matter, are unimportant. It makes a big difference whether a politically active working class or workers' vanguard encounters a party like the Bolshevik Party of, say, March and April 1917, in which it was possible to shift the line of the party from a dangerously opportunist to a revolutionary course, or whether it encounters a party like German Social Democracy in 1918. It is for this reason that I am convinced of the need for democratic centralism. One could perhaps paraphrase Winston Churchill's quip and say that it is a very bad system of organization, but the least bad that has been devised by the working class so far in its history, which is quite rich in organizational forms.

In what does this system consist? The essence of democratic centralism is not really organizational, but political, or better, sociopolitical. The immediate experience of workers is always partial and one-sided. Real workers, as opposed to idealized ones, are active in one factory, in one branch of industry, in one city. The lessons they draw from their immediate experiences are therefore always partial. The spontaneous activity of the working class, while it may be quite varied, is always fragmented and therefore always tends to lead to fragmented consciousness. The essential function of democratic centralism is to overcome that fragmentation by centralizing the experience of the working class as a whole, drawing the proper lessons from it, and organizing a strategy that can unify the proletarian front in its battle for state power.

In this sense, the very essence of democratic centralism lies in the capacity of the individual Bolshevik militant, or at least the individual cells and party units, to take independent initiatives, to enjoy the greatest autonomy. Otherwise, there is nothing to centralize. If marching orders are simply issued by the party leadership in response to reports from the field received after the issuance of prior orders, then there is no need for democratic centralism, for what we are dealing with is merely military organization.

This, by the way, was exactly the splendid, almost magical quality of the Bolshevik Party in its greatest periods of revolutionary initiative and success. It was the ability of the Bolsheviks to integrate and centralize the myriad of independent initiatives being taken by literally thousands of advanced workers that set them off from the other parties. Under Stalin, of course, the entire system was overturned, and this has created great resistance to 'democratic centralism'. The real objection, however, is to bureaucratic centralism, which is the system inaugurated in the Stalinist parties on the ruins of democratic centralism.

Now, it is undoubtedly true that these general principles do not answer all the questions associated with party organization, as we are increasingly discovering as our membership increases. We have now won significant numbers of workers to our organizations in many countries and are therefore facing new and specific problems of which we were insufficiently conscious when we were a tiny vanguard. We have not yet found solutions to all these problems, many of which can only be worked out in the course of long experience. But I will give you some examples, which relate directly to the second part of your question.

The superiority of Bolshevism over Menshevism from the standpoint of party democracy is precisely the fact that Bolshevism requires a higher level of commitment and activity, for this acts as a safeguard against bureaucratic manipulation. The more homogeneous a group is in terms of the level of activity of its membership, the more difficult it is to manipulate that group bureaucratically. This principle is easy enough to apply in a small group; in a small party it becomes more difficult, and in a mass party it is downright impossible. A choice must therefore be made. Either one thinks that the socialist revolution can be led by a party of a few thousand members cleverly directing millions of workers or one recognizes that the future revolutionary party will be a mass party in the real sense of the word, with hundreds of thousands of members and many more close sympathizers. The real difficulty then becomes how to build a larger and larger mass party of the working class without diluting the average level of activity and political education so much that dangers of bureaucratic manipulation arise.

This difficulty is not easily overcome, but it is not impossible. Besides the example of the Bolsheviks, there were other genuine mass Communist parties that had this sort of vibrant internal life, which did manage to combine respect for the formal rules of democratic centralism and multifaceted, independent rank-and-file initiatives. The German Communist Party in the early twenties, for instance, had hundreds of thousands of members and conducted free, public debates that went well beyond anything that has been seen in Social Democratic parties. Even the Italian Communist Party when it was deeply divided between the Bordiga and Gramsci factions, functioning under the early stages of fascist rule, maintained freedom of debate and tendency formation and allowed its rank-and-file militants broad scope for independent initiative. The important point is to recognize the problem; once recognized, it is thorny, but not insoluble.

Finally, there is the problem to which you allude: the contradiction between serious political education and participation in the active life of the revolutionary organization by ordinary workers on the one hand and the material pressures to which the proletariat is constantly subject on the other. What must be avoided at all costs is a social cleavage within the revolutionary party between less politicized workers and hyper-politicized intellectuals, students, and 'professional' revolutionaries, for such a cleavage is inevitably fatal. We have definitely faced this problem in the organizations of the Fourth International, whose members are generally three or four times as active as the members of the reformist mass parties. Industrial workers who spend eight hours or more in a factory every day and have family responsibilities as well cannot maintain a pace of activism that includes several hours of meetings every night. On the other hand, the tasks of the revolutionary party always tend to expand faster than the active forces of the party, and many members are able and eager to maintain what others might consider a feverish pitch of activity. One method of dealing with this problem is to establish special groupings—discussion circles around particular theoretical questions, action groups dealing with specific issues, and so on—which function parallel to one another. This sort of functional division of labour was applied, for example, by the German Communist Party during its best days in cities like Hamburg, Leipzig, and Berlin, where party militants had a choice of as many as five or six meetings or other party activities every night, but were obligated to attend only their cell meetings. It is in this direction that we must look for solutions to this problem, while recognizing that it must be grappled with empirically to a certain extent, that no rigid rules can be laid down. The only general rule that must be defended at all costs is that the norms of democratic centralism must be observed, which means that party militants must have the right to present their views freely and fully and to organize themselves to fight for those views within the party. And that means that the right to form tendencies and factions must not be abridged.

As you have pointed out, the Fourth International has grown significantly since the reunification of 1963, and is presently larger than ever before in its history. Nevertheless, after more than forty years of effort, it has yet to become the mass revolutionary international organization envisaged by its founder, and in no country has it successfully made the transition from relatively small vanguard grouping upholding the continuity of the revolutionary programme, to genuine mass proletarian party. At the same time, the crisis of Stalinism has made it possible for tendencies hostile to both Social Democracy and the official Communist movement to win the leadership of mass struggles and, in at least one case—Cuba—to lead the working class to the seizure of state power. What conclusions would you draw from this mixed balance-sheet? What are the prospects for the Fourth International's finally fulfilling the dreams of its founders?

Two phases must be clearly distinguished in the history of the Fourth International: the first extending from its formation to the late sixties, the second since then, and more particularly since 1968. The growth that has occurred during this second phase should not be underestimated. Our membership has increased manyfold, but our political influence, the circulation of our press, our weight in the trade unions, and even our electoral influence have increased even faster than our actual membership. The FI now has organizations in more than sixty countries, whereas the figure was only thirty or forty in the late sixties. Moreover, there is no indication that this growth is levelling off. Although it would be quite false to maintain that what has happened since 1968 corresponds to the predictions Trotsky made on the eve of the Second World War, and although we have yet to achieve a real breakthrough in any country, it is now possible to glimpse the outlines of the process that could result in the construction of genuine mass revolutionary parties in a number of countries.

The very sorts of factors that prevented the swift growth of the Fourth International at the end of the Second World War have permitted the rapid expansion since 1968. The accumulated effects of the defeats of the world revolution in the twenties and thirties have been gradually eroded by the accumulated effects of the rise of world revolution, geographically and socially limited as it was, during the late fifties and the sixties. The positive effects of the Yugoslav, Chinese, Cuban, and Vietnamese revolutions were compounded by the simultaneous crises of Stalinism and capitalism that erupted after May '68. A new generation of revolutionaries has arisen since then, no longer marked by twenty years of setbacks, but confident in the destiny of revolutionary struggle and prepared to commit themselves to the process of building the revolutionary party precisely because of that confidence.

This is not a linear process, either in time or in space, but it is evident in many countries and on all continents. Most of all, it is linked to the very character of the epoch, which is not one likely to lead to crushing defeats that bury the hopes of revolution for generations, but to overall upswings of struggle and relatively rapid recovery from those setbacks or defeats that are inflicted. In this sense, it is correct to speak of a new period more favourable to the construction of revolutionary parties, a period which began in the second half of the 1960s. This is the only proper Marxist interpretation of the history of the Fourth International thus far, as is proven by two convincing pieces of evidence.

On the one hand, there were not a few who, in the preceding period, had attributed the relative stagnation of the Fourth International to what they called the 'congenital defects' of our movement—its allegedly petty-bourgeois social composition; its 'lack of national roots'; its 'false position on the Russian question'; its alleged revision of the holy writ of Trotsky's writings—and struck off on their own to correct these defects and build a revolutionary movement of their own. But no organization to the left of Stalinism and Social Democracy achieved results qualitatively superior to those of the Fourth International between 1948 and 1968. On the other hand, when objective conditions changed and a new mass vanguard emerged on an international scale, the opposite phenomenon occurred. At the same time as a number of Trotskyist organizations increased their membership five- and tenfold, other organizations to the left of the Communist and Socialist parties also achieved rapid growth, in conformity with these altered objective conditions.

I would contest the proposition that other revolutionary organizations beginning as small groupings have been able to succeed where our movement has failed. The example of the July 26 Movement in Cuba is inappropriate here. Fidel Castro was the leader of a mass organization in Cuba before he became a revolutionary. He stood as a candidate in the legislative elections of 1952 and probably would have been elected but for Batista's coup d'état. He was a leader of one of the major nationalist organizations of the country, the Partido Auténtico. Thus, what happened in Cuba was not at all the transformation of a small revolutionary grouping into a mass party, but rather the opposite: the transformation of a petty-bourgeois, nationalist, and populist mass current into a revolutionary organization through a pragmatic evolution under particular conditions. It was the transformation of a movement commanding mass influence but which was not proletarian in programme or composition into a semi-proletarian movement with mass influence, and then into a mass proletarian party.

But the Cuban revolution did not witness the transformation in just a few years of an isolated revolutionary group into a mass party thanks to the discovery of some miraculous tactic and strategy. For about forty years now, not a few comrades have allowed themselves to be seduced by the search for such miracles. But no one has yet come upon one. Let us add that between 1936 and 1938 there were a number of centrist organizations vastly larger than the sections of the International Left Opposition, precursor of the Fourth International, sometimes as much as twenty times larger, parties with deep roots in the workers' movement in their countries. There was the POUM in Spain, the current led by Brandler in Germany, the Independent Labour Party in Britain, the Bordiga group in Italy, the Revolutionary Socialist Workers Party (RASP) in the Netherlands, the PSOP in France. Each of these organizations was born of a particular phase of the history of the workers' movement of its country and indubitably played a considerable role in the national class struggle, a much more important role than the small sections of the Fourth International. Today, however, most of these organizations have disappeared, and those that survive are smaller and less strongly rooted in the proletariat than the sections of the Fourth International in these countries.

What this simple fact demonstrates is that our movement represents a universal component, an international tendency, of the workers' movement, whereas these various organizations constituted only nationally limited phenomena corresponding to particular moments in the history of contemporary class struggle. One must be quite cautious, then, in attributing the stagnation of our movement up to 1968 to any peculiarities of Trotskyism. There is no doubt that we made mistakes, that accidental organizational factors slowed our growth in some cases, but these are secondary considerations. The fact of the matter is that the vicissitudes of the efforts to construct a genuine revolutionary international are due, in the last analysis, to the evolution of the objective relationship of class forces on a world scale.

There are two additional questions closely related to this one. The first is a reproach often raised against us by far left organizations that otherwise stand close to us politically. Trotskyist obsession with what we call programmatic continuity and what our critics call dogmatism, this argument runs, prevented the unification of the far Left at moments when it would have otherwise been possible to achieve unity. The examples most often cited in this regard are Italy, France, Britain, Portugal, and Germany at varying times between 1970 and 1976. We have always responded, and it is appropriate to repeat this response here, that what prevented this unification was not our fetishistic adherence to the label of the Fourth International, but very precise, concrete political differences on key strategic questions of the ongoing process of class struggle in Europe. It is our view that while new problems always arise, and while there are always changes in objective reality which call for new contributions to Marxist theory and analysis, the old acquisitions of that theory—those which have been proven correct by history—must not be liquidated. On the contrary, the coherence of theory must be preserved. It would have been false to maintain, for example, that Lenin and Trotsky's theory of the united front was inapplicable in Portugal in 1975, or that Leninist and Trotskyist conceptions of transitional demands and of the government slogan that should crown a transitional programme were no longer applicable in France or Italy in 1976 and 1977. The failure of the centrist organizations to understand and apply these correct programmatic positions, usually because they were bending to 'the movement', led to catastrophic mistakes, to their oscillation between sectarianism and opportunist adaptations to the mass organizations of the working class. The ultimate result was a massive loss of both influence and members after what had been a period of rapid growth.

The second remark concerns the more strictly organizational domain. It is no accident that our movement is the only organization that really functions on a world scale and that we identify so strongly with the idea of building national organizations and a world organization simultaneously. This is but the organizational dimension of the theory of permanent revolution and of our opposition to the strategy of socialism in one country. The notion that strong national revolutionary parties must be constructed first and later federated internationally is based on a profound lack of understanding of the organic character of the world economy, world politics, and the world class struggle in the era of imperialism. One must be blind to fail to see that today's multinational corporations are no aberration but the expression of a fundamental feature of the development of the productive forces and the organization of the capitalist economy.

The arguments advanced against this conception in the past have been shown to be not only false but also self-defeating for the very effort to build so-called national organizations. The class struggle today must be waged internationally, in a coordinated manner, not only for moral reasons but for highly pragmatic ones. Consider just one very practical example. Trade-union militants in various European countries have been raising the slogan of the 35-hour week as a means of counteracting unemployment. Employers and labour bureaucrats have answered that this demand, if implemented on a national scale, could actually increase unemployment. Whether or not this is true—and we happen not to think so—the evident reply is clear: fight for it on an international scale, in the first place on a European scale, since it is the only effective means by which to reduce unemployment immediately and radically, and unemployment is the scourge of the working class throughout capitalist Europe today.

To understand this great truth of contemporary communism—that we live in an era of *world* revolution and counter-revolution—is also to understand that a world proletarian organization is required that can centralize and integrate all the aspects of this reality. To understand the disastrous effects of the bureaucratic degeneration of the Communist International is to understand that this world organization must be governed by the norms of genuine democratic centralism. Just as we shall never accept the identification of Leninism on the one hand with Stalinism on the other, of the dictatorship of the proletariat with the dictatorship of the bureaucracy, we shall never accept the identification of international democratic centralism with the bureaucratic conception of a 'guiding centre' with the right to overturn the leaderships of national revolutionary organizations and to impose national tactics that are not accepted by the majority of the militants in a national party. The construction of a democratically centralized revolutionary international that unifies and directs the fight of the world proletariat against its common enemies and for its common interests—that is our purpose.

The Socialism We Want

Let us conclude with a rather general question. The Russian revolution of 1917 opened an era of great hope not only for the international working class, but for millions of oppressed and exploited people throughout the world. More than sixty years later, it must be acknowledged that to a large extent these hopes have been frustrated. You yourself have pointed out on many occasions that the lack of a credible 'model' counterposed to the sad reality of the bureaucratic degeneration of the Soviet Union is a great obstacle to socialist revolution today. Yet the Fourth International does have a 'model' of socialism, and you have also evinced great optimism about the future of that model. The question, then, is twofold. What is the basis for this optimism? What would the Fourth International's vision of socialism look like in practice?

In the final analysis, that optimism is based on the reality of revolutionary developments as an inevitable objective process resulting from the twin crises of world capitalism and of the labour bureaucracy in all its manifestations. Back in 1967 *The Economist* advanced the hypothesis that the 'revolutionary cycle' that began with the French revolution (these gentlemen ignored the English and American revolutions, not to mention others) had come to an end with the failure of Mao's 'cultural revolution'. At the time I wrote an article replying that their perspective was wrong. Since then we have had May '68, the beginning of the political revolution in Czechoslovakia, the victory of the Vietnamese revolution, the Portuguese revolutionary process, the beginning of the Iranian revolution—to mention only the highlights. There can be no doubt that coming years will see many other revolutions, some of them more radical in both mass participation and revolutionary measures than anything that has been seen so far. That is why I am convinced that many of the problems that look so intractable today will be solved by history. The growth of the Fourth International, itself closely linked to the rise of world revolution and of the class consciousness of the proletariat, will also contribute to the resolution of many of these problems.

It is undeniable, however, that the lack of a socialist alternative clearly and convincingly different from the repugnant state of affairs in Russia, Eastern Europe, China, is an important obstacle to the Western proletariat's break with reformism. It is an even greater obstacle to the rise of the Soviet working class out of political apathy. That is why the Fourth International has devoted so much time and effort to defining our socialist goals in the clearest and most unambiguous terms.

Such an endeavour encounters obvious difficulties, for history never unfolds according to a preconceived plan. Many of the features of socialist democracy will depend on such factors as the particular conditions of its birth (in which the most important element is the material resources available, in other words, the concrete economic situation), its rapid geographical extension, the world relationship of forces, the changes it will provoke within the bureaucratized workers' states, the realignment it will cause within the international labour movement, and so on.

Furthermore, one must take care not to fall into a 'Trotskyist' version of socialism in one country. A clear distinction must be made between a democratically-run society in transition from capitalism to socialism and a genuine socialist society, a classless society, which can be established only on a broad international scale, after capitalism has been overthrown in its major bastions.

But even bearing all these problems in mind, we must present the masses today a 'model' of the type of society and state that will emerge from the overthrow of capitalism, and that model has to be an attractive alternative to both capitalism and the bureaucratized workers' states, which have nothing in common with a real socialist, that is classless, society of freely associated producers. Such a model, which must integrate the theoretical heritage of revolutionary Marxism with the experiences of all the proletarian revolutions and struggles of the past sixty years (both successes and failures) and with the conquests of contemporary science and technology, can and will have the sort of effect on the international working class that the firm belief that capitalism was doomed and socialism on the agenda had immediately after the First World War. At the dawn of the era of proletarian revolutions, socialism was seen by the masses of workers as a giant advance in their own conditions of life. It must become so again.

Such a model must be constructed essentially around the following ideas.

The socialist revolution means the overthrow of capitalism and the establishment of the dictatorship of the proletariat, which requires the destruction of the bourgeois state apparatus and the disarming and expropriation of the capitalist class. It does not mean a suppression of democratic liberties, a one-party system, or the rule of bureaucratic despots. Political power will be in the hands of a congress of workers' and people's councils elected by universal suffrage, with a multi-party system to which *all* parties will have access provided they respect socialist legality in practice, which means provided they do not engage in armed struggle against workers' power. All currents and parties will have free access to the mass media in proportion to their membership, and society must enjoy a vigorous pluralist ideological and cultural life. Revolutionary Marxists will fight for political hegemony within the workers' councils by political means—including mass mobilizations—but not through administrative or repressive actions.

Nationalization of the means of production, by which I mean the suppression of both private property and the right to private property in the means of production, is a necessary but not at all sufficient condition for a transition to socialism. A planned economy must strive to eliminate not only unemployment and periodic over-production crises—for that the suppression of private property in the means of production is sufficient—but also social inequality, the oppressive nature of mechanical labour, the alienation of the producers from their labour, and waste of resources and wealth—all of which impose such evils as unnecessary sacrifices in living standards, poverty, frustration of basic needs, inequality of access to information and culture, and so on.

It follows that if the road to socialism is really to be opened, then suppression of private property must be combined with generalized management of the economy by the producers themselves, at all levels at which this is technologically possible: some decisions can be taken on the shop floor, others at the factory level, others at the local or industrial branch level, others nationally, and still others internationally. This generalized workers' management is intimately related to socialist democracy in the sense that key decisions about the division of the national product, priorities in the utilization of scarce resources, social options, and so on, must be taken by those concerned, after open democratic debates in which various alternatives are freely presented. In the long run, such a system will be far less wasteful than either capitalism or the bureaucratized workers' states, because those who make the decisions—who can and will make many mistakes—are also those who will pay for those decisions in their living standards and working conditions, which is generally not the case for Western capitalists and Soviet bureaucrats.

As I have mentioned before, a radical reduction of the working week—probably to half-day working hours—is a material precondition for real workers' management. If the producers work eight hours a day, with an additional two hours or so for commuting, they will simply not have adequate time to manage their own affairs, whether in the factory or office or in the community. Likewise, a radical extension of the process of education, reorganized so as to extend throughout the lifetime of the average producer, and generalized access to centralized information are also preconditions for the accomplishment of one of the central purposes of the social revolution: the elimination of the social division of labour between producers and administrators.

At the same time, no serious advance towards socialism is possible without a radical reduction of the difference in average living standards between the industrialized countries and the dependent countries. Massive aid from the former to the latter is therefore indispensable to progress towards socialism. The question that arises here is whether a radical increase in economic growth in the dependent countries is compatible with a radical reduction of the working week in the developed countries and a consolidation and extension of the material advances of the Western working class. It is my view that the answer to this question is certainly affirmative. Indeed, I think it can be demonstrated rather easily that if the tremendous waste inherent in the present system of allocation of resources were eliminated, if the enormous reserves of the already existing productive apparatus were genuinely and fully tapped, and if the explosion of working-class creativity and inventiveness that would follow a socialist revolution were encouraged and stimulated instead of restricted and blunted, simultaneous accomplishment of these two tasks would be eminently possible. Two examples in this regard are especially obvious. The eradication of the staggering expenditure of social resources on armaments throughout the world, but especially in the imperialist countries, would alone release such quantities of funds, energy, and material resources that they could play a decisive role in the industrialization of the dependent countries, without causing the slightest reduction in the living standards of the workers in the advanced countries. Second, it is perhaps the single most devastating indictment of the capitalist system to observe that masses of people in the world today are hungry *because* there is too much food. This is a point I explained at some length in *The Second Slump*; I will not dwell on it here, except to note that contrary to imperialist propaganda and a widespread belief, the most pressing cause of hunger in the world today is that there has been a typical capitalist *over-production crisis* in foodstuffs.

These two simple examples demonstrate that a rational solution to the problem of equalizing living standards throughout the world entails not the lowering of the living conditions of the exploited classes in the imperialist countries, but the simultaneous improvement of the living conditions of the exploited classes worldwide. The obstacle to this is not material scarcity, but the system of production for private profit. In considering living standards, however, we must distinguish real needs (such as the elimination of hunger, the satisfaction of all basic needs, generalized free education and medical care, massive access to all forms of culture—most of which are far off even for the majority of workers in the imperialist countries) from the consequences of bourgeois-induced consumption patterns, which are not only largely meaningless from the standpoint of realization of individual human possibilities, but strictly harmful from the standpoint of physical and moral health. Our 'model' of socialism implies a radical transformation not only of capitalist technology, but also of habits of consumption. Our responsibility towards future generations not to squander those natural resources which really are rare also points to this conclusion. While we are much less pessimistic about the long-term capacity of human science to solve all major problems of scarcity of energy and raw materials than some current experts, we recognize that such a responsible attitude is imperative. The withering away of market-money relationships in all those areas in which basic needs can be satisfied and a conscious drive against social inequality are therefore part and parcel of any real struggle for socialism (which does not mean that all market phenomena can be suppressed artificially by fiat).

Basic social inequalities like those between men and women, oppressor and oppressed nationalities and races, will of course be legally eliminated by socialist revolution. But their reality and effects will last far beyond the seizure of state power by the proletariat, partly as a result of lingering prejudices in the consciousness of many workers. Key aspects of the transition period, then, will be organized mass struggles for the liberation of women and oppressed nationalities and races, the fight against the repression of children, and so on. All this means, among other things, that it is impossible to build socialism without a gigantic cultural revolution, of which the dissolution of the patriarchal family and of the distinction between particular and general labour are key aspects, but by no means the only ones. Education and health techniques will undergo equally radical changes, as will the urban-rural relationship. The restoration of a healthy natural environment will require even consciously prepared transformations of the earth's geography. Another aspect of this process will be a radical reduction in the level of violence, for one of the first acts of a world socialist federation would be to halt and forbid arms production everywhere and to begin immediately to reduce existing stocks of weapons to a minimal level easily controlled by the mass of people.

All these points can be summarized quite succinctly. Our 'model' of socialism, contrary to what many opponents of Marxism contend, promises neither paradise on earth nor the millennium. We have no illusions about a 'society without conflict' or an 'end of history'. We know very well that hundreds of problems will remain unsolved for centuries—and many new ones will emerge. We are indeed very modest people, with quite modest goals. All we want to do is to solve those half dozen or so problems resulting from the incongruity between the technical and scientific capacities of the human species on the one hand and the system of production for private profit on the other. There is no mystery about what these problems are: hunger, physical misery, social and economic inequality, war, inequality between men and women and between different nationalities and races, exploitation of the labour of others, political repression, socially organized violence. All these obstacles to the self-realization of the human personality can be eliminated through the overturn of the existing relations of production and the political structures that uphold them. All the myriad of other problems, and the future ones that will undoubtedly arise, we make no claim to solve. But these half dozen or so problems have cost the lives of hundreds of millions of people over centuries and have made the lives of thousands of millions of others miserable beyond description. A victorious struggle for socialism would make a seminal contribution to human progress, and it is for this reason that the fight for these goals, modest as they are, is the crucial human endeavour of our age.